Salad Recipes

by Wendy Jo Peterson, MS, RDN

Salad Recipes For Dummies®

Published by: **John Wiley & Sons, Inc.**, 111 River Street, Hoboken, NJ 07030-5774, www.wiley.com

Copyright © 2023 by John Wiley & Sons, Inc., Hoboken, New Jersey

Published simultaneously in Canada

No part of this publication may be reproduced, stored in a retrieval system or transmitted in any form or by any means, electronic, mechanical, photocopying, recording, scanning or otherwise, except as permitted under Sections 107 or 108 of the 1976 United States Copyright Act, without the prior written permission of the Publisher. Requests to the Publisher for permission should be addressed to the Permissions Department, John Wiley & Sons, Inc., 111 River Street, Hoboken, NJ 07030, (201) 748-6011, fax (201) 748-6008, or online at http://www.wiley.com/go/permissions.

Trademarks: Wiley, For Dummies, the Dummies Man logo, Dummies.com, Making Everything Easier, and related trade dress are trademarks or registered trademarks of John Wiley & Sons, Inc., and may not be used without written permission. All other trademarks are the property of their respective owners. John Wiley & Sons, Inc., is not associated with any product or vendor mentioned in this book.

LIMIT OF LIABILITY/DISCLAIMER OF WARRANTY: WHILE THE PUBLISHER AND AUTHORS HAVE USED THEIR BEST EFFORTS IN PREPARING THIS WORK, THEY MAKE NO REPRESENTATIONS OR WARRANTIES WITH RESPECT TO THE ACCURACY OR COMPLETENESS OF THE CONTENTS OF THIS WORK AND SPECIFICALLY DISCLAIM ALL WARRANTIES, INCLUDING WITHOUT LIMITATION ANY IMPLIED WARRANTIES OF MERCHANTABILITY OR FITNESS FOR A PARTICULAR PURPOSE. NO WARRANTY MAY BE CREATED OR EXTENDED BY SALES REPRESENTATIVES, WRITTEN SALES MATERIALS OR PROMOTIONAL STATEMENTS FOR THIS WORK. THE FACT THAT AN ORGANIZATION, WEBSITE, OR PRODUCT IS REFERRED TO IN THIS WORK AS A CITATION AND/OR POTENTIAL SOURCE OF FURTHER INFORMATION DOES NOT MEAN THAT THE PUBLISHER AND AUTHORS ENDORSE THE INFORMATION OR SERVICES THE ORGANIZATION, WEBSITE, OR PRODUCT MAY PROVIDE OR RECOMMENDATIONS IT MAY MAKE. THIS WORK IS SOLD WITH THE UNDERSTANDING THAT THE PUBLISHER IS NOT ENGAGED IN RENDERING PROFESSIONAL SERVICES. THE ADVICE AND STRATEGIES CONTAINED HEREIN MAY NOT BE SUITABLE FOR YOUR SITUATION. YOU SHOULD CONSULT WITH A SPECIALIST WHERE APPROPRIATE. FURTHER, READERS SHOULD BE AWARE THAT WEBSITES LISTED IN THIS WORK MAY HAVE CHANGED OR DISAPPEARED BETWEEN WHEN THIS WORK WAS WRITTEN AND WHEN IT IS READ. NEITHER THE PUBLISHER NOR AUTHORS SHALL BE LIABLE FOR ANY LOSS OF PROFIT OR ANY OTHER COMMERCIAL DAMAGES, INCLUDING BUT NOT LIMITED TO SPECIAL, INCIDENTAL, CONSEQUENTIAL, OR OTHER DAMAGES.

For general information on our other products and services, please contact our Customer Care Department within the U.S. at 877-762-2974, outside the U.S. at 317-572-3993, or fax 317-572-4002. For technical support, please visit https://hub.wiley.com/community/support/dummies.

Wiley publishes in a variety of print and electronic formats and by print-on-demand. Some material included with standard print versions of this book may not be included in e-books or in print-on-demand. If this book refers to media such as a CD or DVD that is not included in the version you purchased, you may download this material at http://booksupport.wiley.com. For more information about Wiley products, visit www.wiley.com.

Library of Congress Control Number: 2022946488

ISBN 978-1-119-90671-1 (pbk); ISBN 978-1-119-90673-5 (ebk); ISBN 978-1-119-90672-8 (ebk)

SKY10036674_101222

Contents at a Glance

Introduction 1

Part 1: Breaking Down the Parts of a Salad 5
CHAPTER 1: Salad Basics 7
CHAPTER 2: Tools and Techniques 15
CHAPTER 3: Going Shopping 23

Part 2: Making a Plan 29
CHAPTER 4: Boosting Nutrition with Salads 31
CHAPTER 5: Making Salad-Inclusive Meal Plans 35

Part 3: Jump-Starting Your Salad Journey 43
CHAPTER 6: Dressings 45
CHAPTER 7: The Classics 63
CHAPTER 8: Weeknight Side Salads 79
CHAPTER 9: Going Global 95
CHAPTER 10: Going Bold with Bowls 119
CHAPTER 11: Plant-Forward Protein Salads 133
CHAPTER 12: Crowd Pleasers 149

Part 4: Getting Creative with Salads 163
CHAPTER 13: Pantry Stars 165
CHAPTER 14: Starchy Salads 173
CHAPTER 15: Fruity Concoctions 187
CHAPTER 16: Sweet Salads 205

Part 5: The Part of Tens 215
CHAPTER 17: Ten (or So) Tips for Building Salads in a Jar 217
CHAPTER 18: Ten Homemade Salad Kits 223
CHAPTER 19: Ten Fun Ways to Add Crunch to a Salad 229
CHAPTER 20: Ten Common Types of Produce and
How to Keep Them Fresh 233

Part 6: Appendixes 239
APPENDIX A: Metric Conversion Guide 241
APPENDIX B: Food Storage Guide 245
APPENDIX C: Food Safety Guide 249

Index 253

Recipes at a Glance

Main-Course Salads

Asian Ground Beef and Rice Bowls 128
☺ Bean Fritters with Pesto Couscous Salad 143
Chinese Chicken Slaw Bowls 126
☺ Cold Ramen Noodle Bowls 132
☺ Cold Soba and Edamame Salad 180
Creamy Coconut Chicken Bowls 125
Crunchy Southwestern Bowls 120
Fiesta Bowls 123
Grilled Chicken Shawarma Bowls 130
☺ Grilled Tofu with Soy and Ginger Salad 135
Italian Arugula and Lox Salad 104
Korean Bun Noodle Salad 109
Laotian Ground Pork Larb 114
☺ Mediterranean Farro Bowls 124
☺ Moroccan Spiced Veggie Bowls 127
☺ Nutty Chinese Noodle Bowls 131
☺ Orange-Glazed Tempeh with Noodles Salad 138
Taco Salad 73
Tangy Barbecue Chicken Bowls 129
Texas-Style Chopped House Bowls 121
☺ Vegetarian Cobb Salad 134
Zesty Thai Steak Bowls 122

Bowls

Asian Ground Beef and Rice Bowls 128
Chinese Chicken Slaw Bowls 126
☺ Cold Ramen Noodle Bowls 132
Creamy Coconut Chicken Bowls 125
Crunchy Southwestern Bowls 120
Fiesta Bowls 123
Grilled Chicken Shawarma Bowls 130
☺ Mediterranean Farro Bowls 124
☺ Moroccan Spiced Veggie Bowls 127

⟳ Nutty Chinese Noodle Bowls 131
⟳ Roasted Veggie Bowls with Peanut Dressing 140
   Tangy Barbecue Chicken Bowls 129
   Texas-Style Chopped House Bowls 121
   Zesty Thai Steak Bowls 122

Side Salads

   Arugula Parmesan Crisps and Bacon-Wrapped Date Salad 159
⟳ Asparagus and Crumbled Egg Salad 86
⟳ Barley and Lemon Chive Salad 184
⟳ Bean and Barley Canadian Salad 90
⟳ Blushed Strawberry and Spinach Salad 72
⟳ Broccoli and Feta Salad 88
   Caesar Salad 65
   Cali BLT Panzanella Salad 181
⟳ Canadian Maple, Cabbage, and Cranberry Salad 116
   Chicken Curry Salad 77
⟳ Chickpea and Cucumber Dill Salad 156
⟳ Chickpea and Sunflower Smashed Salad 171
   Chopped House Salad 68
   Cobb Salad 69
   Crispy Bacon Wedge Salad 67
⟳ Crispy Spring Salad 94
⟳ Crunchy Peanut Zoodle Salad 136
⟳ Cucumber, Tomato, and Goat Cheese Salad 85
⟳ Edamame, Crispy Onions, and Farro Salad 147
⟳ Egyptian Barley and Pomegranate Salad 111
⟳ English Garden Salad 115
   English Pea Salad 71
⟳ Ethiopian Azifa Salad 112
⟳ Fall Harvest Salad 92
⟳ Fennel and Orange Beet Farro Salad 177
⟳ French Endive Salad 108
   French Tuna Niçoise Salad 105
⟳ Green Goddess Salad 70
   Grilled Romaine Salad with Warm Bacon Vinaigrette 160
⟳ Honey Mustard Grated Carrot Salad 84
   Italian Arugula and Lox Salad 104
⟳ Italian Caprese Salad 98
⟳ Italian Radicchio and Blood Orange Salad 107

Italian Tortellini and Bean Salad 179
⟳ Japanese Seaweed Salad 99
⟳ Jump into Summer Salad 91
⟳ Lebanese Tabbouleh Salad 110
⟳ Lemon Miso Quinoa Crunch Salad 139
⟳ Lemony Kale and Parmesan Salad 87
⟳ Lemony Orzo Pasta Salad 81
Loaded Roasted Potato and Kale Salad 186
Mexican Zesty Shrimp Aguachile with Peanuts 118
⟳ The Perfect Side Salad 80
⟳ Pesto Tortellini Salad 89
⟳ Protein-Packed Pasta Salad 142
⟳ Quinoa, Herbed Bean, and Olive Salad 175
⟳ Roasted Butternut Squash, Pumpkin Seed, and Feta Salad 141
⟳ Roasted Mushroom, Arugula, and Buckwheat Salad 182
⟳ Shaved Asparagus and Walnuts Salad 146
⟳ Shaved Brussels Sprouts and White Bean Salad 137
Simple American Pasta Salad 74
⟳ Simple Side Salad 64
⟳ Smoky Sumac and Freekeh Salad 183
⟳ Southwestern Quinoa Salad 176
Spicy Filipino-Style Ceviche 117
⟳ Spring Pea, Bulgur, and Goat Cheese Salad 185
Thai Green Papaya with Shrimp Salad 113
⟳ Tomato and Feta with Dill Salad 82
⟳ Turmeric-Spiced Cauliflower Salad with Tahini Dressing 145
⟳ Warming Winter Salad 93
Wurstsalat (Swiss/German Meat Salad) 103
⟳ Yogurt Cucumber Salad 83
Zesty Tuna Salad 76

Fruit Salads

⟳ Apple and Walnut Salad 189
⟳ Apple, Candied Pecan, and Orange Salad 190
⟳ Balsamic Berry and Mozzarella Salad 191
⟳ Barley and Lemon Chive Salad 184
⟳ Blood Orange, Avocado, and Pistachio Salad 192
⟳ Bold Berry Salad 188
⟳ Canadian Maple, Cabbage, and Cranberry Salad 116
⟳ Citrus Salad 193

◔ Delicata Squash and Apple Salad 200
◔ Fennel and Orange Beet Farro Salad 177
◔ Grilled Fig and Pistachio-Crusted Goat Cheese Salad 203
◔ Italian Radicchio and Blood Orange Salad 107
◔ Jump into Summer Salad 91
◔ Lime, Jicama, and Mango Salad 201
◔ Mediterranean Watermelon Salad 197
◔ Minty Melon Salad 196
◔ Orange Arugula Salad with Pistachio-Crusted Date Croutons 204
◔ Orange Pomegranate Salad 198
◔ Pear Gorgonzola Salad 199
◔ Roasted Grape and Barley Salad 194
◔ Spicy Pineapple and Mango Salad 202
    Thai Green Papaya with Shrimp Salad 113
◔ Tropical Fruit Salad 195

Picnic Salads

◔ Ambrosia 208
◔ Antipasto Pantry Salad 169
    Antipasto Salad 154
◔ Avocado and Crunchy Corn Salad 158
◔ Barley and Lemon Chive Salad 184
◔ Bold Berry Salad 188
◔ Canadian Maple, Cabbage, and Cranberry Salad 116
◔ Cherry Waldorf Salad 207
    Chicken Curry Salad 77
◔ Chickpea and Sunflower Smashed Salad 171
◔ Classic Macaroni Salad 151
◔ Creamy Egg Salad 75
◔ Creamy Green Macaroni Salad 178
    Crunchy Chicken Salad with Orange Ginger Dressing 155
◔ Edamame, Crispy Onions, and Farro Salad 147
◔ English Garden Salad 115
◔ Ethiopian Azifa Salad 112
◔ Fennel and Orange Beet Farro Salad 117
◔ Fiesta Grilled Sweet Potato and Cilantro Salad 161
    French Tuna Niçoise Salad 105
◔ German Radish Salad 102
    German Swabian Potato Salad 100
◔ Grape and Melon Mojito Salad 209

🍳 Greek Salad 66
🍳 Grilled Tofu with Soy and Ginger Salad 135
🍳 Italian Panzanella Salad 106
   Italian Tortellini and Bean Salad 179
🍳 Layered Bean Salad 153
🍳 Lebanese Tabbouleh Salad 110
🍳 Lemon Miso Quinoa Crunch Salad 139
🍳 Lentil Salad 167
🍳 Mayo and Mustard Potato Salad 150
   Mediterranean Potato Salad 174
🍳 Mediterranean Watermelon Salad 197
   Mexican Zesty Shrimp Aguachile with Peanuts 118
🍳 Middle Eastern Fattoush Salad 96
🍳 Minty Melon Salad 196
🍳 Nutty Strawberry Jell-O Salad 212
🍳 Pantry Pasta Salad 170
🍳 Pineapple and Carrot Sweet Slaw 206
🍳 Protein-Packed Pasta Salad 142
🍳 Quinoa, Herbed Bean, and Olive Salad 175
🍳 Southwestern Black Bean Salad 172
🍳 Southwestern Quinoa Salad 176
   Spicy Filipino-Style Ceviche 117
🍳 Spinach and Orzo Salad 157
   Sunflower Seed and Broccoli Salad 152
🍳 Three Bean Salad 168
🍳 Tropical Fruit Salad 195
🍳 Turmeric-Spiced Cauliflower Salad with Tahini Dressing 145
   Wurstsalat (Swiss/German Meat Salad) 103
   Zesty Tuna Salad 76

Sweet Salads

🍳 Ambrosia 208
🍳 Cherry Waldorf Salad 207
🍳 Creamy Filipino Coconut Salad 213
🍳 Fruity Cottage Cheese and Jell-O Salad 214
🍳 Grape and Melon Mojito Salad 209
🍳 Grilled Pineapple and Macadamia Nut Salad 211
🍳 Nutty Strawberry Jell-O Salad 212
🍳 Pear and Amaretti Cookie Salad 210
🍳 Pineapple and Carrot Sweet Slaw 206

Vegetarian Salads

Ambrosia 208

Antipasto Pantry Salad 169

Apple and Walnut Salad 189

Apple, Candied Pecan, and Orange Salad 190

Asparagus and Crumbled Egg Salad 86

Avocado and Crunchy Corn Salad 158

Balsamic Berry and Mozzarella Salad 191

Barley and Lemon Chive Salad 184

Bean and Barley Canadian Salad 90

Bean Fritters with Pesto Couscous Salad 143

Blood Orange, Avocado, and Pistachio Salad 192

Blushed Strawberry and Spinach Salad 72

Bold Berry Salad 188

Broccoli and Feta Salad 88

Canadian Maple, Cabbage, and Cranberry Salad 116

Cherry Waldorf Salad 207

Chickpea and Cucumber Dill Salad 156

Chickpea and Sunflower Smashed Salad 171

Citrus Salad 193

Classic Macaroni Salad 151

Cold Ramen Noodle Bowls 132

Cold Soba and Edamame Salad 180

Creamy Egg Salad 75

Creamy Filipino Coconut Salad 213

Creamy Green Macaroni Salad 178

Crispy Spring Salad 94

Crunchy Peanut Zoodle Salad 136

Cucumber, Tomato, and Goat Cheese Salad 85

Delicata Squash and Apple Salad 200

Edamame, Crispy Onions, and Farro Salad 147

Egyptian Barley and Pomegranate Salad 111

English Garden Salad 115

Ethiopian Azifa Salad 112

Fall Harvest Salad 92

Fennel and Orange Beet Farro Salad 177

Fiesta Grilled Sweet Potato and Cilantro Salad 161

French Endive Salad 108

Fruity Cottage Cheese and Jell-O Salad 214

German Radish Salad 102

⚻ Grape and Melon Mojito Salad 209

⚻ Greek Salad 66

⚻ Green Goddess Salad 70

⚻ Grilled Fig and Pistachio-Crusted Goat Cheese Salad 203

⚻ Grilled Pineapple and Macadamia Nut Salad 211

⚻ Grilled Tofu with Soy and Ginger Salad 135

⚻ Honey Mustard Grated Carrot Salad 84

⚻ Italian Caprese Salad 98

⚻ Italian Panzanella Salad 106

⚻ Italian Radicchio and Blood Orange Salad 107

⚻ Japanese Seaweed Salad 99

⚻ Jump into Summer Salad 91

⚻ Layered Bean Salad 153

⚻ Lebanese Tabbouleh Salad 110

⚻ Lemon Miso Quinoa Crunch Salad 139

⚻ Lemony Kale and Parmesan Salad 87

⚻ Lemony Orzo Pasta Salad 81

⚻ Lentil Salad 167

⚻ Lime, Jicama, and Mango Salad 201

⚻ Mayo and Mustard Potato Salad 150

⚻ Mediterranean Farro Bowls 124

⚻ Mediterranean Watermelon Salad 197

⚻ Middle Eastern Fattoush Salad 96

⚻ Minty Melon Salad 196

⚻ Moroccan Spiced Veggie Bowls 127

⚻ Nutty Chinese Noodle Bowls 131

⚻ Nutty Strawberry Jell-O Salad 212

⚻ Orange Arugula Salad with Pistachio-Crusted Date Croutons 204

⚻ Orange-Glazed Tempeh with Noodles Salad 138

⚻ Orange Pomegranate Salad 198

⚻ Pantry Pasta Salad 170

⚻ Pear and Amaretti Cookie Salad XX

⚻ Pear Gorgonzola Salad 199

⚻ The Perfect Side Salad 80

⚻ Pesto Tortellini Salad 89

⚻ Pineapple and Carrot Sweet Slaw 206

⚻ Protein-Packed Pasta Salad 142

⚻ Quinoa, Herbed Bean, and Olive Salad 175

⚻ Roasted Butternut Squash, Pumpkin Seed, and Feta Salad 141

⚻ Roasted Grape and Barley Salad 194

🍲 Roasted Mushroom, Arugula, and Buckwheat Salad 182
🍲 Roasted Veggie Bowls with Peanut Dressing 140
🍲 Shaved Asparagus and Walnuts Salad 146
🍲 Shaved Brussels Sprouts and White Bean Salad 137
🍲 Simple Side Salad 64
🍲 Smoky Sumac and Freekeh Salad 183
🍲 Southwestern Black Bean Salad 172
🍲 Southwestern Quinoa Salad 176
🍲 Spicy Pineapple and Mango Salad 202
🍲 Spinach and Orzo Salad 157
🍲 Spring Pea, Bulgur, and Goat Cheese Salad 185
🍲 Three Bean Salad 168
🍲 Tomato and Feta with Dill Salad 82
🍲 Tropical Fruit Salad 195
🍲 Turmeric-Spiced Cauliflower Salad with Tahini Dressing 145
🍲 Vegetarian Cobb Salad 134
🍲 Warming Winter Salad 93
🍲 Yogurt Cucumber Salad 83

Meat-Based Salads

Arugula Parmesan Crisps and Bacon-Wrapped Date Salad 159
Cali BLT Panzanella Salad 189
Chicken Curry Salad 77
Crunchy Chicken Salad with Orange Ginger Dressing 155
French Tuna Niçoise Salad 105
Grilled Romaine Salad with Warm Bacon Vinaigrette 160
Italian Arugula and Lox Salad 104
Italian Tortellini and Bean Salad 179
Korean Bun Noodle Salad 109
Laotian Ground Pork Larb 114
Loaded Roasted Potato and Kale Salad 186
Mexican Zesty Shrimp Aguachile with Peanuts 118
Spicy Filipino-Style Ceviche 117
Taco Salad 73
Thai Green Papaya with Shrimp Salad 113
Wurstsalat (Swiss/German Meat Salad) 103
Zesty Tuna Salad 76

Dressings

🍲 Balsamic Vinaigrette 46
🍲 Blue Cheese Dressing 52

 Classic Italian Vinaigrette 47

 Creamy Green Herb Dressing 53

 Creamy Tahini Dressing 54

 Fire-Roasted Tomato Dressing 55

 Honey Dijon Dressing 56

 Poppyseed Dressing 57

 Ranch Dressing 58

 Roasted Carrot Vinaigrette 48

 Sesame and Carrot Dressing 59

 Simple Citrus Vinaigrette 49

 Spicy Cilantro Vinaigrette 50

 Spicy Peanut Dressing 60

 Sweet Raspberry Vinaigrette 51

 Vegan Nutty Dressing 61

 Zesty Avocado Dressing 62

Table of Contents

INTRODUCTION 1

    About This Book. 1
    Foolish Assumptions. 2
    Icons Used in This Book 3
    Beyond the Book. 3
    Where to Go from Here 3

PART 1: BREAKING DOWN THE PARTS OF A SALAD 5

CHAPTER 1: **Salad Basics**. 7
    Types of Salads in This Book 8
        Bursting with greens. 8
        Starchy stars. 8
        Keeping it fresh and fruity 9
        Building salad bowls 10
        Pairing the plate with simple sides. 10
        Crafting party platters. 10
        Composed salads 10
        Sweet salads. 11
    Building a Salad Formula 11
        Greens. 11
        Grains 11
        Protein. 12
        Toppings 12
        Dressing 12
    Seasonal Considerations 12

CHAPTER 2: **Tools and Techniques**. 15
    Time-Saving Tools for Building the Perfect Salad. 15
    Plating a Beautiful Salad. 17
        Sharpening your knife skills. 18
        Making garnishes. 19
        Styling a salad or a bowl. 20

CHAPTER 3: **Going Shopping** 23
    Considering Your Options 23
    Making a List, Checking It Twice 24

PART 2: MAKING A PLAN 29

CHAPTER 4: **Boosting Nutrition with Salads** 31
    Recognizing the Nutritional Benefits of Salads. 32
    Packing a Lunchtime Punch. 34

CHAPTER 5: **Making Salad-Inclusive Meal Plans**.................35

    Savoring Seasonal Goodness...................................35

        Spring...36

        Summer...36

        Fall...37

        Winter..37

    Adding Foreign Flair with Salads from around the World..........38

    Planning Meals When you Follow a Special Diet..................38

        Mediterranean....................................39

        Gluten-free......................................39

        Lower carbohydrate...............................40

        Allergen-free.....................................40

PART 3: JUMP-STARTING YOUR SALAD JOURNEY.........43

CHAPTER 6: **Dressings**..45

CHAPTER 7: **The Classics**...63

CHAPTER 8: **Weeknight Side Salads**..................................79

CHAPTER 9: **Going Global**..95

CHAPTER 10: **Going Bold with Bowls**................................119

CHAPTER 11: **Plant-Forward Protein Salads**.......................133

CHAPTER 12: **Crowd Pleasers**..149

PART 4: GETTING CREATIVE WITH SALADS.................163

CHAPTER 13: **Pantry Stars**...165

CHAPTER 14: **Starchy Salads**...173

CHAPTER 15: **Fruity Concoctions**....................................187

CHAPTER 16: **Sweet Salads**...205

PART 5: THE PART OF TENS.................................215

CHAPTER 17: **Ten (or So) Tips for Building Salads in a Jar**........217

    Start with the Dressing.......................................217

    Know Which Vegetables Can Touch the Dressing 218

    Protect Delicate Ingredients with a Layer of Grains...............219

Pack a Protein Punch 219
Use Nuts and Seeds to Separate the Protein Foods from
the Toppings 220
Think Crunchy for Toppings. 220
Choose Hardy Greens. 221
Finish the Salad with Cheese 221

CHAPTER 18: Ten Homemade Salad Kits 223
Cobb Salad 224
Caesar Salad. 224
Cranberry and Pecan Salad 225
Rancher's Delight Salad 225
Southwestern Salad 226
Mediterranean Salad 226
Thai Salad 227
Harvest Salad 227
Carrot Crunch Salad 228
Orange Poppyseed Salad 228

CHAPTER 19: Ten Fun Ways to Add Crunch to a Salad 229
Croutons. 229
Crispy, Fried Onions 230
Sweet or Savory Nuts 230
Seedy Wonders 231
Roasted Garbanzo Beans. 231
Parmesan Crisps 231
Crunchy Noodles 232
Dried Fruit. 232
Crushed Chips 232
Crisped Bacon 232

**CHAPTER 20: Ten Common Types of Produce and
How to Keep Them Fresh.** 233
Greens. 234
Tomatoes 234
Cucumbers. 234
Mirepoix 235
Herbs. 235
Berries. 236
Tubers 236
Green Beans. 236
Citrus. 237
Salad Toppings. 237

PART 6: APPENDIXES 239

APPENDIX A: **Metric Conversion Guide**............................. 241

APPENDIX B: **Food Storage Guide**.................................. 245

APPENDIX C: **Food Safety Guide** 249
>   Food Temperature 249
>   Cross-Contamination 250

INDEX 253

Introduction

Raise your hand if you love salads? Me, too! It's easy to find yourself in a rut when crafting a salad, though. Bored with your greens? Not sure what to add to the salad? No enticing dressings on hand? Well, cozy up to this book and try something new! Knowing how to build a salad takes some basic knife skills, but most salads can be made quickly and with little extra effort. When you understand the basics of salad making and you have some key ingredients on hand, you're ready to get started. Whether they're made with greens, grains, or gelatin, salads are the perfect addition to any meal or occasion. Consider this book your go-to guide for all things salad, from dressings to desserts. So, grab your cutting board and your chef's knife and let's get chopping!

About This Book

The purpose of this book is to empower you to be a savvy salad maker, from whipping up a dressing, to understanding the variety of salads you can create, and even how to make a dessert salad. This book works with a lot of familiar ingredients and helps you explore new and unique salad ingredients. You discover different ways to cut and serve fruits and vegetables and how to serve up a salad fit for a party. I include recipes from around the globe, from Ethiopia to Thailand, as well as some Southern favorites and classics. This book introduces you to the hows and whys of salad making. Think of it as your own personal coach to crafting the perfect salad!

The recipes in this book are very straightforward and easy to understand. But here are a few notes on the ingredients, which apply to all the recipes:

>> All oven temperatures are given in Fahrenheit. If you're cooking with Celsius, you can find conversions in Appendix A.

>> Vegetarian recipes are marked with a tomato (🍅) in the Recipes in This Chapter lists, as well as in the Recipes in This Book.

>> Whole-fat dairy products are used, from milk to cheese to yogurt, unless specified otherwise in the ingredients list.

- » All eggs are large.

- » All flour is all-purpose flour, unless specified otherwise in the ingredients list.

- » All sugar is granulated sugar, unless specified otherwise in the ingredients list.

- » Salt is table salt unless specified otherwise.

- » Pepper is cracked pepper from a pepper mill, unless specified otherwise.

- » All dry ingredients are measured using nestled dry measuring cups, and all liquids are measured with clear glass measuring cups.

- » Lemon zest or orange zest refers to the outer colored peel, not any of the white pith.

- » Generally, canned, fresh, or frozen fruit can be substituted, unless the recipe specifies one or the other.

- » Many canned ingredients are used in this book. The recipes in this book were created with regular, not low-sodium, canned items. You can use low-sodium or regular, just be sure to test for the flavor profile prior to serving. If the canned item is packed in oil, the recipe will state this.

Within this book, you may note that some web addresses break across two lines of text. If you're reading this book in print and want to visit one of these web pages, simply key in the web address exactly as it's noted in the text, pretending as though the line break doesn't exist. If you're reading this as an e-book, you've got it easy — just click the web address to be taken directly to the web page.

Foolish Assumptions

In writing this book, I made a few assumptions about you, the reader:

- » Your time is important to you, and you want to spend less of it in the kitchen. You're looking for simple, easy, and straightforward recipes.

- » You may be an experienced cook or a beginner. Whichever end of the spectrum you fall on (or somewhere in between), this book is for you!

- » Healthy and delicious meals are important to you and your family, and you don't have a ton of time on your hands to make them.

If this sounds like you, you've come to the right place!

Icons Used in This Book

Throughout this book, you'll see the following icons in the margin. Here's a guide to what the icons mean:

TIP

The Tip icon marks information that can save you time and money as you're planning, shopping for, and prepping meals in advance.

WARNING

I use the Warning icon when I'm filling you in on important safety tips or tricks.

REMEMBER

When offering an important message or reminder, I use the Remember icon.

Beyond the Book

In addition to the book you have in your hands, you can access some helpful extra content online. Check out the free Cheat Sheet by going to www.dummies.com and entering **Salad Recipes For Dummies** in the Search box. You'll find a guide to greens, salad-making tips, and special tips for making delicious dressings.

Where to Go from Here

If you're struggling to put together salads or craft just the right salad combo, spend some time getting to know the process in Part 1. If you're looking for ways to add more salads into your daily routine, check out Part 2. Looking for that go-to salad dressing you can keep on hand? Head over to Part 3! Parts 3 and 4 have all the recipes — page through and earmark ones you're most curious about making. Then make a plan by drafting a grocery list for three or four days and give them a try! You'll even find tips on how long you can keep a salad prepped or fully made in your refrigerator. Part 5 includes The Part of Tens, which is always my favorite part in the *For Dummies* series!

I hope this book helps you fall in love with salads, if you aren't already. I want you to discover recipes here that you'll come back to for a lifetime. I want you to have confidence trying each of these recipes and using them for a special occasion or party. I hope that it's the first book you pick up when you're looking for ways to ramp up your veggies. Salads are fun and delicious, and they can be the star of any meal. So, break out your chef's knife and cutting boards and jump in to salad making!

1

Breaking Down the Parts of a Salad

Discover the different types of salads and how to craft a plated salad.

Stock your kitchen with the right tools and ingredients for simple salad preparation.

Explore the best ways to shop for and store produce.

Chapter **1**

Salad Basics

There are so many different salads out there, and they look and taste different around the world. Some salads are green with vegetables, some are fruity with gelatin, and some are starchy and ready for your favorite picnic. Don't let the diet industry fool you into thinking that salads are rabbit food. They can be filling, comforting, and downright delicious. Salads can be the star of the meal or complete the meal. They can be made in advance or in a split second. They can be complex or incredibly simple. And in this book, I share all my favorite salad recipes with you! This chapter walks you through the variety of salads that exist and takes a deep dive into how to craft your own salad formula. I wrap up with seasonal considerations.

If you were to ask any of my close friends what I'm known for making (besides homemade bread), they would say salads. Salads are my go-to contribution for any school function, picnic, potluck, or meal at a friend's house. I love how a salad can complement almost any meal, from sweet and sour chicken to spaghetti with marinara. I hope this chapter helps you sort through what constitutes a salad, how to build your own, and how to grab seasonal vegetables to craft your own. Let's get started!

Types of Salads in This Book

Defining the varying salads that exist can help with meal planning. Need a grain-centered side? Head to the Chapter 14. Need a quick side dish? Head over to Chapter 8. Knowing what constitutes a salad can help you craft your own recipe from your favorite ingredients. Here's a breakdown of the key salads I tackle in this book.

Bursting with greens

Greens, greens, and more greens, please. From arugula to kale to butter lettuce to iceberg. In many parts of the world, greens are synonymous with salads. You start with a base of your favorite greens and build from there. Think of Caesar, cobb, or taco salads. Each of these classics (see Chapter 7) begins with lettuce greens as the base.

Here are greens to get you started:

>> Arugula

>> Butter lettuce

>> Cabbage

>> Collard greens

>> Endive

>> Iceberg lettuce

>> Kale

>> Mustard greens

>> Romaine lettuce

>> Red leaf lettuce

>> Swiss chard

>> Watercress

Starchy stars

Grain- or starch-based salads are generally served cold and hold up well in the refrigerator for a couple of days. These are often great additions to potlucks and picnics, like potato salads, macaroni salads, pasta salads, bean salads, or whole-grain salads. You can find a lot of these salads in Chapters 12 and 14.

Here are common starches that are the base of starchy salads:

>> Barley

>> Beans

>> Bulgur

>> Farro

>> Freekeh

>> Pasta

>> Potato

>> Rice

>> Sweet potato

Keeping it fresh and fruity

Fruit salads can have fruits as the star of the salad or included in the salad. This is a balancing act of flavors — you need to know how to match up the right fruit for the right grain or green. Certain fruits will hold up better in a salad, whether it's green, grain, or sweet. You can find fruit-focused salads in Chapters 15 and 16.

Favorite fruits for salads include the following:

>> Apples

>> Berries

>> Cherries

>> Citrus

>> Dried fruits

>> Figs

>> Grapes

>> Mangos

>> Peaches

>> Pears

>> Pineapple

>> Pomegranate

>> Watermelon

Building salad bowls

Main dish salads typically have vegetables or greens with a protein and a starch, rounded out with some sauce or dressing. Bowls are essentially salads! Think about Taco Salad (Chapter 7) or Korean Bun Noodle Salad (Chapter 9) — they're both main dish salads in a bowl. If you love simple, bowls may become your new favorite meal! Check out Chapters 10 and 11 for filling main-dish salads.

Pairing the plate with simple sides

Salads don't need to be complex or have a lot of ingredients. In Chapter 6, I highlight simple dressings for delicious vegetables that essentially make them a salad. I grew up eating Yogurt Cucumber Salad as a frequent side dish at our dinner table — you can find that recipe in Chapter 8. Side salads can be a simple green salad (like lettuce, tomato, carrot, and a dressing), or they can be fresh or blanched vegetables that have been dressed with a vinaigrette or sauce. The sky's the limit for which vegetables you dress with a vinaigrette or creamy dressing, from asparagus to kohlrabi to potatoes.

Crafting party platters

Let's get ready for a party! So often, vegetables get overlooked for party platters, at least until charcuterie boards became the next big food trend. Dressed vegetables (whether roasted, grilled, or raw) add color, texture, and bold flavors to the best party platters. You can start with crackers, cheese, and meats, but don't forget the vegetables. You can create a burger board with prepared salads as sides, a taco salad board, or a creative salad bar with all your favorite toppings, which display like a charcuterie board or grazing table. They're fun for the whole family or a group of friends, and they give each person the ability to craft their own meal. Spread out a piece of parchment paper and layer on the toppings — your cleanup will be simple, too!

Composed salads

Composed salads are where the salad is arranged on a platter rather than in a bowl, and they often create symmetry with lines of vegetables. Cobb salads, tuna Niçoise salads, and chop house salads are often served with toppings individually displayed instead of being tossed. This is a great method for serving a salad at parties, because it allows guests to pick their favorite toppings and then serve the dressing on the side.

Sweet salads

Ready for a blast from the past? Break out the Jell-O and make a sweet salad! Why are gelatin-based salads called salads? The addition of fruit, vegetables, cottage cheese, or nuts makes them a molded salad, hence the classification and inclusion in this book. Although I only include a couple of my favorite molded salads, there are other sweet salads with fruit being the main character in the salad. Check out Chapter 16 when you're craving something sweet!

Building a Salad Formula

This section breaks down the basics of what's in a salad:

Greens + Grains + Protein + Toppings + Dressing = Quick Salad

From this formula, you can create your own bowl, salad bar, or basic side dish. Think of this as a guide, not a script. If you don't have one part, you can simply replace it with another or skip it altogether!

Greens

Lettuce is often the go-to green for a salad, but in many parts of the world, lettuce is hard to come by year-round. Hardier greens, such as kale, spinach, and Swiss chard, are great additions when the weather is cool.

As you read through this book, you will find a recurring theme: my love of fresh herbs. Fresh herbs are a green, just like lettuce. They're often stout with nutrition and the star of many salads around the globe. You can make a salad without lettuce. Start with 1 to 2 cups of greens as a base for salads.

Grains

If I want a salad to stick with me as a dinner entree, I always add a grain such as barley, bulgur, croutons, farro, or rice. I tend to make these in large batches and freeze them for easy additions. You can also buy convenient foods such as frozen grains or microwaveable pouches. If a salad calls for a specific grain, you can pretty much swap that grain for another. I use barley, bulgur, farro, freekeh, and rice in many salads and often swap them out with whatever I have on hand. As for amounts, ⅓ to ½ cup per salad makes for a serving.

Protein

Animal-based and plant-based proteins both play a key role in building a salad that will keep you full and not make you feel like you're on a diet or eating rabbit food. Stock your pantry or freezer with quick protein foods to help you build a satisfying salad. If you prep grilled meats or boiled eggs in advance, they can be enjoyed throughout the week in varying salads. You can buy convenience foods such as frozen prepared meats or lunch meats. Paired with a bed of greens, this can be a satisfying and quick dinner. Legumes, such as lentils, garbanzo beans, or edamame, add great texture along with fiber and protein. Nuts and seeds are also great options for boosting protein and nutrition in salads. When adding protein to a salad, think about standard serving sizes, such as 3 to 4 ounces for meats, ½ cup for legumes, and ¼ cup for nuts and seeds.

Toppings

Salad toppings are my favorite! I love a good crunch or sweet and salty addition. Adding in nuts, seeds, fried onions, fried noodles, dried fruits, and cheeses can elevate a salad. All you need is 1 or 2 tablespoons to finish off a salad. Keep items on hand in the pantry for these fun additions.

Dressing

You can make even a boring bowl of lettuce turn into something spectacular with the right dressing. Don't skimp on a good dressing, and keep your favorites on hand. When in hurry, make a Classic Italian Vinaigrette or the Simple Citrus Vinaigrette (both in Chapter 6).

Seasonal Considerations

When it comes to shopping and eating for the season, there are a few things to consider:

>> Certain plants are only available during certain times of the year, which can shape what is on your plate.

>> Running an oven in the summer may heat up your home and raise your electric bill, whereas in winter it may be advantageous.

>> Seasonal produce is often less expensive! If the food doesn't have to travel as far to make it to your plate, there are less costs associated with it.

TIP

COMMUNITY-SUPPORTED AGRICULTURE

Have you heard of a CSA box? In the United States, *CSA* stands for *community-supported agriculture,* and it has to do with local farmers putting together boxes of seasonal produce for consumers. Head to www.localharvest.org, enter your zip code, and you can find out about local farmers' markets and CSA boxes near you! Shopping seasonally and locally can mean fresher, more nutrient-dense produce. Plus, you're supporting local industry and decreasing the distance food travels to reach your plate.

With the use of greenhouses and hydroponics, more produce is available year-round in the United States, so you can find tomatoes in winter and berries throughout the year. Here's a condensed version of seasonal produce around the United States. Check with your local farmer's market to know what and when produce grows best for your area:

>> **Spring:** Apricots, artichokes, arugula, asparagus, butter lettuce, cabbage, citrus, fava beans, fennel, green beans, peas, pineapple, rhubarb, spinach, Swiss chard, watercress

>> **Summer:** Avocados, beets, bell peppers, berries, cherries, corn, cucumber, eggplant, grapes, green beans, melons, okra, peppers, stone fruit, summer squash, tomatoes, watermelon

>> **Fall:** Apples, broccoli, Brussels sprouts, cauliflower, cabbage, grapes, lettuce, pears, plums, turnips, winter squash

>> **Winter:** Citrus, collard greens, kale, kiwi, leeks, sweet potatoes, rutabaga, turnips, winter squash

Seasonal shopping will keep your salad budget in check!

REMEMBER

Chapter **2**

Tools and Techniques

N
ot another kitchen gadget, right? Overall, I am a fan of an excellent knife and solid cutting board for most salad recipes. Tools can help with storage and preparation techniques, and they can enhance your use of ingredients. If you have a tiny kitchen, I get it — be mindful of the tools you have. If you have more space to store kitchen toys and tools, then some of these may speak to you. In this chapter, I break down my favorite tools used in salad making and give you ways to ramp up your presentation skills when serving up salads. Break out your best chef's knife and let's get started!

Time-Saving Tools for Building the Perfect Salad

When you're making a salad, you don't need much — just a good knife, a solid cutting board, and a fun way to serve your salad. Those are the basics. But if you want to create some cool cuts or create salads that have roasted or spiralized vegetables, you may want to grab some more tools.

REMEMBER

If you love stocking up on kitchen gadgets, use this list as your excuse to cut loose! But you don't need all the fancy tools to make a successful salad.

You can find each of the following items (listed roughly in order from most important to least important) at Williams–Sonoma or on Amazon:

TIP

>> **Chef's knife:** A 6- or 8-inch chef's knife is ideal for many tasks when you're making salads. Top-rated knife brands include Mercer, Opinel, Victorinox, Wüsthof, and Zwilling.

One good knife is better than a bunch of cheap knives.

>> **Cutting board:** Many people keep a couple of different colored cutting boards on hand to identify what they use them for — for example, green for produce, red for meats, and white for breads. The advantage of plastic cutting boards is that they're usually dishwasher safe. Wood cutting boards are my favorite, though, and I oil mine with mineral oil every couple of weeks to keep the boards in top shape. IKEA has inexpensive wood cutting boards; if you keep wood cutting boards oiled, they'll hold up to heavy use. Plus, wood cutting boards break down in landfills, unlike plastic.

>> **Paring knife:** A paring knife is handy for smaller knife skills or hand peeling.

>> **Tongs:** A variety of sizes exist. In my kitchen, I keep three sets of tongs on hand for turning meats or tofu in a frying pan, grilling, and tossing salads.

>> **Salad spinner:** Salad spinners really help prolong the life of your greens. Wash them as soon as you get them and spin them dry to have lettuce ready any day of the week. OXO makes a small salad spinner that's a great starting point.

>> **Food processor:** Whether I'm whipping up a dressing or slicing vegetables, I regularly use my food processor. I've had a Cuisinart food processor for almost 30 years, and it still works well. You can find less expensive brands and more expensive brands — just consider your budget and what works best for your kitchen space.

>> **Bread knife:** A well-made serrated knife is great for slicing your favorite crusty French bread to serve with your salad.

>> **Vegetable peeler:** A multifunctional peeler can help with finite cuts, such as a julienne. The Deiss PRO Dual Julienne and Vegetable Peeler is well rated and can be found on Amazon.

>> **Mandoline:** I have owned both a giant mandoline and a hand-held version, but I prefer a simple hand-held mandolin. The OXO Good Grips Simple Mandoline Slicer is easy to use and is dishwasher safe. Be mindful and use the guard when using a mandoline — even experienced chefs have cut the tips of fingers on a mandoline.

TAKING ADVANTAGE OF A MULTICOOKER

Rice, grains, and legumes can be made to perfection in a multicooker like an Instant Pot. Making grains or legumes in bulk and freezing them will help future meals come together quickly. Multicookers are particularly useful when making bowls, which often have a grain, a legume, and raw and roasted vegetables with a dressing. Check out my book *Instant Pot Cookbook For Dummies* (Wiley) for tips on how to use a multicooker, as well as more than a hundred recipes.

>> **Spiralizer:** You can make *zoodles* (vegetable noodles) or curly fries in an instant with a spiralizer. The Spiralizer 7-Blade Vegetable Slicer has earned top marks but is bulky and large. Look for one that fits in your kitchen and works well for your preferred vegetables. Read the reviews before making a purchase.

>> **Blender:** Blenders can be good when whipping up larger batches of dressings or blending soups. If you have a food processor, you may not need a blender.

>> **Sheet pans:** While I was living in Europe, I fell in love with cast-iron and heavy black steel pans. I like how these are versatile and can be used on the stovetop, on a grill, or in the oven. Cast iron also heats evenly. Aluminum pans are lightweight and easy to use in the oven. USA Pan Bakeware is a good brand for lightweight baking sheets and can be found on Amazon.

>> **Digital thermometer:** Many people still cut into meat to check for doneness, but I always encourage the use of a meat thermometer to check for doneness instead. A digital thermometer is inexpensive (ranging from $15 to $30) and quickly registers temperature, giving you an accurate measurement of the food's internal temperature.

Plating a Beautiful Salad

We eat with our eyes first. I'm not suggesting that you need to create a work of art for the plate, but a little effort in meal presentation can encourage even a picky eater to try something new! In this section, I walk you through knife skills and preferred cuts when plating a salad, foods used in garnishing salads, and a variety of ways to style or plate a salad.

Sharpening your knife skills

Learning how to hold a knife and work a knife can make you much more efficient in the kitchen. In culinary schools, knife skills are always taught within the first week and emphasized throughout every course.

TIP

When holding a knife, move your hand up closer to the blade (see Figure 2-1). Have a firm grip, with your index finger over the spine of the knife and your thumb pressed on the flat part of the knife. This grip allows for a solid hold on the knife, creating a safer cut. Plus, it's more efficient when cutting.

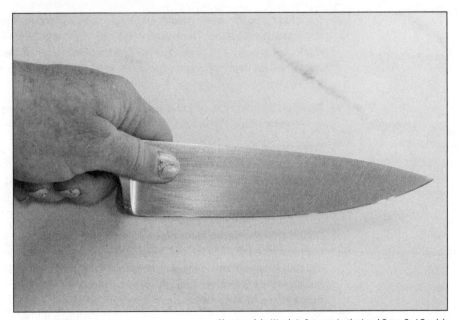

FIGURE 2-1:
How to hold a knife.

Photograph by Wendy Jo Peterson (author) and Grace Geri Goodale

WARNING

Keep your knives sharp! A sharp knife is less likely to cause an accident than a dull blade. A dull blade can slip with pressure, possibly causing injury.

When you're making a salad, a lot of time goes into the aesthetics (the way the salad looks), and although you may not realize it, taste is affected by presentation as well. If you have a giant chunk of bell pepper and a tiny piece of carrot, you may not even taste the carrot. The recipes in this book offer suggestions on how to cut each item, because it does play into the overall taste profile of the salad.

TIP

Here are common cuts I recommend throughout the book:

>> **Brunoise:** A French knife technique creating a tiny dice. Typically, a julienne is cut first, and then the matchsticks are cut into tiny dice. Often used with carrots, cucumbers, and bell peppers in salads.

>> **Dice:** Cutting food items into cube shapes, either small (¼ inch), medium (½ inch), or large (¾ to 1 inch). Often used with potatoes, sweet potatoes, butternut squash, kohlrabi, or beets.

>> **Grate:** Grab your box grater or hand-held grater to create a fine or large grated texture with hard vegetables. Carrots, beets, zucchini, or any hard fruit or vegetable can be grated.

>> **Julienne:** A French knife technique referring to long, thin strips that look like matchsticks. Often used with carrots, cucumbers, and bell peppers.

>> **Spiralize:** A continuous cut around food, creating a long spiral. This cut requires a spiralizer to make. Spiralizing is an attractive way to serve cucumbers, summer squash, carrots, or any other hard vegetable.

>> **Zest:** You can use a microplane or hand-held zesting tool to create a fine grate. Often used with citrus to extract natural oils found in the rind of the citrus peel. You can also zest ginger, carrots, garlic, shallots, onions, and chocolate.

Making garnishes

Garnishes can really elevate your salad game. The general rule is to garnish only with items that are already in your salad. So, you wouldn't want to garnish with parsley if there isn't any parsley in the recipe. In the recipes in this book, you'll find suggestions for garnishes.

TIP

Here's a simple list of garnishes that are frequently used in salads. Keep this list on hand when you want to elevate any dish, including salads:

>> Bacon (crumbled)

>> Berries (thinly sliced and fanned)

>> Cheese (grated)

>> Cilantro (sprig or chopped)

>> Cracked red pepper flakes

>> Cucumbers (sliced and fanned)

>> Dressings

>> Green onions (thinly sliced)

- » Lemon (zest or wedges)

- » Lime (zest or wedges)

- » Mayonnaise

- » Mint (sprig or chopped)

- » Orange (zest, wedges, or sliced)

- » Parsley (sprig or chopped)

- » Peanuts (chopped or whole)

- » Pine nuts

- » Pomegranate arils

- » Rosemary (sprig)

- » Sea salt (large flakes, such as Himalayan pink sea salt or Hawaiian black sea salt)

- » Sesame seeds (black or white)

- » Sriracha sauce

- » Sunflower seeds

- » Vinaigrette

- » Walnuts (chopped or whole)

Styling a salad or a bowl

Styling a salad can be simple or require a bit more patience and skill. The great thing about a salad is that there really isn't a wrong way to serve it up. You can tap into your creative side or simply toss and serve.

If you want to impress your guests or entice your family, try some of the following techniques:

- » **Charcuterie:** This technique is great for a crowd! Charcuterie refers to prepared cold cooked and cured meats served with cheeses, crackers, breads, fruits, and salads. You can also see salads served up this way, allowing for guests to pick and choose their favorite toppings. Many restaurants have started to refer to this as a *grazing table*. Spread out a piece of parchment paper, and let your kids help you artistically design your grazing table!

- » **Circular:** The salad is arranged to form a circle, with the center being the toppings (like cheese, croutons, or dressing). I like to place the dressing in a bowl in the center and create individual ingredients around the dressing bowl. It's best if the ingredients have bold colors that you want to highlight. This technique works well with the French Tuna Niçoise Salad in Chapter 9.

>> **Layered:** Think about the classic Layered Bean Salad (Chapter 12) — each ingredient is a layer, like a lasagne. Often these can be made as an overnight salad with ingredients that hold up well stored for a couple days in the refrigerator.

>> **Linear:** If you look at a round plate filled with lettuce, you use the toppings or additional ingredients to draw lines over the base ingredients. This technique is great in the Cobb Salad or Chopped House Salad (both in Chapter 7). You can also use this technique when making bowls (see Chapter 10).

>> **Tossed:** Tossing a salad may seem obvious, but there is a technique to this serving style as well. I recommend tossing your greens or salad with the dressing in a separate bowl; then place the tossed salad in the serving bowl. This evenly distributes the dressing and allows you to reposition the toppings on top of the dressed greens for presentation while your greens aren't swimming in dressing.

TIP

Styling salads can be fun with kids because it gives them a chance to play with their food! And playing with food can increase their likelihood of trying the food. Sounds like a winning match!

STORING SALADS FOR LATER

Salads can be prepped in advance (either by preparing individual ingredients or by preparing the salads themselves) and stored in the refrigerator. Glass jars (like Mason jars or Pyrex storage containers) are heat- and cold-safe. Glass is incredibly useful for storing meal-prepped items for dinner. Plus, they can be stacked neatly in the refrigerator for clean storage and food identification.

Studies have found that certain chemicals found in plastic can leach out and into the foods or beverages we eat; this connection has also been linked to health issues such as endocrine and fertility issues. For this reason, I recommend glass, aluminum, or silicone for food storage needs instead of plastic.

Chapter **3**

Going Shopping

Navigating grocery stores has changed a lot over the past couple of decades — even more post-pandemic. This chapter explores the different avenues you can take for grocery shopping and how to maintain a grocery list.

Considering Your Options

When it comes to grocery shopping, there are more options today than ever before. From mom-and-pop/local markets to big chains and discount clubs to farmers' markets and more, you can find what you're looking for in many places:

» **Mom-and-pop/local markets:** Supporting local markets can be a great way to find seasonal and local products close to home.

» **Big-box discount stores:** Costco, Sam's Club, Smart & Final, Target, and Walmart often have their own name-brand items for less. Because the stores are bigger, they can purchase in greater quantity, often delivering discounts for consumers.

» **Farmers' markets:** Check to see if your area has a farmers' market, selling locally sourced produce, meat, dairy, or baked goods. Often, local products are fresher, more nutrient dense (due to less travel time), and less expensive. Plus, you can meet local farmers and get to know their practices, which can make you feel more connected to your food and your community.

SHOPPING FOR BARGAINS

Regardless of where you shop, you can find — or at least look for — bargains. If you happen to have a bargain grocery store near you (such as a warehouse market or discount grocery chain), be sure to watch the weekly advertisements to find the best buys. Some of these markets require you to become a member to shop there.

The key to shopping for bargains is checking the unit price of an item (or the price per weight). Sometimes those big cans can *look* like they're a better deal, but if you check the unit price, they could be more expensive. Most markets list the unit price under the price of the item on the shelf. If you can't find it, you can calculate it yourself. To do so, divide the total price by the quantity. For example, if a 28-ounce jar costs $1.29, the unit price would be $1.69 ÷ 28 = $0.06 per ounce. If the 14.5-ounce jar is $1.19, the unit price would be $1.19 ÷ 14.5 = $0.08 per ounce. So, in this case, the larger can is the better price.

Finally, store brands are often a great way to get a bargain, but check the nutrition labels to make sure the product has the same ingredients as your favorite brand.

Remember: Be sure to check the sell-by date! It's easy to overlook that information and realize after you get home that your package of meat needs to be frozen or used by tomorrow! Bargain markets are notorious for selling items that are about to expire.

>> **Community support agriculture (CSA) boxes:** If driving to a farmers' market is tough, consider checking out a CSA. CSAs work in a few different ways. You might buy an annual or biannual share, where you receive various goods throughout the year. You might get a box delivered weekly, with whatever is grown seasonally and harvested that week. If you live in a larger agricultural area, you may even be able to choose what goes into your CSA box each week. My local CSA allows me to add on baked goods, meats, and even prepared foods. During the pandemic, it was a great way to minimize person-to-person contact and still support local farmers. To find out more about CSAs near you, head to www.localharvest.org.

Making a List, Checking It Twice

Before you head out to the grocery store, make a grocery list. Check your pantry, refrigerator, and freezer to make sure you don't have an item before buying extra. This list is a sample of items frequently used in this book for meal prep:

- **Produce**
  - Apples
  - Avocados
  - Bananas
  - Bell peppers
  - Berries
  - Broccoli
  - Cabbage
  - Carrots
  - Citrus
  - Garlic
  - Grapes
  - Herbs, fresh
  - Greens
  - Onions
  - Tomatoes

- **Protein**
  - Beef, ground or steaks
  - Chicken, breast, thighs, or whole
  - Pork, chops, loins, or roasts
  - Seafood, canned, shrimp, or fish
  - Tofu

- **Refrigerator/freezer**
  - Butter
  - Cheese
  - Eggs
  - Fruit, frozen
  - Milk
  - Sour cream

- Vegetables, frozen
- Yogurt

» Pantry staples
- Artichoke hearts, canned
- Baking powder
- Baking soda
- Beans, canned
- Flour
- Herbs, dried
- Olives
- Pickles
- Roasted red bell peppers
- Spices
- Sugar
- Sun-dried tomatoes
- Tomatoes, canned
- Vegetables, canned

» Grains
- Bread
- Couscous
- Farro
- Flatbread
- Oatmeal
- Pasta
- Quinoa
- Rice
- Tortillas

» Fats, oils, and condiments
- Avocado oil

- Barbecue sauce

- Coconut oil

- Honey

- Mayonnaise

- Mustard

- Olive oil, extra-virgin

- Nut butters

- Nuts (almonds, peanuts, walnuts)

- Seeds (chia, flax, hemp, pumpkin, sunflower)

- Soy sauce (low-sodium) or tamari (gluten-free)

SHOPPING SEASONALLY

Seasonal eating promotes health, because seasonal produce doesn't need to be shipped in from other countries. Eating in-season food makes an impact for the following reasons:

- **There's less transit time for the food to make it from the farm to your plate.** The decrease in transit time from farm to plate means produce has greater nutrient density. The longer produce is exposed to oxygen, heat, and light after harvest, the greater the loss of nutrients. Plus, less transit time is also healthy for the environment.

- **You eat an increased variety of produce throughout the year.** Sure, you might be eating a lot of corn, zucchini, and tomatoes in the summer, but you'll eat less of those foods throughout the winter, when you'll eat more broccoli, kale, winter squash, and citrus fruits. It balances out. When you rely on produce that's available year-round at the grocery store, you can easily get stuck in a rut of eating the same standbys throughout the year.

More variety in produce means a greater variety of health-promoting nutrients that aid in disease prevention. Although eating a few different types of fruits and vegetables throughout the year is better than nothing, getting a wide variety is the ultimate goal for good health.

2

Making a Plan

Revamp your lunchbox with simple lunchtime salad hacks.

Prep and plan with seasonal meal plans.

Discover ways to serve up tasty salads while meeting dietary considerations.

Chapter **4**

Boosting Nutrition with Salads

I n this chapter, I break down some of the health attributes of produce, from antioxidants to phytochemicals, and tell you how to boost nutrition with a salad at lunchtime.

Before I dive into this chapter, one note: This chapter is *not* about promoting diet-like behaviors. As a registered dietitian, I love the science behind foods and why certain foods can help you feel better. I also love knowing how to combine ingredients to make them taste amazing! Salads have the potential to add a lot of nutrients to your day and give you a way of combining a variety of ingredients in one bowl to get your daily dose of fruits and vegetables. If you're looking for a tasty way to get more vitamins and minerals, salads taste a lot better than a pill does!

REMEMBER

You don't have to be on a diet to enjoy a salad, and salads don't need to be linked to dieting.

Recognizing the Nutritional Benefits of Salads

Antioxidants, a key component of many plant foods, help slow down the process of oxidation, which occurs when your body's cells burn oxygen. This slowing of oxidation, in turn, decreases the amount of *free radicals* (unstable molecules) that cause damage to your cells, tissues, and DNA.

Antioxidants are a crucial part of your diet because you can't avoid oxidation entirely. Consider the many contaminants you're exposed to every day, from air pollution to sunlight to unhealthy foods. These types of contaminants can cause free radicals to gain speed in your body, damaging everything in their path and leaving you at greater risk of chronic conditions like heart disease and cancer.

Think about slicing an apple. Before you know it, the exposed flesh turns from white to brown. This browning occurs because of oxidation. But adding orange juice or lemon juice to the apple right after you slice it keeps it whiter longer because the antioxidant vitamin C in the juice protects the flesh.

Eating a diet high in antioxidants — such as vitamin C, vitamin E, and beta carotene — gives you better protection for your body and overall health. The benefits of antioxidants aren't just for apples. Here are some antioxidants and some common foods, including lots of fruits and vegetables, where you can find them:

>> **Anthocyanins:** Apples, blueberries, plums, purple grapes, red cabbage, strawberries

>> **Carotenoids (including beta carotene and lycopene):** Broccoli, cantaloupe, carrots, cilantro, collard greens, kale, romaine lettuce, spinach, turnip greens

>> **Catechins:** Apricots, black grapes, black tea, broad beans, cocoa, strawberries

>> **Coumaric acid:** Basil, berries, carrots, garlic, navy beans, peanuts, spices, tomatoes

>> **Quercetin:** Apples, onions, parsley, red wine, sage, tea

>> **Selenium:** Barley, beef, Brazil nuts, brown rice, chicken, fish, shellfish, turkey

>> **Vitamin C:** Asparagus, bell peppers (green and red), broccoli, cantaloupes, cauliflower, collard greens, grapefruits, kale, lemons, oranges, pineapples, spinach, strawberries, tangerines, tomatoes

>> **Vitamin E:** Almonds, chia seeds, collard greens, flaxseeds, mustard greens, peanuts, pine nuts, pumpkin seeds, spinach, sunflower seeds, Swiss chard, turnip greens, walnuts

>> **Zinc:** Beef, cashews, chicken, garbanzo beans, lentils, oysters, pumpkin seeds, sesame seeds, shrimp, turkey

TIP

The National Cancer Institute recommends adults get five to nine servings of fruits and vegetables daily. Eating a salad every day can increase your likelihood of meeting that goal.

Besides vitamins and minerals, plants also contain *phytochemicals* (healthy chemicals that offer your body benefits such as promoting heart health and working to prevent certain cancers). Research in this area is constantly evolving and uncovering a whole side of previously unknown health benefits. To date, certain phytochemicals have been shown to work as antioxidants, contain anti-inflammatory properties, and promote heart health.

TIP

Phytochemicals are the coloring pigment of your fruits and vegetables, so simply looking at the color of your fruits or vegetables can give you insight into which phytochemical you're consuming. Table 4-1 shows a few specific health benefits found in each color.

TABLE 4-1

Decoding Phytochemicals by Color

Color	Health Benefits	Foods
Blue or purple	Reduced risk of some cancers, improved memory, healthy aging	Blueberries, cabbage, eggplants, grapes (purple), and plums
Green	Reduced risk of some cancers, healthy vision, stronger bones and teeth	Arugula, bell peppers (green), broccoli, honeydew melon, kiwi, red leaf lettuce, romaine lettuce, and spinach
Red	Reduced risk of heart disease, reduced risk of some cancers, improved memory	Bell peppers (red), strawberries, watermelon (pink)
White	Reduced risk of heart disease, reduced risk of some cancers	Bananas, garlic, onions
Yellow and orange	Reduced risk of heart disease, reduced risk of some cancers, healthy vision, stronger immune system	Bell peppers (yellow and orange), carrots, oranges, watermelon (yellow)

Packing a Lunchtime Punch

With food prices increasing, you may be feeling more motivated to pack your lunch than to go out to eat. A packed lunch can save money, boost nutrition, and save time. Salads are the perfect lunch-box addition. Here are some ways to boost nutrition at lunchtime:

» **Keep it colorful.** When you're planning your lunches, let the rainbow be your guide — from purple cabbage and deep green kale to red tomatoes and orange carrots.

» **Include protein.** Canned tuna, canned salmon, canned sardines, boiled eggs, and shelf-stable salami sticks are all great ways to boost meat-based proteins in a salad. Also consider adding beans, nuts, and seeds to add protein power.

» **Bring on the toppings.** Salad toppers can add crunch — and they're tasty, too. (Check out Chapter 19 for a list of fun toppings!) Nuts and seeds are packed with fiber, protein, and vitamins. Plus, they're shelf stable.

» **Pile on the microgreens.** *Microgreens* (often referred to as "sprouts") include foods like broccoli sprouts, onion sprouts, and sunflower sprouts. They're bursting with antioxidants.

» **Bring on the beans.** Canned beans are shelf stable, packed with fiber and antioxidants, and boost your protein intake. They make for a great lunch-box salad addition.

Chapter **5**

Making Salad-Inclusive Meal Plans

Planning meals for the week ahead can help you stick to a budget, eat a greater variety of fruits and vegetables, and reduce food waste. Salads are a great addition to any meal — or they can be the main course itself! In this chapter, I offer weekly meal plans based on seasonal considerations, a global meal plan to explore the world through salads, and salads that work well even if you have special dietary needs. If you struggle with setting up a meal plan, let this chapter be your launch pad!

Savoring Seasonal Goodness

Produce availability changes with the seasons, so although it may be fun to eat strawberries in the winter, they may not taste as delicious as they would in summer. This applies to almost all fruits and vegetables. For instance, kale is a cool-weather crop — it can grow in the summer, but it actually has more bitters in the leaves in summertime, so I suggest using kale when the temperatures cool down.

In this section, I take out the guesswork and give you a week's worth of complete dinner ideas based on the seasons.

Spring

Try the following meal plan in springtime:

- » **Monday:** Mediterranean Watermelon Salad (Chapter 15), served with chicken and vegetable kabobs and flatbread
- » **Tuesday:** Spring Pea, Bulgur, and Goat Cheese Salad (Chapter 14), served with rotisserie chicken and steamed green beans
- » **Wednesday:** Crispy Spring Salad (Chapter 8), served with oven-roasted salmon or halibut and steamed rice
- » **Thursday:** Edamame, Crispy Onions, and Farro Salad (Chapter 11), served with green onion pancakes or egg rolls
- » **Friday:** Shaved Asparagus and Walnuts Salad (Chapter 11), served with pan-seared steaks and roasted potatoes
- » **Saturday:** Texas-Style Chopped House Bowls (Chapter 10), served with crunchy bread or garlic bread
- » **Sunday:** Crunchy Chicken Salad with Orange Ginger Dressing (Chapter 12), served as the main course

Summer

The following meal plan knocks it out of the park in the summer:

- » **Monday:** Orange Arugula Salad with Pistachio-Crusted Date Croutons (Chapter 15), served with baked fish and crusty bread
- » **Tuesday:** Grilled Fig and Pistachio-Crusted Goat Cheese Salad (Chapter 15), served with grilled salmon and steamed rice
- » **Wednesday:** Jump into Summer Salad (Chapter 8), served with rotisserie chicken and garlic bread
- » **Thursday:** Creamy Green Macaroni Salad (Chapter 14), served with pork chops and steamed broccoli
- » **Friday:** Cali BLT Panzanella Salad (Chapter 14), served with barbecue chicken
- » **Saturday:** Avocado and Crunchy Corn Salad (Chapter 12), served with spare ribs, sliced cucumbers, and garlic bread
- » **Sunday:** Roasted Veggie Bowls with Peanut Dressing (Chapter 11), served as the main course

Fall

Cozy up to the following meal plan when the weather cools off in the fall:

- » **Monday:** Pear Gorgonzola Salad (Chapter 15), served with oven-roasted chicken, sweet potatoes, and sourdough bread
- » **Tuesday:** Mediterranean Potato Salad (Chapter 14), served with grilled portobello mushrooms and sauteed spinach
- » **Wednesday:** Fall Harvest Salad (Chapter 8), served with meatloaf and mashed potatoes
- » **Thursday:** Loaded Roasted Potato and Kale Salad (Chapter 14), served with bratwurst
- » **Friday:** Grilled Romaine Salad with Warm Bacon Vinaigrette (Chapter 12), served with grilled steaks and crusty bread
- » **Saturday:** Roasted Butternut Squash, Pumpkin Seed, and Feta Salad (Chapter 11), served with rotisserie chicken and sauteed spinach
- » **Sunday:** Zesty Thai Steak Bowls (Chapter 10), served as the main course

Winter

Cozy up to the following meal plan in the winter:

- » **Monday:** Delicata Squash and Apple Salad (Chapter 15), served with lentil soup and crusty bread
- » **Tuesday:** Arugula Parmesan Crisps and Bacon-Wrapped Date Salad (Chapter 12), served with grilled steak and roasted cauliflower
- » **Wednesday:** Warming Winter Salad (Chapter 8), served with baked pork tenderloin
- » **Thursday:** Italian Tortellini and Bean Salad (Chapter 14), served with grilled chicken and steamed green beans
- » **Friday:** Cold Soba and Edamame Salad (Chapter 14), served with teriyaki chicken
- » **Saturday:** Creamy Green Macaroni Salad (Chapter 14), served with pork chops and steamed broccoli
- » **Sunday:** Lentil Salad (Chapter 13), served with grilled cheese and tomato soup

Adding Foreign Flair with Salads from around the World

If I were to pick one chapter in this book as my favorite, it would be Chapter 9. All the recipes in this meal plan are from that chapter, and in many ways, they're the most special to me. Traveling the world has been a culinary adventure for me over the years, and having a place to share my favorite recipes from around the world makes my heart happy!

TIP

If you're creating these recipes for your family, consider looking up the country and talking about cultural customs and geography while savoring the meal. Maybe you'll whet your own appetite for culinary exploration and adventure travel.

Try the following meal plan to get a tour of the world, one salad at a time:

>> **Monday:** Middle Eastern Fattoush Salad (Chapter 9), served with hummus, flatbread, and chicken kabobs

>> **Tuesday:** German Swabian Potato Salad (Chapter 9), served with bratwurst and braised cabbage or sauerkraut

>> **Wednesday:** Japanese Seaweed Salad (Chapter 9), served either with steamed rice and chicken teriyaki or with sushi and edamame

>> **Thursday:** Italian Arugula and Lox Salad (Chapter 9), served with baguettes with olive oil

>> **Friday:** French Tuna Niçoise Salad (Chapter 9), served with crusty French bread and butter or cheese

>> **Saturday:** Korean Bun Noodle Salad (Chapter 9), served with steamed spring rolls

>> **Sunday:** Ethiopian Azifa Salad (Chapter 9), served with flatbread and curried vegetables

Planning Meals When you Follow a Special Diet

If you or someone you love follows a special diet, this section may speak to you. Here, I offer a week of menus that support a Mediterranean diet, gluten-free living, and a lower-carbohydrate diet, as well as a diet for those with allergies.

REMEMBER

This section isn't meant to substitute medical advice, so if you have specific health concerns, talk to your doctor.

Mediterranean

Try the following meal plan for a Mediterranean diet:

>> **Monday:** Greek Salad (Chapter 7), served with sardines marinated in lemon and olive oil, flatbread, hummus, walnuts, and olives

>> **Tuesday:** Tomato and Feta with Dill Salad (Chapter 8), served with yogurt-marinated grilled chicken, roasted potatoes with lemon zest, and crusty baguettes

>> **Wednesday:** Lebanese Tabbouleh Salad (Chapter 9), served with hummus, *tzatziki* (cucumber yogurt dip), grilled lamb, and flatbread

>> **Thursday:** Italian Caprese Salad (Chapter 9), served with spaghetti with marinara and The Perfect Side Salad (Chapter 8)

>> **Friday:** Italian Panzanella Salad (Chapter 9), served with rotisserie chicken

>> **Saturday:** Moroccan Spiced Veggie Bowls (Chapter 10), served with crusty bread

>> **Sunday:** Mediterranean Farro Bowls (Chapter 10), served as the main course

REMEMBER

The Mediterranean diet consists mostly of fruits, vegetables, legumes, olive oil, nuts, seeds, olives, and seafood. Keep this in mind while menu planning. Check out *Mediterranean Diet Cookbook For Dummies*, 3rd Edition, which I wrote with Meri Raffetto (Wiley), for more information and loads of recipes!

Gluten-free

If you're gluten-free, check out the following meal plan:

>> **Monday:** Asian Ground Beef and Rice Bowls (Chapter 10), served as the main course

>> **Tuesday:** Tangy Barbecue Chicken Bowls (Chapter 10), served as the main course (***Note:*** Be sure to check that the barbecue sauce is gluten-free.)

>> **Wednesday:** Laotian Ground Pork Larb (Chapter 9), served as the main course (***Note:*** Be sure the fish sauce is gluten-free.)

>> **Thursday:** Korean Bun Noodle Salad (Chapter 9), served as the main course (***Note:*** Use a gluten-free breaded chicken, and be sure the fish sauce is gluten-free.)

>> **Friday:** French Tuna Niçoise Salad (Chapter 9), served as the main course

>> **Saturday:** Crunchy Southwestern Bowls (Chapter 10), served as the main course

>> **Sunday:** Zesty Thai Steak Bowls (Chapter 10), served as the main course

Lower carbohydrate

If you're limiting carbohydrates, the following meal plan may be a good fit for you:

>> **Monday:** Zesty Thai Steak Bowls (Chapter 10), served as the main course

>> **Tuesday:** Cobb Salad (Chapter 7), served as the main course

>> **Wednesday:** Chicken Curry Salad (Chapter 7), served inside butter lettuce with blackberries and sliced tomatoes

>> **Thursday:** Lemony Kale and Parmesan Salad (Chapter 8), served with grilled chicken and quinoa

>> **Friday:** Wurstsalat (Swiss/German Meat Salad; Chapter 9), served with sauerkraut and sliced cucumbers

>> **Saturday:** Blushed Strawberry and Spinach Salad (Chapter 7), served with grilled steak and Asparagus and Crumbled Egg Salad (Chapter 8)

>> **Sunday:** Mexican Zesty Shrimp Aguachile with Peanuts (Chapter 9), served with shredded cabbage and tortilla chips

Allergen-free

The top allergens are dairy, eggs, shellfish, fish, tree nuts, peanuts, wheat, soy, and sesame. Here are sample meals that address each of these concerns:

>> **Dairy:** Blood Orange, Avocado, and Pistachio Salad (Chapter 15), served with grilled fish and crusty bread

>> **Eggs:** Roasted Grape and Barley Salad (Chapter 15), served with barbecue chicken and rolls

>> **Shellfish/fish:** Lime, Jicama, and Mango Salad (Chapter 15), served with chicken or beef tacos and Fiesta Grilled Sweet Potato and Cilantro Salad (Chapter 12)

>> **Tree nuts/peanuts:** Avocado and Crunchy Corn Salad (Chapter 12), served with barbecue ribs and biscuits

» **Wheat:** Lemon Miso Quinoa Crunch Salad (Chapter 11), served with stir-fried chicken

» **Soy:** Protein-Packed Pasta Salad (Chapter 11), served with grilled steak and steamed broccoli

» **Sesame:** Edamame, Crispy Onions, and Farro Salad (Chapter 11), served with fried chicken

WARNING

Although I've done my best to list recipes that can be made without allergens, when it comes to food allergies, you *must* do your own research and read food labels. Allergens can appear in foods where you wouldn't expect them. You can find an extensive list to better identify potentially contaminated foods at www.kidswithfoodallergies.org/top-food-allergens.aspx.

3

Jump-Starting Your Salad Journey

Discover how to make the perfect salad dressing.

Make salad classics, from Caesar to the Wedge.

Ramp up your weeknight veggies with simple side salads.

Explore salads from around the world, from the Mediterranean Sea to Thailand.

Jump on the bowl bandwagon and foster family meals with salad bowls.

Pack a protein punch without relying on meat.

Kick up your picnic game with salads that can serve large crowds.

Chapter **6**

Dressings

RECIPES IN THIS CHAPTER

- ℧ **Balsamic Vinaigrette**
- ℧ **Classic Italian Vinaigrette**
- ℧ **Roasted Carrot Vinaigrette**
- ℧ **Simple Citrus Vinaigrette**
- ℧ **Spicy Cilantro Vinaigrette**
- ℧ **Sweet Raspberry Vinaigrette**
- ℧ **Blue Cheese Dressing**
- ℧ **Creamy Green Herb Dressing**
- ℧ **Creamy Tahini Dressing**
- ℧ **Fire-Roasted Tomato Dressing**
- ℧ **Honey Dijon Dressing**
- ℧ **Poppyseed Dressing**
- ℧ **Ranch Dressing**
- ℧ **Sesame and Carrot Dressing**
- ℧ **Spicy Peanut Dressing**
- ℧ **Vegan Nutty Dressing**
- ℧ **Zesty Avocado Dressing**

Dressings make a salad! You can put lettuce on a plate, and if you have a great dressing, you can call it a side dish. And if the dressing is a flop, your level of excitement instantly goes down. Over the years, I've traveled the globe and tried a variety of salad dressings, from warm vinaigrettes to creamy herb dressings to sweet and fruity vinaigrettes. In this chapter, I share a variety of my favorites — and ones that are too popular to leave out!

TIP

If you have lettuce on hand, dip a piece in to taste the dressing as you make it. This is a great way to adjust for seasonings from salt to vinegar. If a dressing is too sharp in vinegar, try balancing it with citrus or sugar to help balance the flavor profile.

TIP

When dressing a salad, place your greens in a bowl, drizzle your dressing over the top, and toss. Then plate your greens and add your favorite salad toppings, like goat cheese and toasted nuts.

My family's favorite dressings are the Roasted Carrot Vinaigrette, the Creamy Green Herb Dressing, and the Zesty Avocado Dressing. My dad declared that my Blue Cheese Dressing is the best he's ever tasted. I hope you feel the same about one of these dressings as well!

REMEMBER

You can always half or double any of these recipes to meet your needs.

Balsamic Vinaigrette

INGREDIENTS

⅓ cup balsamic vinegar

2 teaspoons brown sugar or honey

½ teaspoon sea salt

½ teaspoon cracked pepper

1 garlic clove, minced

1 tablespoon Dijon mustard

½ cup extra-virgin olive oil

DIRECTIONS

1 In a small saucepan, add the vinegar and brown sugar or honey. Heat over medium-low heat, stirring occasionally, for 5 minutes.

2 Remove from the heat and whisk in the salt, pepper, garlic, and mustard. While continuously whisking, drizzle in the olive oil.

PER SERVING: *Calories 134 (From Fat 122); Fat 14g (Saturated 2g); Cholesterol 0mg; Sodium 141mg; Carbohydrate 3g (Dietary Fiber 0g); Protein 0g.*

NOTE: Store in an airtight container in the refrigerator for up to 2 weeks.

NOTE: Balsamic vinegars hail from Italy and are made from Trebbiano grapes. Buy a good balsamic vinegar and store it in a dark, cool place for up to 3 years. Be sure to taste a freshly opened bottle so that you know how fresh balsamic should taste. Costco sells a good balsamic vinegar for less than $25.

VARY IT! Swap out half of the olive oil with walnut oil for a more robust flavor profile. Add chopped fresh herbs, such as basil, oregano, tarragon, or thyme. Replace the balsamic vinegar with white balsamic vinegar for a milder dressing.

TIP: Reducing the balsamic vinegar with a little bit of sugar thickens the vinegar and enhances the sweetness. You can continue reducing the vinegar to make a thick reduction, one without all the fillers and unnecessary ingredients found in store-bought varieties.

Classic Italian Vinaigrette

PREP TIME: ABOUT 5 MIN | COOK TIME: NONE | YIELD: 8 SERVINGS

INGREDIENTS

3 cloves garlic

¼ cup red wine vinegar or white wine vinegar

1 tablespoon lemon juice

1 tablespoon dried or 1 teaspoon fresh oregano

1 tablespoon dried or 1 teaspoon fresh parsley

1 tablespoon dried or 1 teaspoon fresh basil

¼ teaspoon cracked pepper

1 tablespoon Dijon mustard

1 teaspoon honey or sugar

⅓ cup extra-virgin olive oil

½ teaspoon sea salt

DIRECTIONS

1 In a blender, place the garlic, vinegar, lemon juice, oregano, parsley, basil, pepper, mustard, and honey or sugar. Blend until smooth, about 1 minute. While the blender is running, drizzle in the olive oil. Season with salt.

PER SERVING: *Calories 90 (From Fat 82); Fat 9g (Saturated 1g); Cholesterol 0mg; Sodium 141mg; Carbohydrate 2g (Dietary Fiber 1g); Protein 0g.*

NOTE: Store in an airtight container in the refrigerator. If you're using dried herbs, it'll keep up to 2 weeks; if you're using fresh herbs, it'll keep for 5 to 7 days.

TIP: Dried herbs help extend the shelf life of dressings while being cost effective and packed with flavor.

VARY IT! Add in roasted red bell peppers or sun-dried tomatoes for a zesty spin on this vinaigrette.

TIP: Taste the olive oil before using to make sure that it's fruity and fresh.

TIP: If you don't have fresh garlic, you can use 1 teaspoon granulated garlic instead.

Roasted Carrot Vinaigrette

PREP TIME: ABOUT 5 MIN	COOK TIME: 20 MIN	YIELD: 8 SERVINGS

INGREDIENTS

2 carrots, washed, trimmed, and cut into 1-inch pieces

¼ cup extra-virgin olive oil

2 cloves garlic

1 shallot, sliced

1 tablespoon fresh rosemary

2 teaspoons walnut oil

3 tablespoons sherry vinegar

1 tablespoon honey

½ teaspoon sea salt

DIRECTIONS

1 Preheat the oven to 400 degrees. Line a baking sheet with parchment paper.

2 On the parchment paper, place the carrots, olive oil, garlic, shallots, and rosemary. Roast until the carrots are beginning to brown and soften, about 15 to 20 minutes.

3 Transfer the roasted carrots (including the olive oil and rosemary) to a food processor or blender. Add the walnut oil, vinegar, honey, and salt, and blend until smooth, about 1 to 2 minutes.

PER SERVING: *Calories 89 (From Fat 72); Fat 8g (Saturated 1g); Cholesterol 0mg; Sodium 129mg; Carbohydrate 5g (Dietary Fiber 1g); Protein 0g.*

NOTE: Store in an airtight container in the refrigerator for 5 to 7 days.

NOTE: Roasting vegetables elevates the flavor exponentially. This vinaigrette is delicious over grilled fish or chicken, pasta, or your favorite baby greens.

TIP: If you can't find walnut oil, add 4 walnuts and increase the amount of olive oil by 1 teaspoon.

VARY IT! Replace the rosemary with tarragon or thyme.

Simple Citrus Vinaigrette

INGREDIENTS

2 tablespoons fresh
lemon juice

¼ cup fresh orange juice

1 tablespoon white wine
vinegar or champagne vinegar

2 teaspoons Dijon mustard

3 tablespoons brown sugar
or honey

¼ teaspoon garlic powder

¼ teaspoon sea salt

¼ teaspoon cracked pepper

¼ cup extra-virgin olive oil

DIRECTIONS

1   In a medium bowl, whisk together the lemon juice, orange juice, vinegar, mustard, brown sugar or honey, garlic powder, salt, and pepper. While continuing to whisk, drizzle in the olive oil until combined.

PER SERVING: *Calories 86 (From Fat 61); Fat 7g (Saturated 1g); Cholesterol 0mg; Sodium 75mg; Carbohydrate 6g (Dietary Fiber 0g); Protein 0g.*

NOTE: Store in an airtight container in the refrigerator for 5 to 7 days.

VARY IT! Each variety of citrus will lend a different flavor profile. Try using the juice of a Meyer lemon or Cara Cara oranges for a sweet twist. Replace the orange juice with grapefruit juice or tangerine juice.

VARY IT! Chives, shallots, and tarragon are great additions to this dressing.

TIP: Taste as you go. If your lemon is very sour, add a pinch more sugar. If your oranges are super sweet, reduce the sugar. Find the flavor profile that suits your taste buds!

Spicy Cilantro Vinaigrette

PREP TIME: ABOUT 5 MIN	COOK TIME: 20 MIN	YIELD: 16 SERVINGS

INGREDIENTS

1 cup fresh cilantro

1 jalapeño, seeds removed

1 small garlic clove

2 limes, zested and juiced

2 teaspoons sugar or honey

½ teaspoon cumin

¼ teaspoon coriander

1 tablespoon white wine vinegar

¾ teaspoon sea salt

½ cup avocado oil or extra-virgin olive oil

DIRECTIONS

1 In a food process or blender, place the cilantro, jalapeño, garlic, lime zest, lime juice, sugar or honey, cumin, coriander, vinegar, and salt; blend for 1 minute. Drizzle in the avocado oil or olive oil while blending. Continue to blend until smooth, about 1 to 2 minutes.

PER SERVING: *Calories 64 (From Fat 61); Fat 7g (Saturated 1g); Cholesterol 0mg; Sodium 89mg; Carbohydrate 1g (Dietary Fiber 0g); Protein 0g.*

NOTE: Store in an airtight container in the refrigerator for 5 to 7 days.

TIP: You can use granulated garlic in place of fresh garlic — just use ¼ teaspoon ground garlic instead.

VARY IT! If cilantro isn't your favorite herb, you can use fresh mint and/or parsley instead.

Sweet Raspberry Vinaigrette

PREP TIME: ABOUT 10 MIN	COOK TIME: NONE	YIELD: 16 SERVINGS

INGREDIENTS

1 cup fresh or frozen (thawed) raspberries

2 tablespoons sugar

¼ cup white balsamic vinegar or red wine vinegar

1 teaspoon Dijon mustard

¼ teaspoon sea salt

½ cup extra-virgin olive oil or avocado oil

DIRECTIONS

1 In a food processor or blender, place the raspberries, sugar, vinegar, mustard, and salt; blend for 1 minute. While continuing to blend, drizzle in the olive oil or avocado oil.

PER SERVING: *Calories 71 (From Fat 61); Fat 7g (Saturated 1g); Cholesterol 0mg; Sodium 33mg; Carbohydrate 3g (Dietary Fiber 1g); Protein 0g.*

NOTE: Store in an airtight container in the refrigerator for 3 to 5 days.

NOTE: If you use frozen raspberries, be sure to defrost them first, or else you'll make a vinaigrette smoothie! Frozen raspberries are great to use all year long!

VARY IT! Replace the vinegar with 2 tablespoons sherry vinegar, which has a smooth and great flavor profile and enhances the sweetness. My favorite brands are O Aged Sherry Vinegar and Napa Valley Naturals Sherry Vinegar.

TIP: Serve with your favorite spinach salad or over grilled chicken breasts.

Blue Cheese Dressing

PREP TIME: ABOUT 10 MIN	COOK TIME: NONE	YIELD: 12 SERVINGS

INGREDIENTS

3 ounces blue cheese

½ cup whole-fat Greek yogurt

⅓ cup real mayonnaise

2 tablespoons chopped fresh parsley

1 tablespoon lemon juice or white wine vinegar

½ teaspoon sea salt

½ teaspoon cracked pepper

¼ teaspoon garlic powder

¼ cup buttermilk (or more as needed to thin out to desired consistency)

DIRECTIONS

1 In a medium bowl, add the blue cheese; mash with a fork. Whisk or stir in the yogurt and mayonnaise until combined. Stir in the parsley, lemon juice or vinegar, salt, pepper, and garlic powder. Drizzle in the buttermilk while whisking to your desired consistency.

PER SERVING: *Calories 60 (From Fat 42); Fat 5g (Saturated 2g); Cholesterol 8mg; Sodium 235mg; Carbohydrate 2g (Dietary Fiber 0g); Protein 3g.*

NOTE: Store in an airtight container in the refrigerator up to 5 days.

TIP: Serve as a dip for vegetables, wings, or on your favorite burgers.

Creamy Green Herb Dressing

INGREDIENTS

2 tablespoons extra-virgin olive oil

2 cloves garlic, chopped

1 shallot, thinly sliced

½ cup whole Greek yogurt

½ cup buttermilk

1 cup fresh parsley

¼ cup fresh basil

¼ cup fresh dill

¼ cup fresh mint

½ lemon, zested and juiced

½ teaspoon sea salt

¼ teaspoon cracked pepper

DIRECTIONS

1 In a small skillet, heat the olive oil, garlic, and shallots over medium–low heat for 2 minutes. Set aside.

2 In a blender or food processor, add the yogurt, buttermilk, parsley, basil, dill, mint, lemon zest, lemon juice, salt, and pepper; blend for 30 seconds. Drizzle in the olive oil, garlic, and shallots, and continue to blend until creamy and smooth, about 1 minute. Taste for seasoning, and adjust the salt and pepper as desired.

PER SERVING: Calories 30 (From Fat 20); Fat 2g (Saturated 1g); Cholesterol 1mg; Sodium 70mg; Carbohydrate 2g (Dietary Fiber 0g); Protein 1g.

NOTE: Store in an airtight container in the refrigerator up to 3 days.

NOTE: This dressing is similar to a green goddess dressing. You can make it thicker by using all Greek yogurt or thin it out by adding in more buttermilk instead of Greek yogurt.

VARY IT! This recipe is versatile! Do you have other herbs on hand? Use chives, cilantro, rosemary, tarragon, or any other green herb you enjoy. Make it more zesty with lime juice, a jalapeño, and cilantro for a Tex-Mex version. Channel your inner Frenchman by using white wine vinegar instead of lemon and using chives, tarragon, and thyme.

TIP: Do you want to make a dip? Replace the buttermilk with sour cream. This is my daughter's favorite veggie dip. We serve it with bell peppers, carrots, cucumbers, jicama, and tomatoes.

Creamy Tahini Dressing

| PREP TIME: ABOUT 5 MIN | COOK TIME: NONE | YIELD: 8 SERVINGS |

INGREDIENTS

½ lemon, juiced

3 tablespoons tahini

1 clove garlic, minced

2 teaspoons honey

1 teaspoon Dijon mustard

1 teaspoon sea salt

½ teaspoon cracked pepper

2 tablespoons water

⅓ cup extra-virgin olive oil

DIRECTIONS

1 In a medium bowl, whisk together the lemon juice, tahini, garlic, honey, mustard, salt, pepper, and water. While whisking, drizzle in the olive oil, and whisk until combined.

PER SERVING: *Calories 119 (From Fat 108); Fat 12g (Saturated 2g); Cholesterol 0mg; Sodium 248mg; Carbohydrate 3g (Dietary Fiber 1g); Protein 1g.*

NOTE: Store in an airtight container in the refrigerator for 3 to 5 days.

NOTE: Tahini is sesame butter and, like most nuts, can become rancid. Store it in your refrigerator, and be sure to taste it before using to make sure it hasn't become rancid.

TIP: Serve over roasted vegetables, like carrots or cauliflower.

Fire-Roasted Tomato Dressing

PREP TIME: ABOUT 5 MIN | COOK TIME: 20 MIN | YIELD: 8 SERVINGS

INGREDIENTS

4 Roma tomatoes, cut in half lengthwise

4 cloves garlic

1 shallot

¼ cup extra-virgin olive oil

2 tablespoons red wine vinegar

1 teaspoon lemon juice

½ teaspoon sea salt

½ teaspoon cracked pepper

1 teaspoon dried tarragon or thyme

DIRECTIONS

1 Preheat the oven to 400 degrees.

2 In a baking dish, place the tomatoes, garlic, and shallot. Drizzle with the olive oil. Bake for 20 minutes.

3 Transfer the roasted vegetables to a blender and pulse for 30 seconds. Add the vinegar, lemon juice, salt, pepper, and tarragon or thyme. Blend to the desired consistency, about 1 minute. Serve warm or chilled in the refrigerator.

PER SERVING: *Calories 70 (From Fat 61); Fat 7g (Saturated 1g); Cholesterol 0mg; Sodium 120mg; Carbohydrate 2g (Dietary Fiber 0g); Protein 0g.*

NOTE: Store in an airtight container in the refrigerator for 3 to 5 days.

NOTE: Canned fire-roasted tomatoes can be used in this recipe. If the recipe tastes too acidic (canned tomatoes can sometimes be more acidic), add in 1 to 2 teaspoons sugar.

VARY IT! Canola oil can be used in place of olive oil for a milder flavor.

TIP: This recipe is delicious on taco salads or served warm on a spinach and boiled egg salad.

Honey Dijon Dressing

PREP TIME: ABOUT 5 MIN	COOK TIME: NONE	YIELD: 8 SERVINGS

INGREDIENTS

3 tablespoons apple cider vinegar

1 tablespoon lemon juice

1 garlic clove, minced

3 tablespoons Dijon mustard

¼ teaspoon cracked pepper

½ teaspoon sea salt

2 tablespoons honey

⅓ cup olive oil or avocado oil

DIRECTIONS

1 In a medium bowl, whisk together the vinegar, lemon juice, garlic, mustard, pepper, salt, and honey. While whisking continuously, drizzle in the olive oil or avocado oil. Sample on a piece of lettuce and adjust for salt or honey, as desired.

PER SERVING: *Calories 101 (From Fat 82); Fat 9g (Saturated 1g); Cholesterol 0mg; Sodium 182mg; Carbohydrate 5g (Dietary Fiber 0g); Protein 0g.*

NOTE: Store in an airtight container. If you're using dried herbs, the dressing will keep in the refrigerator up to 2 weeks; if you're using fresh herbs, it'll keep for 5 to 7 days.

NOTE: If you don't have fresh garlic on hand, opt for ½ teaspoon granulated garlic powder.

NOTE: Not all mustards are created equal. Dijon mustards are creamier than bright yellow mustards and contain less vinegar. The taste is often spicier than prepared mustards. Grey Poupon and Maille Dijon Original were used for most recipes calling for Dijon mustard in this book.

VARY IT! Replace the honey with maple syrup. You can also use canola oil in place of the olive oil or avocado oil for a milder flavor.

TIP: Honey mustard dressing can vary based on sweetness and spiciness. Add more honey for a sweeter version, or use a milder prepared mustard for less spice.

Poppyseed Dressing

PREP TIME: ABOUT 5 MIN | COOK TIME: NONE | YIELD: 8 SERVINGS

INGREDIENTS

½ cup real mayonnaise

¼ cup whole milk

3 tablespoons sugar

2 tablespoons white wine vinegar

¼ teaspoon onion powder

¼ teaspoon dry mustard

1 tablespoon poppy seeds

⅛ teaspoon sea salt

DIRECTIONS

1 In a Mason jar, place all the ingredients. Secure with a lid, and shake for 1 minute to combine.

PER SERVING: *Calories 87 (From Fat 50); Fat 6g (Saturated 1g); Cholesterol 5mg; Sodium 138mg; Carbohydrate 9g (Dietary Fiber 0g); Protein 1g.*

NOTE: Store in an airtight container in the refrigerator for 3 to 5 days.

NOTE: Poppyseed dressing is commonly served with fruit-focused salads and on fruit salads. This dressing is a bit sweeter than most, and it can be made even sweeter with more sugar; you can reduce the sweetness by reducing the amount of sugar used or by using a sugar alternative like Stevia.

Ranch Dressing

PREP TIME: ABOUT 10 MIN	COOK TIME: NONE	YIELD: 16 SERVINGS

INGREDIENTS

3 tablespoons extra-virgin olive oil

2 cloves garlic

1 shallot

2 tablespoons chopped basil

¼ cup chopped parsley

1 tablespoon dried or 3 tablespoons fresh dill

1 tablespoon lemon juice

1 tablespoon Dijon mustard

1 cup real mayonnaise

½ cup sour cream or Greek yogurt

½ cup buttermilk

1 teaspoon sea salt

1 teaspoon cracked pepper

DIRECTIONS

1 In a small skillet, heat the olive oil, garlic, and shallot over medium-low heat for 2 minutes. Set aside.

2 In a blender or food processor, place the basil, parsley, dill, lemon juice, mustard, mayonnaise, sour cream or yogurt, buttermilk, salt, and pepper; blend for 30 seconds. Drizzle in the olive oil (including the garlic and shallots) and continue to blend until creamy and smooth, about 1 minute. Taste for seasoning, and adjust the salt and pepper as desired.

PER SERVING: *Calories 101 (From Fat 82); Fat 9g (Saturated 2g); Cholesterol 8mg; Sodium 246mg; Carbohydrate 5g (Dietary Fiber 0g); Protein 1g.*

NOTE: Store in an airtight container in the refrigerator for 3 to 5 days.

NOTE: Creamy ranch dressing is quintessential in American cuisine. You can use dried herbs in place of fresh; just use 2 teaspoons dried basil and 2 tablespoons dried parsley instead.

VARY IT! Add in 1 tablespoon of taco seasoning for a creamy taco salad!

TIP: Do you want to make a dip? Swap out the buttermilk with more sour cream. Serve with your favorite raw vegetables.

Sesame and Carrot Dressing

PREP TIME: ABOUT 10 MIN	COOK TIME: NONE	YIELD: 10 SERVINGS

INGREDIENTS

2 carrots, grated

3 tablespoons soy sauce
or tamari

1 tablespoon sesame oil

¼ cup rice wine vinegar

2 teaspoons honey or sugar

⅓ cup avocado oil

2 tablespoons sesame seeds

1 green onion, thinly sliced

DIRECTIONS

1 In a food processor or blender, place the carrots, soy sauce or tamari, sesame oil, vinegar, and honey or sugar; blend for 30 seconds. Drizzle in the avocado oil while continuing to blend until smooth. Transfer to a Mason jar, and stir in the sesame seeds and green onion.

PER SERVING: *Calories 100 (From Fat 85); Fat 9g (Saturated 1g); Cholesterol 0mg; Sodium 282mg; Carbohydrate 3g (Dietary Fiber 1g); Protein 1g.*

NOTE: Store in an airtight container in the refrigerator for 3 to 5 days.

VARY IT! Canola, peanut, or safflower oil can be used in place of avocado oil.

TIP: Serve with fresh spring rolls, tossed with butter lettuce, or over chicken and rice bowls.

Spicy Peanut Dressing

PREP TIME: ABOUT 5 MIN | COOK TIME: NONE | YIELD: 16 SERVINGS

INGREDIENTS

½ cup creamy peanut butter

1 tablespoon lime juice

3 tablespoons rice wine vinegar

2 tablespoons soy sauce or tamari

1 tablespoon Sriracha or red chili sauce

1 tablespoon sugar or honey

1 clove garlic

¼ cup chopped cilantro

¼ cup roasted peanut oil or avocado oil

DIRECTIONS

1 In a blender or food processor, place the peanut butter, lime juice, vinegar, soy sauce or tamari, Sriracha or red chili sauce, sugar or honey, garlic, and cilantro; blend for 1 minute. Drizzle in the peanut oil or avocado oil while continuing to blend.

PER SERVING: *Calories 82 (From Fat 67); Fat 7g (Saturated 1g); Cholesterol 0mg; Sodium 38mg; Carbohydrate 3g (Dietary Fiber 1g); Protein 2g.*

NOTE: Store in an airtight container in the refrigerator for 5 to 7 days.

NOTE: Sriracha is a specific brand of hot chili sauce, frequently found in the Asian section of grocery stores. If you can't find it, substitute hot sauce.

NOTE: Move over olive oil — roasted peanut oil is moving in! Rich in vitamin E, this robust oil is perfect for salad dressings or light sautéing. Look for a cold-pressed peanut oil or a roasted peanut oil for the best flavor profile.

TIP: If you're using natural peanut butter, be sure to stir it before adding it to the recipe. This recipe was prepared with regular creamy peanut butter.

TIP: Serve with grilled chicken, roasted carrots, sweet potatoes, or fresh spring rolls.

Vegan Nutty Dressing

PREP TIME: ABOUT 25 MIN   COOK TIME: NONE   YIELD: 16 SERVINGS

INGREDIENTS

1 cup dry roasted peanuts or cashews

2 cups warm water (for soaking)

2 tablespoons rice wine vinegar

2 tablespoons tamari

1 shallot, chopped

1 clove garlic, chopped

1 tablespoon fresh lemon juice

2 teaspoons maple syrup

½ teaspoon crushed red pepper flakes

1 teaspoon sea salt

⅓ cup extra-virgin olive oil

DIRECTIONS

1 In a medium bowl, add the nuts and warm water; soak for 20 minutes, and then drain completely.

2 In a food processor or blender, place the soaked nuts, vinegar, tamari, shallot, garlic, lemon juice, maple syrup, red pepper flakes, and salt; blend for 1 minute. Add the olive oil in a slow drizzle while continuing to blend until creamy. Add water if you want a thinner consistency.

PER SERVING: *Calories 98 (From Fat 81); Fat 9g (Saturated 1g); Cholesterol 0mg; Sodium 317mg; Carbohydrate 3g (Dietary Fiber 1g); Protein 2g.*

NOTE: Store in an airtight container in the refrigerator for 5 to 7 days.

NOTE: Soaked nuts create a uniquely creamy texture in a vegan dressing.

VARY IT! Add in 1 to 2 tablespoons fresh herbs and 1 tablespoon nutritional yeast for a ranch-like flavor profile. Add in a pinch of curry powder for Indian flavor.

Zesty Avocado Dressing

PREP TIME: ABOUT 5 MIN	COOK TIME: NONE	YIELD: 16 SERVINGS

INGREDIENTS

1 large Hass avocado

1 lime, zested and juiced, or 2 tablespoons lemon juice

2 teaspoons seeded and minced jalapeño (or more if desired)

¼ cup sour cream, Greek yogurt, or buttermilk

½ cup chopped fresh cilantro

½ teaspoon ground cumin

¼ teaspoon onion powder

¼ teaspoon garlic powder

½ teaspoon sea salt

¼ cup water

¼ cup extra-virgin olive oil or avocado oil

DIRECTIONS

1 In a blender or food processor, place the avocado; lime zest and lime juice (or the lemon juice); jalapeño; sour cream, yogurt, or buttermilk; cilantro; cumin; onion powder; garlic powder; salt; and water. Blend for 1 minute. Drizzle in the olive oil or avocado oil while continuing to blend for 30 seconds. Taste for seasoning and adjust with salt, as desired.

PER SERVING: Calories 52 (From Fat 49); Fat 5g (Saturated 1g); Cholesterol 2mg; Sodium 62mg; Carbohydrate 1g (Dietary Fiber 1g); Protein 0g.

NOTE: Store in an airtight container in the refrigerator for 2 to 3 days.

NOTE: If cilantro isn't your favorite herb, you can replace it with parsley or skip it all together.

VARY IT! Cumin and cilantro are typical Mexican flavors. If you want to swing over to the Mediterranean, use lemon instead of the lime, parsley instead of the cilantro, and coriander instead of the cumin.

TIP: Do you want to make a dip? Skip the water and olive oil or avocado oil to keep this a thick and creamy dip instead!

Chapter **7**

The Classics

RECIPES IN THIS CHAPTER

- Simple Side Salad
- Caesar Salad
- Greek Salad
- Crispy Bacon Wedge Salad
- Chopped House Salad
- Cobb Salad
- Green Goddess Salad
- English Pea Salad
- Blushed Strawberry and Spinach Salad
- Taco Salad
- Simple American Pasta Salad
- Creamy Egg Salad
- Zesty Tuna Salad
- Chicken Curry Salad

There's a reason we call them classics: From the Cobb Salad to the Chopped House Salad, classic salads have held the test of time. When researching and testing recipes for this chapter, I sampled many salads at restaurants and at friends' homes. These recipes include salads from around the world — from the Mexican classic Caesar Salad to the authentic Greek Salad. Now you can make them at home, too!

Classic salads are a great addition to a simple meal of grilled steak, baked chicken, or pan-seared salmon. Simply add bread, a baked potato, rice, or beans, and you have a complete meal in 30 minutes.

Also included are three of my favorite salads that go great between two pieces of bread: Creamy Egg Salad, Zesty Tuna Salad, and Chicken Curry Salad. Some of my secret additions are sure to excite your taste buds!

This chapter also includes my dad's favorite, Crispy Bacon Wedge Salad; my mom's Blushed Strawberry and Spinach Salad; and the recipe I get asked for all the time, my Taco Salad.

Simple Side Salad

PREP TIME: ABOUT 10 MIN | COOK TIME: NONE | YIELD: 8 SERVINGS

INGREDIENTS

8 cups romaine lettuce, torn

1 cup grated carrots

½ cucumber, cut lengthwise and thinly sliced

¼ cup thinly sliced red onion

1 cup halved cherry tomatoes or chopped tomatoes

1 cup croutons

½ cup dressing of choice (see Chapter 6)

DIRECTIONS

1 In a large serving bowl, layer the lettuce, carrots, cucumbers, onions, tomatoes, and croutons. Serve with dressing on the side, or place the lettuce in a bowl and toss with the dressing; then top with the remaining ingredients. After the salad is tossed, it needs to be eaten within 15 to 30 minutes.

PER SERVING: *Calories 111 (From Fat 74); Fat 8g (Saturated 1g); Cholesterol 4mg; Sodium 185mg; Carbohydrate 8g (Dietary Fiber 2g); Protein 2g.*

NOTE: This recipe represents a basic American side salad. In most restaurants, dressings include ranch, blue cheese, Italian, or honey mustard.

VARY IT! The sky's the limit on salad toppings, from sliced avocado, baby corn, black beans, corn kernels, kidney beans, olives, sliced celery, sliced radishes, or toasted nuts. Create a salad bar of your family's favorite toppings, and let each person craft their own!

TIP: If you want to save the salad, keep it undressed and separate the tomatoes and cucumbers from the greens. Tomatoes and cucumbers can wilt lettuce greens and make for a less appetizing leftover salad.

Caesar Salad

INGREDIENTS

2 eggs

½ cup extra-virgin olive oil

2 cloves garlic, chopped

2 anchovy fillets, chopped, or 2 tablespoons Worcestershire sauce

1 tablespoon Dijon mustard

3 tablespoons lemon juice

¼ cup avocado oil

½ teaspoon cracked pepper

Salt, to taste

2 heads romaine lettuce, cleaned and torn

¼ cup finely grated Parmigiano-Reggiano cheese

3 cups croutons

DIRECTIONS

1 Fill a small pot with water, and bring to a gentle simmer (not a rapid boil). Place the eggs in the water, and cook for 6 minutes on a simmer. Remove the eggs and place them into ice cold water for 2 minutes. (This creates soft-boiled eggs.)

2 Meanwhile, in a small skillet, heat the olive oil and garlic over medium-low heat for 2 minutes. Remove from the heat and allow the oil to cool slightly.

3 Next, crack the eggs open and place the yolks into a medium bowl. (Save the whites for another use.) Whisk in the anchovies or Worcestershire sauce, mustard, lemon juice, and avocado oil. Drizzle in the warm garlic oil a little at a time; this should take about 2 minutes of whisking. Add the pepper and adjust the seasoning with salt.

4 Place the torn romaine leaves into a large bowl. Pour the dressing over the greens, and toss to coat. Top with the cheese and croutons, tossing to coat. Place the salad on a serving dish, and serve immediately.

PER SERVING: *Calories 397 (From Fat 288); Fat 32g (Saturated 5g); Cholesterol 75mg; Sodium 299mg; Carbohydrate 23g (Dietary Fiber 5g); Protein 9g.*

NOTE: Ready for a shocker? This dish is originally from Tijuana, Mexico — not Italy! Chef Cesare Cardini was living in San Diego and working at a restaurant in Tijuana when he crafted this gastronomic masterpiece! This dressing has been presented many ways over the years, but this recipe is definitely my favorite.

VARY IT! Grilled romaine lettuce makes for a stunning presentation. Top with sun-ripened tomatoes for a pop of color.

TIP: Making soft-boiled eggs is still a hazard for salmonella. If you prefer to avoid this risk or feel unsure about the quality or safety of your eggs, you can use ¼ cup mayonnaise or pasteurized egg yolks instead. Also, Worcestershire sauce is made from anchovies, so if the tiny fish make you squirm, stick with Worcestershire sauce instead.

Greek Salad

PREP TIME: ABOUT 5 MIN	COOK TIME: NONE	YIELD: 6 SERVINGS

INGREDIENTS

4 Roma tomatoes, quartered lengthwise

1 cucumber, peeled and diced

12 pitted kalamata olives, halved

¼ large white onion, thinly sliced

½ green bell pepper, thinly sliced

2 ounces Greek feta block

¼ cup red wine vinegar

½ cup extra-virgin olive oil

2 teaspoons dried oregano

¼ cup chopped fresh parsley

1 teaspoon sea salt

½ teaspoon cracked pepper

One 16-ounce crusty baguette

DIRECTIONS

1 On a serving platter, place the tomatoes, cucumbers, olives, onion, and bell pepper. Place the block of feta on top of the vegetables. Drizzle the vinegar over the top, followed by the olive oil. Sprinkle the oregano, parsley, salt, and pepper over the top. Serve with the crusty bread.

PER SERVING: *Calories 454 (From Fat 220); Fat 24g (Saturated 5g); Cholesterol 8mg; Sodium 1,179mg; Carbohydrate 49g (Dietary Fiber 4g); Protein 11g.*

NOTE: This recipe doesn't actually have lettuce in it! Traditional Greek salads *don't* have lettuce. Lettuce grows well in cool climates or in fall and spring, but Greece is a warm and sunny climate, so it's no surprise that lettuce is not as commonly seen there. The trick to making this salad amazing lies in the quality of ingredients. Use sun-ripened tomatoes, really good olive oil, authentic Greek feta, and the best baked baguette you can get your hands on. The simplicity of this dish will shine!

VARY IT! If your heart craves greens, you can serve this salad on a bed of torn romaine lettuce. Using a variety of fresh herbs is also encouraged, from rosemary to basil. Thinly sliced carrots make a great addition to this salad, too!

Crispy Bacon Wedge Salad

INGREDIENTS

8 slices bacon

1 head iceberg lettuce, cut into 8 wedges

1 cup Blue Cheese Dressing (see Chapter 6)

8 teaspoons chopped chives or 2 green onions, thinly sliced

2 large tomatoes, seeded and diced

½ cup croutons, crushed

DIRECTIONS

1 Preheat the oven to 350 degrees. Line a baking sheet with parchment paper or foil.

2 Place the bacon strips onto the baking sheet, not touching. Bake for 20 minutes or until crispy. Slightly cool the bacon and then crumble or rough chop it.

3 Discard the tough outer leaves of the iceberg lettuce. Place the wedges onto a serving platter. Drizzle the dressing over the top of the wedges, sprinkle 1 teaspoon of chives or onions over each wedge. Top with the tomatoes and crumbled bacon. Finish with the croutons and serve.

PER SERVING: *Calories 219 (From Fat 174); Fat 19g (Saturated 4g); Cholesterol 18mg; Sodium 495mg; Carbohydrate 8g (Dietary Fiber 2g); Protein 5g.*

NOTE: As much as I love a good dark lettuce, the crispness of iceberg lettuce can't be beat for this salad.

VARY IT! Vegetarian bacon can be used for a meat-free alternative.

Chopped House Salad

PREP TIME: ABOUT 10 MIN | COOK TIME: 20 MIN | YIELD: 8 SERVINGS

INGREDIENTS

8 slices center-cut bacon

1 cup sour cream

½ cup mayonnaise

¼ cup extra-virgin olive oil

¼ cup fresh lemon juice

1 clove garlic, minced

¼ cup finely chopped fresh parsley

1 teaspoon sea salt

½ teaspoon cracked pepper

8 cups romaine lettuce, thinly sliced in ½-inch strands

1 cup cherry tomatoes, halved

One 14-ounce can hearts of palm, drained and chopped

½ cup crumbled blue cheese or grated cheddar cheese

4 hard-boiled eggs, peeled and chopped

1 cup crispy fried onions, such as French's

DIRECTIONS

1 Preheat the oven to 350 degrees. Line a baking sheet with parchment paper.

2 Place the bacon onto the parchment paper. Bake until crispy and fully cooked, about 15 to 20 minutes. Slightly cool the bacon and then crumble it; set aside.

3 Prepare dressing. In a small bowl, whisk together the sour cream, mayonnaise, olive oil, lemon juice, garlic, parsley, salt, and pepper; set aside.

4 In a large bowl, place the lettuce, tomatoes, hearts of palm, cheese, eggs, and crumbled bacon. Toss with the dressing. Plate the tossed salad and top with crispy fried onions. Serve immediately.

PER SERVING: *Calories 344 (From Fat 268); Fat 30g (Saturated 10g); Cholesterol 140mg; Sodium 776mg; Carbohydrate 11g (Dietary Fiber 3g); Protein 10g.*

NOTE: Think of your favorite steak-house salads. This salad is simple to pull together. Grab a good knife and a cutting board, and you're halfway there!

VARY IT! Add your favorite additional toppings, such as olives, grated carrots, thinly sliced onions, radishes, or croutons.

TIP: To make hard-boiled eggs, place the eggs in a large pot, cover with cold water, and bring to a boil. Cover the pot and remove from heat. Allow the eggs to sit for 9 minutes. Remove the eggs from the hot water and place them into an ice bath for 3 minutes.

Cobb Salad

PREP TIME: ABOUT 30 MIN | COOK TIME: 35 MIN | YIELD: 8 SERVINGS

INGREDIENTS

½ cup red wine vinegar

2 tablespoons Dijon mustard

2 teaspoons honey

2 garlic cloves, minced

1 teaspoon sea salt

1 teaspoon cracked pepper

1 cup extra-virgin olive oil

2 skinless, boneless chicken breasts

8 slices bacon, crumbled or chopped

6 cups romaine lettuce, chopped

3 hard-boiled eggs, chopped

1 ripe avocado, cubed

2 Roma tomatoes, seeded and diced

½ cup crumbled blue cheese or grated cheddar cheese

2 green onions, thinly sliced

DIRECTIONS

1 Preheat the oven to 400 degrees. Line a baking sheet with parchment paper.

2 In a medium bowl, whisk together the vinegar, mustard, honey, garlic, salt, pepper, and olive oil. Transfer 1 cup of this salad dressing to another bowl, and place the chicken breasts into that bowl. Allow the chicken to marinade for 30 minutes, flipping to coat both sides of the chicken.

3 Meanwhile, place the bacon on the parchment paper and bake until crispy, about 15 minutes. Remove the bacon from the parchment paper, and add the marinated chicken breasts. Bake until the chicken reaches an internal temperature of 165 degrees, about 20 minutes. Let the chicken rest for 5 minutes; then cube the chicken into small, bite-size pieces.

4 In a large bowl, toss the lettuce with the remaining dressing. Adjust the salt and pepper as needed. With tongs, remove the dressed lettuce to a serving plate. In lines, top with the eggs, avocado, tomatoes, cheese, onions, crumbled bacon, and chicken. Serve immediately.

PER SERVING: *Calories 432 (From Fat 348); Fat 39g (Saturated 8g); Cholesterol 117mg; Sodium 644mg; Carbohydrate 6g (Dietary Fiber 2g); Protein 16g.*

NOTE: Cobb salads are decorative in design. Place the toppings in lines or around the edges, or toss it all together if you prefer!

VARY IT! Add sliced cucumbers, chopped bell pepper, grated carrot, or croutons, too!

TIP: The chicken breast can be marinated up to 8 hours. If you prefer grilled chicken, grill for 8 to 10 minutes on each side over medium-high heat until cooked to an internal temperature of 165 degrees.

Green Goddess Salad

PREP TIME: ABOUT 10 MIN | COOK TIME: NONE | YIELD: 6 SERVINGS

INGREDIENTS

2 cups thinly sliced green cabbage

2 cups thinly sliced romaine lettuce

2 cucumbers, peeled, seeded, and finely diced

1 green bell pepper, finely diced

½ cup Creamy Green Herb Dressing (see Chapter 6)

DIRECTIONS

1   In a large bowl, toss together all the ingredients until the vegetables are coated with dressing. Serve immediately.

PER SERVING: *Calories 65 (From Fat 31); Fat 3g (Saturated 1g); Cholesterol 1mg; Sodium 100mg; Carbohydrate 6g (Dietary Fiber 2g); Protein 3g.*

NOTE: Boost your greens, literally, with this green salad! Packed with fiber and zing, this dressing is a great side dish, whether you're barbecuing or picking up a rotisserie chicken.

VARY IT! Add green olives, peas, finely diced kohlrabi or jicama, kale, canned artichokes, or hearts of palm to keep with the green theme!

TIP: Going to a picnic or a potluck? This salad is easy to increase servings, as needed. Layer the salad in a large salad bowl, cover, and keep the dressing separate. When you're ready to serve, pour in the dressing, toss, and serve.

English Pea Salad

INGREDIENTS

4 slices bacon

3 tablespoons mayonnaise

2 tablespoons buttermilk

½ teaspoon Worcestershire sauce

1 tablespoon fresh lemon juice

2 tablespoons finely chopped parsley

¼ teaspoon garlic powder

½ teaspoon sea salt

10 ounces (about 2 cups) frozen peas, defrosted, or blanched fresh peas

2 green onions, thinly sliced

½ cup grated sharp cheddar cheese

2 hard-boiled eggs, finely chopped

DIRECTIONS

1 Preheat the oven to 350 degrees. Line a baking sheet with parchment paper.

2 Place the bacon onto the parchment paper. Bake until crispy and fully cooked, about 15 to 20 minutes. Cool slightly and crumble the cooked bacon; set aside.

3 Meanwhile, in a small bowl, whisk together the mayonnaise, buttermilk, Worcestershire sauce, lemon juice, parsley, garlic powder, and salt; set aside.

4 In a medium bowl, stir together the peas, onions, cheese, eggs, and bacon. Pour the dressing over the salad; stir. Refrigerate for at least 30 minutes or up to several hours before serving.

PER SERVING: *Calories 168 (From Fat 84); Fat 9g (Saturated 3g); Cholesterol 86mg; Sodium 662mg; Carbohydrate 11g (Dietary Fiber 2g); Protein 10g.*

NOTE: English pea salads are not from the United Kingdom; instead, this salad is popular in the southern United States. You'll find it served at picnics, church gatherings, or barbecues. When peas are fresh in the spring, this is a great way to serve them.

TIP: To blanch fresh peas, place them in boiling water for 1 minute. Drain and place into an ice bath for 1 minute.

Blushed Strawberry and Spinach Salad

PREP TIME: ABOUT 5 MIN	COOK TIME: 5 MIN	YIELD: 8 SERVINGS

INGREDIENTS

⅓ cup red wine vinegar

2 tablespoons sugar

3 strawberries, mashed

2 teaspoons lemon juice

⅔ cup avocado oil

¼ teaspoon sea salt

6 cups baby spinach

2 cups strawberries, thinly sliced

½ cup sliced almonds, chopped walnuts, or toasted pine nuts

4 ounces crumbled goat cheese or feta

DIRECTIONS

1 In a small saucepan, heat the vinegar, sugar, and strawberries over medium–low heat until the sugar is dissolved, about 3 to 5 minutes. Remove from the heat and whisk in the lemon juice, avocado oil, and salt. Test the seasoning with a spinach leaf and adjust as needed. Cool the dressing in the refrigerator while you prepare the remaining ingredients, about 10 minutes.

2 In a large bowl, place the spinach. Pour the dressing over the greens and toss to coat. Transfer the dressed greens to a serving bowl. Top with the strawberries, nuts, and cheese. Serve immediately.

PER SERVING: *Calories 268 (From Fat 220); Fat 24g (Saturated 4g); Cholesterol 13mg; Sodium 236mg; Carbohydrate 10g (Dietary Fiber 2g); Protein 4g.*

NOTE: Heating the red wine vinegar with the sugar and strawberries softens the bite of the vinegar. You can skip this part, but I think it really helps the dressing's flavor.

VARY IT! Use your favorite nuts or seeds, add in thinly sliced red onions, or top with croutons.

TIP: Avocado oil is a neutral-tasting oil. If you can't find it, you can use canola or safflower oil instead. The flavor of olive oil is too bold for this delicate flavor profile.

TIP: Toasting the nuts intensifies their flavor. Use a skillet, and heat the nuts over medium-low heat, stirring constantly until you begin to smell them. Remove from the pan immediately, and let the nuts cool. You don't want to burn the nuts or leave them in the pan to cool.

Taco Salad

INGREDIENTS

1 pound ground beef

1 tablespoon chili powder

2 teaspoons ground cumin

½ teaspoon garlic powder

½ teaspoon onion powder

1 teaspoon dried oregano

1 can pinto beans, drained and rinsed

1 lime, juiced

6 cups romaine lettuce, torn or chopped

2 cups red cabbage, thinly shredded

4 cups crushed tortilla chips

½ small red onion, thinly sliced or diced

4 small tomatoes, seeded and diced

½ cup canned corn, drained and rinsed

1 cup chopped fresh cilantro

1 avocado, diced

1 cup grated cheddar cheese or Monterey Jack cheese

½ cup Greek yogurt or sour cream

2 teaspoons hot sauce (more if desired)

1 tablespoon lime juice

¼ teaspoon sea salt

DIRECTIONS

1 In a skillet, brown the ground beef over medium-high heat until fully cooked, about 10 minutes; drain if necessary. Add the chili powder, cumin, garlic powder, onion powder, oregano, and pinto beans. Stir to combine and continue to cook for 2 minutes. Remove from the heat and stir in the lime juice.

2 In a large salad bowl, layer the lettuce, cabbage, tortilla chips, onion, tomatoes, and corn. Top with the ground beef, cilantro, avocado, and cheese.

3 In a small bowl, place the yogurt or sour cream, hot sauce, lime juice, and salt. Drizzle over the top of the salad, toss, and serve immediately.

PER SERVING: Calories 445 (From Fat 20); Fat 22g (Saturated 7g); Cholesterol 59mg; Sodium 570mg; Carbohydrate 42g (Dietary Fiber 7g); Protein 22g.

NOTE: The meat mixture also acts like a dressing. Adding the lime juice balances the fat of the ground beef and enhances the taco seasonings.

NOTE: If you use a higher-fat ground beef, consider draining off the extra liquid after the meat browns. Buy the meat that fits your budget.

VARY IT! I make this salad with many different vegetables, from grated carrots to olives to julienned bell peppers. Add your favorites to the list! Replace the pinto beans with black beans or lentils. It's okay to swap out vegetables based on seasonal freshness — taco salad is great in all seasons!

TIP: Layering the salad with the ground beef closer to the top allows for the juices to coat the rest of the salad, pulling in all the flavors.

Simple American Pasta Salad

PREP TIME: ABOUT 10 MIN PLUS 30 MIN FOR RESTING	COOK TIME: 15 MIN	YIELD: 8 SERVINGS

INGREDIENTS

½ cup extra-virgin olive oil

2 cloves garlic, minced

1 shallot, finely diced

1 teaspoon dried oregano

1 teaspoon Dijon mustard

1 teaspoon honey

2½ teaspoons sea salt, divided

½ teaspoon cracked pepper

2 tablespoons lemon juice

¼ cup red wine vinegar

1 pound dried fusilli, farfalle, or penne pasta

1 medium red bell pepper, julienned

2 cups broccoli florets

1 cup halved cherry tomatoes

¼ cup finely chopped parsley

¼ pound salami, cubed

¼ pound provolone cheese or mozzarella cheese, cubed

DIRECTIONS

1 In a small skillet or saucepan, heat the olive oil and garlic over low heat until the garlic becomes fragrant, about 3 minutes. The garlic should not brown or toast. Remove from the heat and whisk in the shallot, oregano, mustard, honey, ½ teaspoon of the salt, pepper, lemon juice, and vinegar.

2 In a large pot, bring water to a boil with the remaining 2 teaspoons of salt. Add the pasta and cook according to the package instructions.

3 Meanwhile, in a large salad bowl, place the bell pepper and broccoli. After draining the pasta, immediately pour the hot pasta over the vegetables, and stir. Pour half the dressing over the top of the pasta and vegetables. Let the mixture sit for 5 minutes. Next, add in the tomatoes, parsley, salami, and cheese, stirring to combine. Pour the remaining dressing over the top, cover, and refrigerate until ready to serve. Let the salad sit for at least 30 minutes prior to serving.

PER SERVING: *Calories 246 (From Fat 111); Fat 12g (Saturated 3g); Cholesterol 11mg; Sodium 432mg; Carbohydrate 26g (Dietary Fiber 2g); Protein 8g.*

NOTE: Pasta salad can be kept in the refrigerator for at least 3 days.

VARY IT! Add canned artichokes, canned beans, corn, green beans, red onions, zucchini, or peas.

TIP: If heating olive oil on the stovetop is tedious, you can heat it in the microwave for 30 seconds instead.

Creamy Egg Salad

PREP TIME: ABOUT 5 MIN	COOK TIME: NONE	YIELD: 4 SERVINGS

INGREDIENTS

10 hard-boiled eggs

½ cup mayonnaise

2 teaspoons prepared mustard

1 teaspoon pickle juice

½ teaspoon dried dill

⅛ teaspoon paprika or cayenne

1 tablespoon minced chives

1 stalk celery, finely diced

Salt, to taste

Pepper, to taste

DIRECTIONS

1 Peel and finely chop the eggs.

2 In a medium bowl, whisk together the mayonnaise, mustard, pickle juice, dill, paprika or cayenne, and chives. Gently stir in the eggs and celery. Season with salt and pepper, cover, and refrigerate until ready to serve.

PER SERVING: *Calories 313 (From Fat 209); Fat 23g (Saturated 6g); Cholesterol 538mg; Sodium 405mg; Carbohydrate 9g (Dietary Fiber 0g); Protein 16g.*

TIP: Use older eggs instead of fresh ones. If you wait a week after purchasing the eggs, they'll be easier to peel when you hard-boil them.

NOTE: Egg salad is versatile and a simple way to boost protein in a meal. Top your favorite torn lettuce or an English muffin with egg salad. My family's favorite after-school snack is egg salad on crackers!

VARY IT! This salad can go many ways, but this is a good starting point. Add in diced bell pepper, cucumbers, or onion for added crunch and color.

Zesty Tuna Salad

PREP TIME: ABOUT 15 MIN | COOK TIME: NONE | YIELD: 4 SERVINGS

INGREDIENTS

½ cup mayonnaise

1 tablespoon pickle juice

¼ teaspoon garlic powder

¼ teaspoon onion powder

½ teaspoon sea salt

¼ teaspoon cracked pepper

One 12-ounce can chunk light tuna packed in water, drained

¼ cup finely diced celery

2 tablespoons thinly sliced green onions

3 tablespoons pickle relish (dill or sweet)

DIRECTIONS

1 In a medium bowl, whisk together the mayonnaise, pickle juice, garlic powder, and onion powder until combined. Stir in the salt and pepper. Stir in the tuna, celery, onions, and pickle relish. Let sit for 30 minutes, covered, in the refrigerator; then taste and adjust the seasoning, as needed.

PER SERVING: *Calories 223 (From Fat 95); Fat 11g (Saturated 2g); Cholesterol 31mg; Sodium 806mg; Carbohydrate 11g (Dietary Fiber 0g); Protein 20g.*

NOTE: Tuna salad can be kept in the refrigerator for 3 to 5 days.

NOTE: Chunk light tuna is a lower-mercury choice, whereas canned white albacore or yellowfin tuna are higher in mercury. All are still great sources of protein, selenium, and omega-3 fatty acids. Choose the canned tuna you prefer.

VARY IT! Everyone has their favorite additions to tuna salad, whether it's boiled eggs, chopped pickles or relish, grated carrots, or diced cucumbers. Serve this salad on toast, crackers, or a bed of greens.

Chicken Curry Salad

PREP TIME: ABOUT 15 MIN | COOK TIME: 30 MIN | YIELD: 6 SERVINGS

INGREDIENTS

3 skinless, boneless chicken breasts

3 cups chicken stock or broth

2 teaspoons curry powder, divided

½ cup golden raisins

⅔ cup mayonnaise

1 tablespoon lemon juice

¼ cup finely diced onion

½ teaspoon sea salt

½ teaspoon cracked pepper

1 large tart apple (like Granny Smith), finely diced

¼ cup finely diced celery

½ cup chopped toasted almonds

DIRECTIONS

1 In a large saucepan, place the chicken breasts, stock or broth, 1 teaspoon of the curry powder, and raisins. Bring the mixture to a boil over high heat; then reduce the heat to medium and simmer, covered, until cooked to an internal temperature of 165 degrees, about 20 minutes. Remove the chicken breasts and raisins. Chop the chicken breasts into bite-size cubes.

2 Meanwhile, in a medium bowl, stir together the mayonnaise, the remaining 1 teaspoon of curry powder, lemon juice, onion, salt, pepper, apple, celery, and almonds; stir. Stir in the chicken and raisins. Cover and refrigerate for at least 1 hour prior to serving.

PER SERVING: *Calories 349 (From Fat 161); Fat 18g (Saturated 3g); Cholesterol 56mg; Sodium 600mg; Carbohydrate 28g (Dietary Fiber 3g); Protein 21g.*

NOTE: To gain the health benefits of turmeric, which gives the curry powder its orange hue, it needs to be combined with black pepper. They work synergistically together.

VARY IT! Replace the almonds with pecans or cashews, replace the apple with dried apricots, or replace the onion with chopped chives.

TIP: Serve on a toasted croissant, crusty baguette, crackers, or your favorite bed of greens.

TIP: Canned chicken breasts work as well. Kirkland's canned chicken breast has won taste tests, so find a good-quality product to use.

» Completing your dinner plate with a simple side salad

» Exploring creative ways to dress your favorite veggies

» Prepping ahead with pasta salads

Chapter **8**

Weeknight Side Salads

RECIPES IN THIS CHAPTER

- The Perfect Side Salad
- Lemony Orzo Pasta Salad
- Tomato and Feta with Dill Salad
- Yogurt Cucumber Salad
- Honey Mustard Grated Carrot Salad
- Cucumber, Tomato, and Goat Cheese Salad
- Asparagus and Crumbled Egg Salad
- Lemony Kale and Parmesan Salad
- Broccoli and Feta Salad
- Pesto Tortellini Salad
- Bean and Barley Canadian Salad
- Jump into Summer Salad
- Fall Harvest Salad
- Warming Winter Salad
- Crispy Spring Salad

We all know how crazy weeknights can be — eating enough fruits and vegetables can be a challenge! Don't sweat it — I have you covered! The simple side salad is a staple in my kitchen and a quick solution for the weeknight mayhem. Don't just think green salads — salads can be a compilation of many great vegetables tossed together with a vinaigrette or dressed with something creamy.

In this chapter, I share my fast and favorite side dishes, from pasta salads to bean salads, including the simplest of vegetables dressed for the side of the plate. Side salads are that extra dose of vegetables we all need. They add texture and color to your dinner plate, and they're versatile. Don't forget to read the notes at the end of each recipe — I will share ways to re-create side dishes with varying dressings or vegetables.

Get your taste buds ready! My family's go-to sides include The Perfect Side Salad, Lemony Kale and Parmesan Salad, Yogurt Cucumber Salad, and Lemony Orzo Pasta Salad. Which will be your favorites?

The Perfect Side Salad

PREP TIME: ABOUT 3 MIN	COOK TIME: NONE	YIELD: 1 SERVING

INGREDIENTS

1½ cups baby green lettuce

2 tablespoons grated carrots

1 tablespoon chopped walnuts, almonds, or pecans

⅛ teaspoon garlic powder

⅛ teaspoon onion powder

⅛ teaspoon dried oregano

⅛ teaspoon sea salt

⅛ teaspoon cracked pepper

½ lemon or 2 teaspoons red wine vinegar

1 tablespoon extra-virgin olive oil

DIRECTIONS

In a salad bowl, place the lettuce. Top with the carrots and nuts. Sprinkle with garlic powder, onion powder, oregano, salt, and pepper. Squeeze the lemon over the top of the salad, catching the seeds with your hands (or if using vinegar, drizzle that over the top). Toss the greens with a fork, drizzle with olive oil, and serve.

PER SERVING: *Calories 188 (From Fat 166); Fat 18g (Saturated 2g); Cholesterol 0mg; Sodium 253mg; Carbohydrate 5g (Dietary Fiber 2g); Protein 2g.*

NOTE: This salad is my go-to. I'm constantly asked what I put on the salad and given rave reviews from my friends. Always make sure that you dress with the acid (lemon juice or vinegar) first; then put on the oil. If you don't, the salad greens will be like a slip-and-slide, and the acid will slip right off the oil-coated greens. And even though this makes just one salad, you can double the salad or make it for a crowd with ease.

VARY IT! Grab a handful of pumpkin seeds, sunflower seeds, or pine nuts instead of chopped nuts, or use cucumbers, tomatoes, or bell pepper in place of the carrots. Or add all of the above!

TIP: Use boxed salad greens and pre-grated carrots to keep this super simple!

Lemony Orzo Pasta Salad

PREP TIME: ABOUT 10 MIN	COOK TIME: 10 MIN	YIELD: 8 SERVINGS

INGREDIENTS

1 tablespoon salt (for boiling pasta)

1½ cups dried orzo pasta

2 lemons, zested and juiced (about 6 tablespoons)

½ teaspoon sea salt

½ teaspoon cracked pepper

¼ cup finely chopped fresh parsley

4 green onions, thinly sliced

3 Roma tomatoes, seeded and diced

½ English cucumber, diced

¼ cup extra-virgin olive oil

½ cup crumbled Greek feta

DIRECTIONS

1   Fill a large pot with water and add the 1 tablespoon of salt; bring to a boil. Add the pasta and cook according to package directions. Drain and place the pasta in a serving dish or storage container.

2   To the pasta, add the lemon juice, lemon zest, sea salt, pepper, and parsley. Stir to coat.

3   Add the onions, tomatoes, and cucumber, tossing to coat. Stir in the olive oil and check for seasonings; adjust as desired. Top with feta and refrigerate until ready to serve.

PER SERVING: *Calories 201 (From Fat 86); Fat 10g (Saturated 2g); Cholesterol 8mg; Sodium 382mg; Carbohydrate 24g (Dietary Fiber 2g); Protein 6g.*

NOTE: This salad can be kept in the refrigerator for up to 5 days. If you're serving the salad over the next week, top with feta just as you serve it — this will help the salad stay fresh.

NOTE: One of my best friends from college shared this recipe with me, and it instantly became a favorite. You want to have the right ratio of vegetables to pasta, which makes this more of a vegetable side, not just a starchy pasta dish.

VARY IT! Add chopped bell peppers, olives, or artichoke hearts. If you don't have fresh lemon, use ¼ cup red wine or white wine vinegars instead. If your garden is overflowing with herbs, use basil or mint in place of the parsley — or use a combination of all three!

TIP: Adding the acid and seasonings to the hot pasta helps the pasta soak up the zingy flavors.

Tomato and Feta with Dill Salad

PREP TIME: ABOUT 10 MIN | COOK TIME: NONE | YIELD: 4 SERVINGS

INGREDIENTS

1 shallot, finely diced

1 clove garlic, minced

3 tablespoons red wine vinegar

½ teaspoon sea salt

¼ teaspoon cracked pepper

4 large heirloom tomatoes or 8 Roma tomatoes, sliced or cut into wedges

¼ cup chopped fresh dill

2 tablespoons chopped fresh parsley

¼ cup extra-virgin olive oil

2 ounces crumbled French feta

DIRECTIONS

1   In a small bowl, whisk together the shallot, garlic, vinegar, salt, and pepper.

2   On a serving platter, place the tomatoes. Drizzle the dressing over the tomatoes. Top the tomatoes with dill and parsley. Drizzle the olive oil over the top. Top with feta and serve.

PER SERVING: *Calories 185 (From Fat 151); Fat 17g (Saturated 4g); Cholesterol 13mg; Sodium 401mg; Carbohydrate 6g (Dietary Fiber 2g); Protein 3g.*

NOTE: Imagine yourself sitting along the Mediterranean Sea as you savor the flavors. French feta is milder in flavor than Greek feta. It's also less salty with a creamier texture. Valbreso is my favorite brand of French feta.

VARY IT! Add thinly sliced cucumbers or raw zucchini.

TIP: After the salad is dressed, eat it within 30 minutes. If you want to prep ahead, slice the tomatoes and cover with plastic wrap; then dress the salad right before serving.

Yogurt Cucumber Salad

INGREDIENTS

2 English cucumbers, thinly sliced

1 teaspoon sea salt, divided

1 shallot, finely diced

2 teaspoons white wine vinegar

1 teaspoon sugar

½ teaspoon cracked pepper

½ cup plain Greek yogurt

2 tablespoons extra-virgin olive oil

¼ cup finely chopped dill

DIRECTIONS

1 In a bowl, place the cucumbers and sprinkle with ½ teaspoon of the salt; stir. Let the cucumbers sit for 15 minutes.

2 Meanwhile, in a medium bowl, whisk together the remaining ½ teaspoon of salt, shallot, vinegar, sugar, pepper, yogurt, and olive oil.

3 Drain the cucumbers, rinse with cold water, and pat dry. Put the cucumbers into the yogurt mixture and stir. Add the dill, stir, and serve.

PER SERVING: *Calories 51 (From Fat 37); Fat 4g (Saturated 1g); Cholesterol 0mg; Sodium 241mg; Carbohydrate 2g (Dietary Fiber 0g); Protein 2g.*

NOTE: This salad can be served immediately or the next day but it tastes best when consumed within 24 hours.

VARY IT! Raw zucchini can be used in place of cucumbers.

TIP: Salting the cucumbers prior to mixing helps draw out extra moisture from the cucumbers. The extra moisture can make your salad have a lot of liquid, so don't skip this step unless you plan on eating the salad immediately.

Honey Mustard Grated Carrot Salad

PREP TIME: ABOUT 10 MIN	COOK TIME: NONE	YIELD: 6 SERVINGS

INGREDIENTS

2 shallots, finely chopped

½ cup chopped fresh parsley or mint (or ¼ cup of both)

1 tablespoon lemon juice

1 tablespoon white wine vinegar

2 teaspoons Dijon mustard

4 teaspoons honey

¼ cup extra-virgin olive oil

¾ teaspoon sea salt

¼ teaspoon cracked pepper

6 medium carrots, grated

DIRECTIONS

In a medium bowl, whisk together the shallots, parsley or mint, lemon juice, vinegar, mustard, honey, olive oil, salt, and pepper. Add the carrots, toss to coat, and serve.

PER SERVING: *Calories 125 (From Fat 83); Fat 9g (Saturated 1g); Cholesterol 0mg; Sodium 299mg; Carbohydrate 11g (Dietary Fiber 2g); Protein 1g.*

NOTE: This salad is great all year long because carrots can be found year-round. It's an all-season win!

VARY IT! Grated carrot salads are my jam! Try it with cilantro and cumin for a southwestern flavor. If you don't have honey, try brown sugar or maple syrup instead.

TIP: The longer the salad sits, the juicier it becomes because the salt draws out the moisture. This salad is delicious at room temperature or chilled.

Cucumber, Tomato, and Goat Cheese Salad

INGREDIENTS

One 14.5-ounce can diced tomatoes or 3 Roma tomatoes, diced

1 cucumber, peeled, seeded and diced

¼ cup finely chopped onion

1 tablespoon lemon juice

¼ cup extra-virgin olive oil

¼ teaspoon sea salt

¼ teaspoon cracked pepper

¼ cup chopped fresh parsley or 2 tablespoons dried parsley

¼ cup crumbled goat cheese

DIRECTIONS

1 Drain the tomatoes, reserving the juice for another use.

2 In a medium bowl, stir together the tomatoes, cucumber, onion, lemon juice, olive oil, salt, pepper, and parsley. Taste and adjust for seasoning as needed. Top with the goat cheese and serve.

PER SERVING: *Calories 179 (From Fat 146); Fat 16g (Saturated 4g); Cholesterol 7mg; Sodium 162mg; Carbohydrate 7g (Dietary Fiber 1g); Protein 3g.*

NOTE: Canned vegetables have their place! Canned tomatoes are a great choice in winter when fresh tomatoes fall short on flavor. Canned tomatoes are canned at the peak of their season, ensuring maximum flavor. I grew up eating my mom's canned tomatoes and truly appreciate canned tomatoes all year long. Adding fresh vegetables, like cucumbers and parsley, will make it taste like summer!

VARY IT! Add chopped bell pepper, capers, and croutons.

TIP: Boost the flavor with quality ingredients such as fresh herbs and fresh lemon juice. Serve with a toasted baguette or warmed flatbread.

Asparagus and Crumbled Egg Salad

PREP TIME: ABOUT 10 MIN	COOK TIME: 3 MIN	YIELD: 4 SERVINGS

INGREDIENTS

1 tablespoon salt (for boiling)

1 pound asparagus, woody ends trimmed

2 tablespoons finely diced red bell pepper

1 shallot, finely chopped

1 tablespoon chopped parsley

¼ cup mayonnaise

1 tablespoon lemon juice

1 tablespoon Dijon mustard

½ teaspoon sea salt

¼ teaspoon cracked pepper

2 hard-boiled eggs, peeled

DIRECTIONS

1 In a large pot, place 8 cups of water and the 1 tablespoon of salt; bring to a boil. Add the asparagus and blanch for 2 minutes. Immediately remove from the heat and place the asparagus into ice water for 1 minute.

2 Meanwhile, in a small bowl, whisk together the bell pepper, shallot, parsley, mayonnaise, lemon juice, mustard, salt, and pepper.

3 Plate the asparagus and drizzle the mayonnaise mixture over the top. With a box grater, grate the eggs over the top of the asparagus. Serve.

PER SERVING: *Calories 122 (From Fat 71); Fat 8g (Saturated 2g); Cholesterol 110mg; Sodium 416mg; Carbohydrate 9g (Dietary Fiber 2g); Protein 6g.*

NOTE: Perfect at brunch or dinner, asparagus and boiled eggs just go together. I was first served this type of dish in France in the spring when asparagus are at the height of their season. Every time I make this salad, it instantly brings me back to that café in Strasbourg. I love how food connects us to our memories.

VARY IT! You can use basil, tarragon, or thyme in place of parsley.

TIP: Grating boiled eggs give a great aesthetic appeal to the dish, but if that seems cumbersome, just give the eggs a quick chop instead.

Lemony Kale and Parmesan Salad

PREP TIME: ABOUT 5 MIN	COOK TIME: NONE	YIELD: 4 SERVINGS

INGREDIENTS

10 large kale leaves, large center stems removed

1 lemon, juiced

½ teaspoon onion powder

½ teaspoon garlic powder

½ teaspoon sea salt

⅓ cup extra-virgin olive oil

½ cup finely grated Parmesan cheese

½ cup crushed croutons

DIRECTIONS

1 Place the kale leaves on top of one another on a cutting board. Roll up the kale like a fat, rolled cigar. Using a sharp knife, thinly slice the kale into thin strands. Place the kale into a medium bowl.

2 Squeeze the lemon over the kale, catching the seeds with your hand. Using your hands, massage the lemon juice into the kale. Sprinkle with onion powder, garlic powder, and salt. Drizzle with olive oil and toss to coat. Sprinkle the Parmesan over the top and toss. Top with crushed croutons and serve.

3 Secure the lids onto jars and store up to 5 days in the refrigerator.

PER SERVING: *Calories 263 (From Fat 199); Fat 22g (Saturated 5g); Cholesterol 11mg; Sodium 481mg; Carbohydrate 11g (Dietary Fiber 2g); Protein 8g.*

NOTE: This salad always gets requests for the recipe. I grow a lot of kale, so we end up eating this salad weekly and often serve it to guests. Even people who've declared a hatred of kale have enjoyed this recipe.

VARY IT! Arugula, spinach, and Swiss chard also pair well with this dressing.

TIP: If you're new to kale, try using the Lucinato kale (also known as Italian kale or dinosaur kale). This variety has a flatter leaf and is more tender than traditional kale.

Broccoli and Feta Salad

PREP TIME: ABOUT 5 MIN	COOK TIME: 20 MIN	YIELD: 4 SERVINGS

INGREDIENTS

4 cups broccoli florets

4 tablespoons extra-virgin olive oil, divided

1 teaspoon sea salt, divided

¼ cup pine nuts

1 lemon, zested and juiced

3 tablespoons crumbled feta

⅛ teaspoon crushed red pepper

DIRECTIONS

1   Preheat the oven to 400 degrees. Line a baking sheet with parchment paper.

2   Place the broccoli on the parchment paper, and toss with 2 tablespoons of the olive oil and ½ teaspoon of the salt. Bake until the broccoli begins to lightly brown on the edges, about 18 to 22 minutes.

3   In a small skillet, heat the pine nuts over medium–low heat until they become fragrant, about 2 to 3 minutes.

4   In a small bowl, whisk together the remaining 2 tablespoons of olive oil, the remaining ½ teaspoon of salt, lemon zest, lemon juice, feta, and red pepper.

5   In a medium bowl, toss the roasted broccoli with the pine nuts and dressing and serve.

PER SERVING: *Calories 228 (From Fat 189); Fat 21g (Saturated 3g); Cholesterol 6mg; Sodium 574mg; Carbohydrate 8g (Dietary Fiber 3g); Protein 5g.*

NOTE: Roasting vegetables gives them a whole new flavor profile. The roasting process enhances and intensifies the flavor while also giving them a slight sweetness. The broccoli should still have a crispness to it and not be soggy.

VARY IT! Asparagus, bell peppers, carrots, cauliflower, kohlrabi, and sweet potatoes all roast beautifully and would pair well with this dressing.

TIP: Toasting nuts should be quick. Don't allow the nuts to brown or over-toast. Move the pan or stir frequently to avoid overheating. Remove the nuts from the pan immediately after they become fragrant.

Pesto Tortellini Salad

PREP TIME: ABOUT 5 MIN | COOK TIME: 20 MIN | YIELD: 8 SERVINGS

INGREDIENTS

1 teaspoon sea salt (for boiling pasta)

One 10-ounce package fresh cheese tortellini pasta

½ cup prepared pesto

10 seeded kalamata olives, halved

One 12-ounce container fresh mozzarella balls, drained

1 cup halved grape or cherry tomatoes

1 shallot, thinly sliced

One 6-ounce jar marinated artichoke hearts, drained and quartered

DIRECTIONS

1 Bring a large pot of water to a boil with 1 teaspoon salt. Add the pasta and cook per package instructions, around 3 to 5 minutes. Drain and place in a medium bowl.

2 Add the remaining ingredients and stir to mix well. Serve.

PER SERVING: *Calories 365 (From Fat 221); Fat 25g (Saturated 9g); Cholesterol 51mg; Sodium 603mg; Carbohydrate 21g (Dietary Fiber 1g); Protein 16g.*

NOTE: This salad can be kept in the refrigerator for up to 3 days.

VARY IT! Raw zucchini, raw or canned bell peppers, canned pepperoncini, raw cucumbers, and blanched green beans can all be added to this salad.

TIP: Fresh mozzarella is different from block mozzarella. Block mozzarella can be used but cut it into small cubes before adding to the salad.

Bean and Barley Canadian Salad

PREP TIME: ABOUT 10 MIN | **COOK TIME: 30 MIN** | **YIELD: 6 SERVINGS**

INGREDIENTS

½ cup pearl barley, rinsed

½ cup brown lentils, rinsed

2 tablespoons apple cider vinegar

1 tablespoon lemon juice

⅓ cup safflower oil

2 teaspoons Dijon mustard

1 tablespoon maple syrup

¾ teaspoon sea salt

1 medium red bell pepper, finely diced

One 14.5-ounce can navy beans, drained and rinsed

½ cup dried cranberries

2 green onions, thinly sliced

½ cup pumpkin seeds or ¼ cup sunflower seeds

4 cups baby arugula or spinach

DIRECTIONS

1 Cook the barley according to package directions.

2 In a small saucepan, place 2 cups of water. Add the lentils and bring to a boil. Cover and simmer for 20 minutes. Drain and set aside.

3 Meanwhile, in a Mason jar, place the vinegar, lemon juice, oil, mustard, maple syrup, and salt. Seal the jar with a lid and shake for 1 minute.

4 In a medium bowl, place the cooked barley, cooked lentils, bell pepper, beans, cranberries, onions, and seeds; stir to mix. Add the dressing and toss to combine. Serve on a bed of arugula or spinach.

PER SERVING: *Calories 384 (From Fat 162); Fat 18g (Saturated 1g); Cholesterol 0mg; Sodium 525mg; Carbohydrate 47g (Dietary Fiber 11g); Protein 12g.*

NOTE: This salad can be made and refrigerated for up to 5 days. Place over the arugula or spinach only when ready to eat.

VARY IT! Try any variety of beans in this mixture. Replace the bell peppers with broccoli. Try raisins or currants in place of the cranberries.

TIP: This salad is a hearty side dish, packed with fiber. Serve with grilled chicken breasts or roasted pork tenderloin.

Jump into Summer Salad

PREP TIME: ABOUT 15 MIN	COOK TIME: NONE	YIELD: 6 SERVINGS

INGREDIENTS

1 cup blueberries, divided

2 tablespoons red wine vinegar

1 tablespoon lemon juice

1 teaspoon honey

½ teaspoon sea salt

¼ teaspoon cracked pepper

3 tablespoons extra-virgin olive oil

6 cups baby lettuce greens or watercress

1 cup sliced peaches

½ cup chopped walnuts

¼ cup crumbled goat cheese or blue cheese

DIRECTIONS

1 Place ½ cup of the blueberries, the vinegar, lemon juice, honey, salt, and pepper in a blender or food processor. Pulse for 1 minute; then blend for 1 to 2 minutes while slowly drizzling in the olive oil.

2 Next, place the lettuce or watercress on a serving platter or in a bowl. Dress the lettuce or watercress with the blueberry vinaigrette, tossing to coat. Top with the remaining ½ cup of blueberries, peaches, walnuts, and cheese. Serve immediately.

PER SERVING: *Calories 183 (From Fat 137); Fat 15g (Saturated 3g); Cholesterol 4mg; Sodium 185mg; Carbohydrate 10g (Dietary Fiber 3g); Protein 4g.*

NOTE: Nothing says summer more than fresh berries. This salad is festive, perfect for the Fourth of July with the red, white, and blue theme!

VARY IT! Any berry can replace the blueberries in the vinaigrette. You can use frozen blueberries for the dressing as well.

Fall Harvest Salad

PREP TIME: ABOUT 15 MIN | COOK TIME: 20 MIN | YIELD: 6 SERVINGS

INGREDIENTS

1 large sweet potato, scrubbed clean and cubed

2 teaspoons dried or fresh rosemary, chopped

¼ cup extra-virgin olive oil, divided

1 teaspoon sea salt, divided

1 teaspoon cracked pepper, divided

6 slices center-cut bacon

1 tablespoon apple cider vinegar

1 tablespoon lemon juice

2 teaspoons maple syrup or honey

1 teaspoon Dijon mustard

6 cups baby spinach

1 Honeycrisp apple, thinly sliced

¼ cup pumpkin seeds or sunflower seeds

¼ cup grated Parmesan cheese

DIRECTIONS

1 Preheat the oven to 400 degrees. Line a baking sheet with parchment paper.

2 In a medium bowl, season the sweet potato with the rosemary, 1 tablespoon of the olive oil, ½ teaspoon of the salt, and ½ teaspoon of the pepper. Place the bacon and sweet potato onto the baking sheet. Bake until the sweet potatoes are golden and the bacon is crisp, about 20 minutes. Cool the bacon for 5 minutes, chop, and set aside.

3 In a small bowl, whisk together the vinegar, lemon juice, maple syrup or honey, mustard, the remaining ½ teaspoon of salt, and the remaining ½ teaspoon of pepper. While whisking, add the remaining 3 tablespoons of olive oil until combined.

4 Place the greens in a large bowl or on a serving platter. Top with the sweet potatoes, bacon, apple, seeds, and Parmesan. Pour the dressing over the top, toss, and serve immediately.

PER SERVING: *Calories 311 (From Fat 217); Fat 24g (Saturated 6g); Cholesterol 19mg; Sodium 642mg; Carbohydrate 19g (Dietary Fiber 3g); Protein 7g.*

NOTE: Pumpkin seeds, sweet potatoes, and apples make this a festive fall salad addition to your table.

VARY IT! Pears can be used in place of the apples; delicata squash or butternut squash can be used in place of the sweet potatoes; and thinly sliced kale or a combination of radicchio and butter lettuce can be used in place of the spinach.

TIP: Serve with a cheddar sourdough.

Warming Winter Salad

PREP TIME: ABOUT 15 MIN	COOK TIME: 20 MIN	YIELD: 6 SERVINGS

INGREDIENTS

12 carrots, about 1 inch in diameter at the top, cut lengthwise

1 teaspoon dried thyme

¼ cup extra-virgin olive oil, divided

1 teaspoon sea salt, divided

1 teaspoon cracked pepper, divided

½ cup Creamy Tahini Dressing (see Chapter 6)

1 cup shredded purple cabbage

1 cup shredded green cabbage

2 cups thinly sliced kale

1 navel orange, peel and pith removed and thinly sliced

2 tablespoons sunflower seeds

2 tablespoons pumpkin seeds

¼ cup crumbled feta

DIRECTIONS

1 Preheat the oven to 425 degrees. Line a baking sheet with parchment paper.

2 On the baking sheet, season the carrots with the thyme, 1 tablespoon of the olive oil, ½ teaspoon of the salt, and ½ teaspoon of the pepper, tossing to mix. Bake until the carrots are golden, about 20 to 30 minutes.

3 Place the Creamy Tahini Dressing in a large bowl. Add the purple cabbage, green cabbage, and kale, and toss to coat. Place the dressed greens on a serving platter. Top with the roasted carrots. Lay the oranges around the edge of the salad. Sprinkle the sunflower seeds, pumpkin seeds, and feta over the top. Serve immediately.

PER SERVING: *Calories 207 (From Fat 122); Fat 14g (Saturated 3g); Cholesterol 6mg; Sodium 503mg; Carbohydrate 20g (Dietary Fiber 6g); Protein 4g.*

NOTE: If your carrots are big, slice lengthwise down the center. Keep the carrots all about the same size for easy baking.

VARY IT! Persimmons, dried apricots, or dried cherries can be used in place of the oranges.

Crispy Spring Salad

PREP TIME: ABOUT 15 MIN	COOK TIME: 20 MIN	YIELD: 6 SERVINGS

INGREDIENTS

1 teaspoon salt (for blanching vegetables)

2 tablespoons lemon juice

1 tablespoon white wine vinegar

1 teaspoon Dijon mustard

1 shallot, minced

1 tablespoon chopped fresh dill

¼ cup extra-virgin olive oil

1 cup asparagus tips

1 cup sugar snap peas

4 cups mixed baby greens

4 radishes, thinly sliced

½ cup roasted and salted Marcona almonds

1 cup croutons

DIRECTIONS

1 In a large saucepan, bring 4 cups of water to a boil with the salt.

2 While the water is coming to a boil, make the dressing. In a small bowl, whisk together the lemon juice, vinegar, mustard, shallot, dill, and olive oil.

3 Blanch the asparagus tips and peas for 1 minute in the boiling water; then strain and place them in ice water for 1 minute to halt the cooking. Place the asparagus on a towel so as not to carry any excess water to the salad. The vegetables will be crisp and vibrant in color.

4 Place the baby greens in a serving bowl or on a platter, top with the radishes and blanched vegetables, and dress with the vinaigrette. Toss the salad and top with the almonds and croutons. Serve immediately.

PER SERVING: *Calories 207 (From Fat 155); Fat 17g (Saturated 2g); Cholesterol 0mg; Sodium 165mg; Carbohydrate 10g (Dietary Fiber 3g); Protein 5g.*

NOTE: Blanching vegetables is a great way to slightly soften them while intensifying the color and still leaving them crisp in texture.

VARY IT! I frequently use boiled eggs, artichokes, and sprouts in this salad. Tarragon and red wine vinegar can be used in the dressing as well.

Chapter 9

Going Global

RECIPES IN THIS CHAPTER

Middle Eastern Fattoush Salad

Italian Caprese Salad

Japanese Seaweed Salad

German Swabian Potato Salad

German Radish Salad

Wurstsalat (Swiss/German Meat Salad)

Italian Arugula and Lox Salad

French Tuna Niçoise Salad

Italian Panzanella Salad

Italian Radicchio and Blood Orange Salad

French Endive Salad

Korean Bun Noodle Salad

Lebanese Tabbouleh Salad

Egyptian Barley and Pomegranate Salad

Ethiopian Azifa Salad

Thai Green Papaya with Shrimp Salad

Laotian Ground Pork Larb

English Garden Salad

Canadian Maple, Cabbage, and Cranberry Salad

Spicy Filipino-Style Ceviche

Mexican Zesty Shrimp Aguachile with Peanuts

Most people are familiar with Italy's Caprese Salad and France's famed Tuna Niçoise Salad, but have you heard of Ethiopia's Azifa Salad or Mexico's Aguachile? This chapter is near and dear to my heart, because throughout all my travels, I've spent years filing away recipes of salads I've enjoyed around the globe. Each of these recipes holds a memory of exploration and wonder. Food is magical, a cultural celebration, and each bite can transport you to another place around the globe.

This chapter explores salads of Middle Eastern, African, European, North American, Central American, South American, and Asian roots. I can't claim to be from these wonderful areas of the globe, but I have researched and spoken to friends who are from varying countries to share their treasured recipes and added my own spin on foods I've tasted during my travels. These salads may be very different from what your palate is familiar with, but I have no doubt they'll pique your interest and excite your taste buds. Perhaps this chapter will inspire you to visit another country or at least explore more recipes from around the globe.

How do I even begin to pick my favorites? Although you may jump to the recipes you're most familiar with, I encourage you to try the Middle Eastern Fattoush Salad, Ethiopian Azifa Salad, Laotian Ground Pork Larb, and Mexican Zesty Shrimp Aguachile with Peanuts. I still dream about these recipes when I think back to my travels and culinary explorations.

Middle Eastern Fattoush Salad

PREP TIME: ABOUT 10 MIN	COOK TIME: 30 MIN	YIELD: 10 SERVINGS

INGREDIENTS

2 Middle Eastern flatbreads or pita, cut into bite-size pieces

½ cup extra-virgin olive oil, divided

2 teaspoons sumac, divided

2 teaspoons sea salt, divided

½ cup pomegranate juice

1 teaspoon sugar

4 cups chopped purslane or thinly sliced romaine lettuce

½ cup diced radishes

1 cup diced Persian or English cucumbers

1 cup diced Roma tomatoes

½ bell pepper (any color), diced

½ cup thinly sliced mint leaves

½ cup finely chopped parsley

2 tablespoons lemon juice

½ teaspoon cracked pepper

1 clove garlic, minced, or ½ teaspoon garlic powder

2 teaspoons toasted sesame seeds

DIRECTIONS

1 Preheat the oven to 400 degrees.

2 On a baking sheet, toss the bread with 3 tablespoons of the olive oil, 1 teaspoon of the sumac, and ½ teaspoon of the sea salt. Bake until golden and toasted, about 15 to 20 minutes. Set aside to cool.

3 Meanwhile, in a small saucepan, heat the pomegranate juice with the sugar over medium-low heat until reduced in half and thickened to a syrup, about 20 minutes, stirring occasionally. After it's reduced, remove from the heat to cool. (See the Note at the end of this recipe for storage of leftover pomegranate syrup.)

4 To assemble the salad, on a large serving platter or bowl, layer the lettuce, radishes, cucumbers, tomatoes, bell pepper, mint, and parsley. Top with the toasted bread pieces.

5 In a small bowl, whisk together the remaining 1 tablespoon of olive oil, the remaining 1 teaspoon of sumac, and the remaining 1½ teaspoons of salt. Whisk in the lemon juice, cracked pepper, garlic, and 1 tablespoon of the pomegranate syrup. Drizzle dressing over the salad and top with sesame seeds. Serve immediately.

PER SERVING: *Calories 149 (From Fat 111); Fat 12g (Saturated 2g); Cholesterol 3mg; Sodium 413mg; Carbohydrate 9g (Dietary Fiber 1g); Protein 2g.*

NOTE: If you have a farmers' market nearby or a knack for growing things, try purslane. This highly nutrient-dense weed (as it's often referred to) is delicious, nutritious, and worth trying.

NOTE: This salad hails from Lebanon and uses leftover flatbreads. The breads are often fried instead of baked, but I think it's easier to toast them in the oven, allowing you time to make the pomegranate syrup.

NOTE: Pomegranate molasses is a thickened reduction of pomegranate juice. If you happen to have a Middle Eastern market nearby, you'll find this product there and you can skip making the pomegranate reduction. Store the remaining syrup in the refrigerator for 1 to 2 months. The syrup also tastes wonderful over ice cream.

VARY IT! Add feta, diced avocado, roasted garbanzo beans (see Chapter 19), or thin slices of lemon.

Italian Caprese Salad

PREP TIME: ABOUT 12 MIN | **COOK TIME: NONE** | **YIELD: 4 SERVINGS**

INGREDIENTS

4 heirloom tomatoes

One 8-ounce ball buffalo mozzarella, drained and patted dry

¼ cup loose-leaf basil leaves

⅓ cup extra-virgin olive oil

½ teaspoon sea salt

DIRECTIONS

Core the tomatoes with a paring knife. Cut the tomatoes in ¼-inch slices and arrange in a circle around the circumference of a plate. Slice the mozzarella in similar slices and arrange between the tomatoes, to alternate tomatoes and mozzarella. Tear the basil leaves in half and sprinkle over the top of the salad. Drizzle with olive oil and sprinkle with salt. Serve immediately.

PER SERVING: *Calories 361 (From Fat 278); Fat 31g (Saturated 10g); Cholesterol 45mg; Sodium 599mg; Carbohydrate 8g (Dietary Fiber 2g); Protein 14g.*

NOTE: Buffalo mozzarella hails from Campania, Italy, and is made from Italian water buffalo's milk. It's creamier, softer, and slightly tangier than traditional mozzarella. The cheese is stored in liquid, so look for mozzarella balls in a tub. Any size can work.

NOTE: Use high-quality ingredients. This salad is very simple and requires the best quality of ingredients, from vine-ripened tomatoes to high-quality extra-virgin olive oil.

VARY IT! Using multicolored heirloom tomatoes helps this dish stand out.

Japanese Seaweed Salad

PREP TIME: ABOUT 15 MIN | COOK TIME: 10 MIN | YIELD: 8 SERVINGS

INGREDIENTS

One 2.1-ounce package wakame seaweed

1 tablespoon mirin

1 tablespoon soy sauce

1 teaspoon grated fresh ginger

1 garlic clove, minced

¼ teaspoon red pepper flakes

1 teaspoon sugar

1 small Persian cucumber

1 tablespoon toasted sesame oil

1 tablespoon toasted sesame seeds

DIRECTIONS

1 Thinly slice the dry wakame and place it into a mixing bowl. Top with warm water and let the seaweed reconstitute for at least 10 minutes. Then place the seaweed into ice water for 6 minutes. The seaweed should be tender and pliable when reconstituted. Drain off the excess water, squeezing to remove the excess liquid from the seaweed. Cut any large pieces of seaweed.

2 Top the reconstituted seaweed with the mirin, soy sauce, ginger, garlic, red pepper flakes, and sugar, stirring to coat the seaweed.

3 Cut the ends off the cucumber; then cut the cucumber lengthwise. Cut the cucumber into thin half-moon slices and add the cucumber to the wakame. Stir in the sesame oil and sesame seeds. Cover and refrigerate for 30 minutes prior to serving.

PER SERVING: Calories 219 (From Fat 160); Fat 18g (Saturated 5g); Cholesterol 22mg; Sodium 475mg; Carbohydrate 8g (Dietary Fiber 2g); Protein 8g.

NOTE: Wakame is a species of kelp; it's often referred to as a "sea vegetable." It's nutrient-rich, particularly in iodine, iron, phosphorous, copper, and vitamins A, C, E, and K. Wakame is widely used in Japanese and Korean dishes. You can find it in many health-food markets, most Asian markets, and online. Wakame is different from nori, which is used in sushi rolls. It is also different from the seasoned snacking seaweed found in most grocery stores. Look in specialty markets or on Amazon for dried wakame seaweed.

NOTE: You can store this salad in an airtight container in the refrigerator for up to 3 days.

NOTE: Mirin is a type of rice wine often found in Japanese cooking.

VARY IT! Add 1 cup edamame (soybeans), ¼ cup julienned daikon radish, ¼ cup julienned carrots, ¼ cup cherry tomato halves, and 1 diced avocado.

TIP: This salad makes a delicious side dish for Korean barbecue, chicken wings, teriyaki chicken, or sushi.

German Swabian Potato Salad

PREP TIME: ABOUT 30 MIN	COOK TIME: 30 MIN	YIELD: 8 SERVINGS

INGREDIENTS

2 pounds baby Yukon gold potatoes

1 tablespoon plus 1 teaspoon salt, divided

1 large yellow onion, finely diced

⅓ cup plus 1 tablespoon safflower oil, divided

1 cup beef broth

½ teaspoon white pepper

⅓ cup malt vinegar or apple cider vinegar

2 tablespoons chopped fresh parsley

DIRECTIONS

1 Place the potatoes in a large pot of water with 1 tablespoon of the salt. Bring to a boil, cover, and reduce the heat to a simmer until fork tender, about 15 minutes.

2 While the potatoes are coming to a boil, in a medium skillet, sauté the onions in 1 tablespoon of the safflower oil over medium heat until translucent, about 5 minutes. Add the broth. Bring to a boil and lower to a simmer for 10 minutes. Remove from the heat.

3 Drain the cooked potatoes. Using a paring knife (and perhaps a pot holder to protect your hands from the heat), peel the potatoes and thinly slice. Place the sliced potatoes in a large mixing or serving bowl. Pour the warm onion beef broth over the potatoes and stir. Add the remaining 1 teaspoon of salt, the white pepper, the vinegar, and the parsley. Stir to combine. Let the mixture sit at room temperature for 15 minutes. Add the remaining ⅓ cup of oil and stir. Serve immediately, or let the potato salad refrigerate for an hour. The salad is typically served at room temperature.

PER SERVING: *Calories 203 (From Fat 97); Fat 11g (Saturated 1g); Cholesterol 0mg; Sodium 324mg; Carbohydrate 24g (Dietary Fiber 2g); Protein 3g.*

NOTE: Swabian potato salad is probably quite different from what you imagined a German *Kartoffelsalat* (potato salad) to be. This potato salad starts with a rich beef and onion broth and uses tiny golden potatoes that are steamed, peeled while hot, sliced thin, and mixed. It's simplistic and delicious. Swabians often serve this potato salad beneath green salads, so as you stick your fork into the salad you get this creamy, delicious potato bite with crisp field greens. While living in the heart of Swabia, I took time to learn these subtle culinary tricks to re-creating our favorite dishes, this being one of them.

NOTE: You can store this salad in an airtight container in the refrigerator for up to 3 days.

VARY IT! Some of our neighbors added finely diced and fried *speck* (which is like bacon), German mustard, finely diced chives, and boiled eggs. Play with it and see how you enjoy it!

TIP: Serve this wherever you'd serve potato salad, or do as the Germans do and serve it as the base of your favorite side salad.

German Radish Salad

PREP TIME: ABOUT 15 MIN | COOK TIME: NONE | YIELD: 6 SERVINGS

INGREDIENTS

½ daikon radish or 12 red radishes

1 teaspoon salt, divided

½ cup quark, sour cream, or full-fat Greek yogurt

¼ cup finely chopped chives

2 tablespoons finely chopped parsley

¼ teaspoon cracked pepper

DIRECTIONS

1 If using a daikon radish, peel the outer skin. Then thinly slice and julienne the radish in 2-inch pieces. If using red radishes, thinly slice and cut into thin strips. Place cut radish into a bowl and sprinkle with ½ teaspoon of the salt. Let the radishes sit for 10 minutes. Rinse the radishes with cold water; then pat dry.

2 In a medium bowl, whisk together the quark, sour cream, or yogurt; the chives; the parsley; the remaining ½ teaspoon of salt; and the pepper. Stir in the radishes and serve immediately or store in an airtight container in the refrigerator until serving.

PER SERVING: *Calories 39 (From Fat 34); Fat 4g (Saturated 2g); Cholesterol 10mg; Sodium 332mg; Carbohydrate 1g (Dietary Fiber 0g); Protein 1g.*

NOTE: Although I referred to this as a German radish salad, the truth is, you can find this type of salad throughout much of Europe, from France to Russia. German beer radishes are typically the radish of choice for this dish; they're an heirloom variety that I've only seen in Germany. Daikon makes for a great substitute, as does the more common red radish.

NOTE: You can store this salad in an airtight container in the refrigerator for up to 3 days.

VARY IT! If a spicy radish is not your thing, try the salad with thinly sliced cucumbers instead. The German cucumber salad is very similar to this. Now you have two recipes in one!

TIP: This dish is commonly served with roasted meats or with bratwurst and breads.

Wurstsalat (Swiss/German Meat Salad)

PREP TIME: ABOUT 15 MIN	COOK TIME: NONE	YIELD: 8 SERVINGS

INGREDIENTS

2 tablespoons malt vinegar

2 tablespoons apple cider vinegar

1 tablespoon Dijon mustard

¼ cup finely chopped fresh parsley

2 teaspoons sugar

1 tablespoon pickle juice

1 small white onion, thinly sliced

½ pound sliced *lyoner* (German bologna), bologna, or ham

½ pound sliced Swiss cheese

1 cup baby dill pickles

3 tablespoons safflower oil or canola oil

DIRECTIONS

1 Make the vinaigrette: In a medium bowl, whisk together the malt vinegar, apple cider vinegar, mustard, parsley, sugar, pickle juice, and onions. Set aside.

2 Next, stack the bologna or ham and slice it into julienned strips. Do the same with the Swiss cheese. Thinly slice and julienne the pickles. Place all the ingredients, including the vinaigrette and oil into a bowl, tossing to mix. Serve immediately or cover and refrigerate until ready to serve.

PER SERVING: *Calories 271 (From Fat 196); Fat 22g (Saturated 8g); Cholesterol 51mg; Sodium 588mg; Carbohydrate 8g (Dietary Fiber 1g); Protein 11g.*

NOTE: This salad may create some debate, which is why I chose to refer to it as Swiss/German. In Bavaria (the southern part of Germany near the Swiss and Austrian border), you'll frequently see this salad on the menu; however, it can come with or without cheese. In Switzerland, this salad has cheese. I enjoy the balance of both cheese and meats, and you're welcome to make it how you like it, too. *Lyoner* is similar to an American high-quality bologna, such as Boar's Head, but it's still subtly different. *Lyoner* is made with both pork and beef and looks much like a bologna.

NOTE: Store this salad in an airtight container in the refrigerator for up to 3 days.

VARY IT! Add chives, green onions, or fresh dill for pops of green and flavor.

TIP: Serve this salad with a hearty piece of rye bread or pumpernickel.

Italian Arugula and Lox Salad

PREP TIME: ABOUT 10 MIN | COOK TIME: NONE | YIELD: 6 SERVINGS

INGREDIENTS

8 cups baby arugula or rocket

1 lemon

1 teaspoon sea salt

½ teaspoon cracked pepper

2 tablespoons capers, drained

6 ounces smoked salmon, thinly sliced

¼ cup toasted pine nuts or chopped walnuts

¼ cup extra-virgin olive oil

DIRECTIONS

Place the greens in a medium bowl. Squeeze the lemon over the top, catching the seeds and discarding. Toss the greens with the lemon juice, gently massaging the greens. Sprinkle with salt and pepper and toss. Place the greens on a serving platter. Top with the capers, salmon, and nuts, and drizzle with the olive oil. Serve immediately.

PER SERVING: *Calories 155 (From Fat 123); Fat 14g (Saturated 2g); Cholesterol 7mg; Sodium 627mg; Carbohydrate 2g (Dietary Fiber 1g); Protein 7g.*

NOTE: As much as I'd love to add fresh Parmesan onto this salad, my Italian friends would slap me if I did. In Italy, there is a strong belief that seafood is not mixed with cheese. My dear friends tell me that the strong flavors of cheese do not mix well with the delicate flavors of seafood. If you add cheese, I promise not to tell on you, though.

NOTE: Although 6 ounces of salmon can seem like a small amount, the flavor is powerful and best in smaller portions.

VARY IT! Add cherry tomato halves, sliced avocados, thinly sliced red onion, croutons, or thin slices of lemon.

TIP: Serve this salad with a crunchy baguette or focaccia.

French Tuna Niçoise Salad

PREP TIME: ABOUT 20 MIN	COOK TIME: 20 MIN	YIELD: 6 SERVINGS

INGREDIENTS

1 pound small Yukon gold potatoes

1 tablespoon salt (for boiling)

½ pound haricot verts (small French green beans), trimmed

½ lemon, zested and juiced

2 tablespoons white wine vinegar

1 tablespoon Dijon mustard

⅓ cup extra-virgin olive oil

1 teaspoon capers, crushed

1 clove garlic, minced

½ teaspoon cracked pepper

1 teaspoon sea salt

2 shallots, thinly sliced

6 leaves butter lettuce or red leaf lettuce

2 medium tomatoes, quartered

½ cup Niçoise olives or black oil-cured olives

½ English cucumber, thinly sliced

One 6-ounce can oil-packed tuna, drained

3 hard-boiled eggs, quartered lengthwise

3 tablespoons chopped parsley

DIRECTIONS

1 Place the potatoes in a large pot of water with 1 tablespoon salt. Bring to a boil over high heat; then reduce the heat to a simmer and cover until the potatoes are tender, about 15 minutes. Remove the potatoes, setting aside to cool. Bring the water back to a boil and add the haricot verts and boil for 3 minutes. Remove and immediately place haricot verts into an ice bath for 1 minute. Drain and set aside.

2 Meanwhile, in a small bowl, whisk together the lemon zest, lemon juice, vinegar, mustard, olive oil, capers, garlic, pepper, salt, and shallots.

3 On a serving platter, arrange the lettuce leaves. Arrange the boiled potatoes on one side of the platter and the green beans on the other. In a composed fashion, arrange the tomatoes, olives, cucumbers, tuna, and eggs between the cooked vegetables. Drizzle dressing over the top of the composed salad and sprinkle with parsley. Serve immediately.

PER SERVING: *Calories 303 (From Fat 165); Fat 18g (Saturated 3g); Cholesterol 111mg; Sodium 596mg; Carbohydrate 21g (Dietary Fiber 3g); Protein 15g.*

NOTE: Yet another controversial salad. Historical references share versions without potatoes, without green beans, and with anchovies instead of tuna. But all along my travels and explorations, I found that some version of this salad is served like this. Any way you choose to serve it is delicious, and you have the freedom to make changes as you see fit!

VARY IT! Replace the green beans with asparagus or baby artichokes. You can also use traditional green beans in place of the haricot verts.

TIP: Serve with a crusty French baguette.

Italian Panzanella Salad

PREP TIME: ABOUT 10 MIN	COOK TIME: 15 MIN	YIELD: 6 SERVINGS

INGREDIENTS

½ pound day-old French bread or other crusty bread

2 cloves garlic

½ cup extra-virgin olive oil, divided

2 tablespoons capers, drained

¼ cup red wine vinegar

½ small red onion, sliced thin

4 large tomatoes, large diced

1 English cucumber or 2 Persian cucumbers, seeded and diced

8 basil leaves, sliced into long strips or torn

Salt to taste

Pepper to taste

DIRECTIONS

1 Preheat the oven to 425 degrees.

2 Cut a baguette lengthwise in half. Bake on the oven rack until the bread is golden, about 10 minutes. Remove from the oven and rub the bread with the raw garlic cloves to infuse the garlic into the bread. Cube the bread and toss with ¼ cup olive oil and capers. Return to the oven for 5 to 8 minutes. The bread should be a deep golden brown and crunchy. Let the bread cool completely, tossing occasionally to help it cool and not become soggy from steam.

3 Meanwhile, in a serving bowl, mix the red wine vinegar and onions. Add the tomatoes, and cucumbers. Add the toasted bread, stirring to coat with the vinegar. Drizzle the remaining ¼ cup of olive oil over the top and stir. Top with the basil and season the salad with salt and pepper. Stir and serve immediately.

PER SERVING: *Calories 306 (From Fat 171); Fat 19g (Saturated 3g); Cholesterol 0mg; Sodium 339mg; Carbohydrate 29g (Dietary Fiber 3g); Protein 6g.*

NOTE: Panzanella is a traditional bread salad hailing from Italy, but this type of salad can be seen throughout the Mediterranean. Breads are not traditionally made with preservatives so they turn stale faster than store-bought breads. This salad is one of the many ways Italians use up day-old bread. A well-toasted bread won't get soggy as this salad sits in the refrigerator, and it can be kept covered up to 3 days.

VARY IT! Add olives, bell peppers, and avocado to expand this salad.

TIP: Serve with grilled fish or chicken.

Italian Radicchio and Blood Orange Salad

PREP TIME: ABOUT 10 MIN	COOK TIME: NONE	YIELD: 4 SERVINGS

INGREDIENTS

2 tablespoons red wine vinegar

2 teaspoons honey

¼ cup extra-virgin olive oil

½ teaspoon sea salt

¼ teaspoon cracked pepper

3 cups baby arugula

1 head red radicchio, thinly sliced

2 blood oranges, peeled and sliced into ¼-inch rounds

¼ cup chopped toasted walnuts

DIRECTIONS

1 In a small bowl, whisk together the vinegar, honey, olive oil, salt, and pepper.

2 On a serving platter, arrange the arugula on the base of the platter. Top with the radicchio and oranges. Sprinkle the walnuts over the top and drizzle with the dressing. Serve immediately.

PER SERVING: *Calories 217 (From Fat 167); Fat 19g (Saturated 2g); Cholesterol 0mg; Sodium 241mg; Carbohydrate 13g (Dietary Fiber 2g); Protein 2g.*

NOTE: Both radicchio and arugula have a bite and bitterness in flavor. Pairing them with blood oranges adds a pop of color and mellows the bitterness with the sweetness of the orange. Radicchio is adored throughout Italy and seen in many dishes; you may also find it labeled *Italian chicory.*

NOTE: To toast walnuts, heat over medium-high heat in a skillet, stirring regularly. When the nuts become fragrant, remove from the heat and from the pan. Be careful not to burn or scorch the nuts.

VARY IT! Sliced avocados, black olives, thinly sliced fennel, thinly sliced apples, toasted almonds or pine nuts, and crumbled goat cheese or blue cheese would all make delicious additions to this salad.

French Endive Salad

INGREDIENTS

1 tablespoon champagne vinegar

2 teaspoons lemon juice

1 teaspoon honey

1 teaspoon Dijon mustard

¼ teaspoon white pepper

½ teaspoon sea salt

1 teaspoon dried tarragon

¼ cup extra-virgin olive oil

3 heads pale yellow endive, leaves pulled apart and chopped

1 green apple or pear, thinly sliced

¼ cup chopped hazelnuts or walnuts

2 tablespoons chopped chives

DIRECTIONS

1 In a small bowl, whisk together the vinegar, lemon juice, honey, mustard, white pepper, salt, and tarragon. While whisking continuously, drizzle in the olive oil until combined.

2 Arrange the endive on a serving platter. Top with the apple or pear, nuts, and chives. Drizzle the dressing over the top and serve immediately.

PER SERVING: *Calories 259 (From Fat 173); Fat 19g (Saturated 3g); Cholesterol 0mg; Sodium 334mg; Carbohydrate 20g (Dietary Fiber 13g); Protein 6g.*

NOTE: Endive is grown in northern France and is a cherished vegetable throughout the country. Pairing it with a mild vinaigrette and sweet apples makes for a balanced flavor profile.

VARY IT! Persimmons, green plums, or cherries can be used in place of the apples.

TIP: Serve with Camembert and crusty French baguettes or croissants.

Korean Bun Noodle Salad

INGREDIENTS

1 pound frozen crispy chicken strips

8 ounces rice vermicelli noodles

2 tablespoons fish sauce

1 bird's-eye chili, sliced

½ cup water

¼ cup lime juice

2 tablespoons brown sugar

2 tablespoons rice wine vinegar

1 teaspoon grated fresh ginger

1 clove garlic, minced

4 cups butter lettuce leaves

2 Persian cucumbers, thinly sliced

2 small carrots, julienned

1 cup mung bean sprouts

1 jalapeño, thinly sliced

½ cup fresh mint leaves

½ cup fresh Thai basil leaves

½ cup fresh cilantro leaves

1 cup chopped salted roasted peanuts

Lime wedges, for garnish

DIRECTIONS

1   Cook the chicken strips according to package instructions. Cook the rice vermicelli noodles according to package instructions.

2   In a small bowl, whisk together the fish sauce, bird's-eye chili, water, lime juice, brown sugar, rice wine vinegar, ginger, and garlic.

3   Gather 4 serving bowls. In each bowl, place the lettuce leaves in the base of the bowl. In half of each bowl, place the vermicelli noodles. In the other half, place the cucumbers, carrots, sprouts, jalapeños, mint, basil, and cilantro. Top the salad with the chopped peanuts and the sauce.

PER SERVING: *Calories 807 (From Fat 309); Fat 34g (Saturated 9g); Cholesterol 59mg; Sodium 1,992mg; Carbohydrate 92g (Dietary Fiber 8g); Protein 37g.*

NOTE: Bun is a Vietnamese salad that is traditionally made with nuoc cham sauce, rice noodles, herbs, and vegetables. I've had well-executed and poorly executed versions of this salad. This recipe has been my spin on one of my favorites, and I love the addition of the fried chicken fingers! Pork sausage balls or grilled steak also work well.

TIP: You can find nuoc cham sauce in a bottle if you want to further simplify this recipe. Just don't skip the fresh herbs — they really elevate the salad flavors!

Lebanese Tabbouleh Salad

PREP TIME: ABOUT 15 MIN | **COOK TIME: 20 MIN** | **YIELD: 6 SERVINGS**

INGREDIENTS

¼ cup fine bulgur (uncooked)

2 large tomatoes, finely diced

2 Persian cucumbers, finely diced

½ small onion, finely chopped

¼ teaspoon cinnamon

⅛ teaspoon cloves

1 tablespoon sesame seeds

4 cups finely chopped parsley

¼ cup chopped fresh mint leaves

1 lemon, juiced

½ teaspoon sea salt

¼ teaspoon cracked pepper

¼ cup extra-virgin olive oil

DIRECTIONS

In a medium bowl, mix all the ingredients together. Let the salad sit at room temperature for 1 hour prior to serving. Refrigerate after 1 hour.

PER SERVING: *Calories 153 (From Fat 93); Fat 10g (Saturated 1g); Cholesterol 0mg; Sodium 188mg; Carbohydrate 14g (Dietary Fiber 4g); Protein 3g.*

NOTE: Fine bulgur is a small grain typically used in tabbouleh. The juices from the tomatoes, lemon juice, and herbs reconstitute the bulgur, making it unnecessary to cook the bulgur first. If you can only find the larger grain, allow the salad to sit longer to reconstitute the grain.

VARY IT! Trying adding garbanzo beans, olives, or capers to the salad.

NOTE: Serve tabbouleh wrapped in pita bread or as a side salad, or serve grilled meat on top.

Egyptian Barley and Pomegranate Salad

PREP TIME: 15 MIN	COOK TIME: 6 MIN	YIELD: 6 SERVINGS

INGREDIENTS

8 ounces halloumi cheese

¼ cup sesame seeds

½ cup olive oil (for frying)

2 cups cooked pearl barley

1 cup chopped fresh parsley

¼ cup chopped fresh dill

3 green onions, finely chopped

4 dates, pitted and thinly sliced

1 celery stalk, thinly sliced

½ cup pomegranate arils

½ lemon, juiced

2 tablespoons pomegranate molasses

½ teaspoon ground cumin

¼ teaspoon ground allspice

1 clove garlic, minced

¼ cup extra-virgin olive oil

Salt to taste

Pepper to taste

¼ cup pistachios

DIRECTIONS

1 Cut the halloumi into ½-inch fingers. Press the halloumi into the sesame seeds to coat. In a heavy skillet, heat the olive oil over medium heat. Pan-fry the halloumi until golden, about 2 to 3 minutes per side. Set aside and assemble the salad.

2 In a serving bowl, stir together the barley, parsley, dill, onions, dates, celery, and pomegranate arils.

3 In a small bowl, whisk together the lemon juice, pomegranate molasses, cumin, allspice, garlic, and olive oil. Pour the dressing over the salad. Season with salt and pepper to taste. Top with halloumi and pistachios to serve.

PER SERVING: *Calories 447 (From Fat 260); Fat 29g (Saturated 9g); Cholesterol 27mg; Sodium 440mg; Carbohydrate 39g (Dietary Fiber 6g); Protein 12g.*

NOTE: To make pomegranate molasses from scratch, see the Middle Eastern Fattoush Salad recipe at the beginning of this chapter for instructions.

NOTE: Halloumi is a firm, mild cheese from Cyprus, traditionally made from sheep or goat milk. It's similar to queso blanco cheese or queso panela. Halloumi holds up to being pan-fried, and the firm texture and high protein make it a great meat substitute, too.

VARY IT! Almonds, walnuts, or pine nuts can be used in place of pistachios. You can also try other combinations of herbs, from fresh mint to cilantro.

TIP: You can buy pomegranate arils in the freezer section of specialty markets. In season, you may find them fresh.

Ethiopian Azifa Salad

PREP TIME: ABOUT 15 MIN	COOK TIME: 20 MIN	YIELD: 6 SERVINGS

INGREDIENTS

1 cup green lentils, washed

2½ cups cold water (for cooking)

2 Roma tomatoes

1 serrano pepper or 1 small green bell pepper

1 small red onion

¼ cup lime juice

1 tablespoon black mustard seed, ground

3 tablespoons vegetable oil

Salt to taste

DIRECTIONS

1 In a medium saucepan, place the lentils and cold water. Bring to a boil; then cover and simmer until just tender, about 15 to 20 minutes. Keep the lentils slightly firm and not soggy. Drain and set aside.

2 Meanwhile, dice the tomatoes, pepper, and onion and add to a medium serving bowl. Stir in the lime juice, mustard seed, and oil. Add the lentils, stir, and season with salt. Refrigerate the salad at least 1 hour prior to serving.

PER SERVING: *Calories 192 (From Fat 68); Fat 8g (Saturated 1g); Cholesterol 0mg; Sodium 4mg; Carbohydrate 23g (Dietary Fiber 11g); Protein 9g.*

NOTE: This salad can be kept refrigerated for up to 5 days.

NOTE: Azifa is a green lentil salad often served as a snack or side dish throughout Ethiopia. I first had this at an Ethiopian restaurant in Washington, D.C., and I've tried to capture the flavors here.

NOTE: Mustard seeds have a distinct flavor. They're often used in Indian cuisine as well.

VARY IT! You can also use cumin, coriander, and cilantro if it's more convenient than mustard seeds.

TIP: Serve with *teff injera* (Ethiopian flatbread) or Middle Eastern flatbreads.

Thai Green Papaya with Shrimp Salad

PREP TIME: ABOUT 15 MIN	COOK TIME: 20 MIN	YIELD: 4 SERVINGS

INGREDIENTS

1 green papaya

1 pound raw shrimp, shells removed and deveined

6 cloves garlic, minced and divided

4 bird's-eye peppers, divided

1 teaspoon sea salt

2 tablespoons butter

2 tablespoons vegetable oil

¼ cup fish sauce

¼ cup lime juice

2 tablespoons palm sugar or brown sugar

2 Roma tomatoes, seeded and diced

½ cup chopped fresh cilantro

½ cup chopped fresh Thai basil

¼ cup chopped fresh mint

1 cup chopped peanuts

DIRECTIONS

1 Peel the green papaya with a vegetable peeler. Cut the papaya in half and remove seeds. Slice the papaya into 1/4-inch slices, then julienne the papaya. Place the papaya in ice water for 5 minutes.

2 Meanwhile, season the shrimp with 2 teaspoons of the garlic, 1 finely chopped bird's-eye pepper, and the sea salt. In a large skillet, melt the butter and oil over medium-high heat. Add the shrimp in batches, cooking until pink in color, about 2 to 3 minutes per side. Remove and set aside while finishing the salad.

3 In a food processor, pulse 3 of the bird's-eye peppers with the remaining garlic, fish sauce, lime juice, and sugar for 1 minute.

4 Drain the julienned papaya and pat dry. In a medium bowl, place the papaya and use tongs to toss the papaya with the dressing, tomatoes, cilantro, basil, mint, and peanuts. Plate the salad and serve the shrimp over the top of the salad.

PER SERVING: *Calories 514 (From Fat 303); Fat 34g (Saturated 8g); Cholesterol 188mg; Sodium 2,191mg; Carbohydrate 22g (Dietary Fiber 5g); Protein 35g.*

NOTE: A green papaya is simply an unripened papaya. Green papayas are used throughout many Asian countries and cherished particularly in Thai food. When I prepared this salad at a cooking class in Indonesia, we used a stone mortar to grind the garlic and chilies. I've found that I had similar results pulsing with my food processor. If you have a mortar and pestle, give it a try. Green papaya is typically hand-cut thinly and julienned; alternatively, you can use a green papaya peeler, which is a specific tool often found in Asian markets or online stores.

NOTE: Soaking the papaya helps remove the milky white juice, keeping the salad crispier.

NOTE: Palm sugar comes from coconut nectar and toddy palm trees. It's a staple in Thai cuisine. Brown sugar is a decent substitute if you can't find palm sugar.

TIP: Serve with steamed jasmine rice to complete the meal.

Laotian Ground Pork Larb

PREP TIME: ABOUT 15 MIN | **COOK TIME: 25 MIN** | **YIELD: 6 SERVINGS**

INGREDIENTS

2 cups water (to cook the rice)

1 cup jasmine rice

2 tablespoons ground white rice flour (glutinous rice)

1½ pounds ground pork

2 tablespoons fish sauce

1 tablespoon palm sugar

1 small red onion, thinly sliced

2 bird's-eye chilies, sliced in half, or 1 serrano pepper, sliced in half

¼ cup lime juice

½ cup chopped fresh cilantro

½ cup chopped fresh Thai basil

¼ cup chopped fresh mint leaves

18 butter lettuce leaves (for lettuce cups)

½ cup chopped peanuts

Sriracha sauce, for serving

DIRECTIONS

1 In a medium saucepan, bring the water to a boil. Add the rice, stir, cover, lower the heat to a low simmer, and cook for 20 to 25 minutes.

2 In a skillet, toast the rice flour for 3 minutes over medium heat, stirring constantly. Remove from the pan and set aside. Add the ground pork to the pan and cook until fully cooked, about 12 minutes, stirring frequently to break up clumps. Drain off the excess liquid, and add the fish sauce, palm sugar, onions, and toasted rice flour. Continue to cook over low heat for 5 minutes. Stir in the lime juice, cilantro, basil, and mint. Remove from the heat.

3 To serve, fill the lettuce cups with the rice and ground pork mixture, similar to a lettuce wrap. Top with the chopped peanuts and Sriracha.

PER SERVING: Calories 644 (From Fat 278); Fat 31g (Saturated 10g); Cholesterol 82mg; Sodium 522mg; Carbohydrate 63g (Dietary Fiber 4g); Protein 28g.

NOTE: Larb is a meat salad from Laos. It's enjoyed throughout many Asian countries.

VARY IT! Larb can be made with ground chicken, ground turkey, or chopped mushrooms. Try a plant-forward approach by using 1 pound chopped mushrooms with 1 pound ground chicken. You can also add edamame, grated carrots, and sliced green onions to boost the vegetables in this recipe.

TIP: Serve larb as a side dish or make it the main dish!

English Garden Salad

PREP TIME: ABOUT 15 MIN | COOK TIME: 20 MIN | YIELD: 6 SERVINGS

INGREDIENTS

1 pound new potatoes

1 tablespoon salt (for boiling)

1 cup cut green beans

½ cup green peas

3 tablespoons mayonnaise

1 tablespoon mustard

2 teaspoons white wine vinegar

1 shallot, minced

½ teaspoon sugar

½ teaspoon sea salt

½ teaspoon cracked pepper

4 cups butter lettuce leaves

3 tablespoons chopped chives

3 radishes, thinly sliced

¼ cup chopped fresh parsley

DIRECTIONS

1 Place the potatoes in a large saucepan, cover with water, and add the 1 tablespoon of salt. Bring the potatoes to a boil; then simmer with the lid on for 15 minutes. Add the green beans to the potatoes, cover, and continue cooking for 4 minutes. Then add the peas and cook for 1 minute. The potatoes should be fork tender at this point. Drain and run cold water over the vegetables for 2 minutes; set aside.

2 Next, whisk together the mayonnaise, mustard, vinegar, shallot, sugar, salt, and pepper. Cut the cooked potatoes in quarters.

3 To serve the salad, lay the torn lettuce leaves on the base of a plate. Top the lettuce leaves with the potatoes, green beans, peas, chives, and radishes. Drizzle the dressing over the top and garnish with parsley. Serve immediately.

PER SERVING: *Calories 110 (From Fat 25); Fat 3g (Saturated 0g); Cholesterol 2mg; Sodium 94mg; Carbohydrate 19g (Dietary Fiber 2g); Protein 3g.*

TIP: Serve with a dense brown or whole-grain bread.

Canadian Maple, Cabbage, and Cranberry Salad

PREP TIME: ABOUT 30 MIN	COOK TIME: NONE	YIELD: 8 SERVINGS

INGREDIENTS

½ cup fresh or frozen and defrosted cranberries

2 tablespoons maple syrup

2 tablespoons apple cider vinegar

1 teaspoon mustard

¼ cup canola oil

1 teaspoon salt

4 cups shredded purple cabbage

1 carrot, grated

1 green apple, thinly sliced

¼ cup pumpkin seeds

2 tablespoons chopped fresh mint

DIRECTIONS

1 Using a blender or food processor, blend the cranberries, maple syrup, vinegar, and mustard for 1 minute, scraping down the sides as needed. While blending, drizzle in the oil and salt.

2 Next, place the cabbage, carrot, apple, and pumpkin seeds in a serving bowl. Toss the vegetables with the cranberry maple vinaigrette and stir in the fresh mint. Let the salad rest for 15 minutes, adjust the seasoning as desired, and serve immediately.

PER SERVING: *Calories 125 (From Fat 80); Fat 9g (Saturated 1g); Cholesterol 0mg; Sodium 249mg; Carbohydrate 11g (Dietary Fiber 2g); Protein 2g.*

NOTE: Store the salad in an airtight container in the refrigerator for up to 3 days.

NOTE: Cranberries grow well throughout Canada and the United States. This dressing is tangy and bright in flavor and sweetened with a hint of maple.

TIP: Serve this slaw alongside pork chops or a pork tenderloin and crusty rye bread.

Spicy Filipino-Style Ceviche

PREP TIME: 15 MIN PLUS 1 HR FOR RESTING	COOK TIME: NONE	YIELD: 6 SERVINGS

INGREDIENTS

1 pound sushi-grade yellowfin tuna

¼ cup full-fat coconut milk

One 3-inch piece ginger, minced

1 small red onion, thinly sliced

3 bird's-eye chilies or 2 serrano peppers, thinly sliced

½ cup calamansi juice or lime juice

2 firm Filipino mangos, diced (Ataulfo mangos)

2 green onions, thinly sliced

DIRECTIONS

Cube the tuna into 1-inch pieces and place in a glass bowl. Stir in the coconut milk, ginger, red onion, chilies, calamansi juice or lime juice, mangos, and green onions. Refrigerate for 1 to 2 hours before serving.

PER SERVING: *Calories 144 (From Fat 9); Fat 1g (Saturated 1g); Cholesterol 34mg; Sodium 34mg; Carbohydrate 15g (Dietary Fiber 2g); Protein 18g.*

NOTE: Calamansi is a Filipino lime, but it has an orange flesh and a tart orange and lime flavor. I've had this dish many times, because while my husband was working in the Philippines, it quickly became his favorite. We prefer more citrus flavors, but I've had it made with coconut vinegar as well. If the citrus is too strong, try using half coconut vinegar (found in Asian markets) and half lime juice.

NOTE: *Sushi-grade* refers to fish that has been cleaned immediately upon being caught and flash frozen at –35 degrees for at least 15 hours to ward off unwanted parasites.

NOTE: This salad should be consumed the same day you make it.

TIP: If using raw fish makes you squeamish, try using cooked shrimp instead.

TIP: Serve with sticky rice and fried wonton chips.

Mexican Zesty Shrimp Aguachile with Peanuts

PREP TIME: ABOUT 20 MIN	COOK TIME: NONE	YIELD: 8 SERVINGS

INGREDIENTS

2 pounds large uncooked shrimp, peeled and deveined

¾ cup lime juice

¼ cup orange juice

1 bunch cilantro, divided

2 serrano peppers

1 teaspoon sea salt

1 jalapeño, thinly sliced

1 small red onion, thinly sliced

3 Persian cucumbers, thinly sliced

½ cup chopped roasted peanuts

DIRECTIONS

1 Place the raw shrimp in a large glass bowl for mixing.

2 In a blender, place the lime juice, orange juice, cilantro stems, ½ of the cilantro leaves, serrano peppers, and salt. Blend until smooth, about 2 to 3 minutes. Pour the mixture over the shrimp, stir, and refrigerate for at least 15 minutes. Next, stir in the remaining cilantro leaves, jalapeño, onion, cucumbers, and peanuts. Stir to coat and serve immediately.

PER SERVING: *Calories 196 (From Fat 59); Fat 7g (Saturated 1g); Cholesterol 172mg; Sodium 449mg; Carbohydrate 8g (Dietary Fiber 2g); Protein 26g.*

NOTE: Aguachile is a spicy, green shrimp ceviche from Mexico.

VARY IT! Replace the raw shrimp with cooked shrimp if you prefer to use cooked seafood. Sushi-grade yellowfin tuna, halibut, or squid can also be used in this dish. If you prefer a less spicy dish, omit the serrano peppers and use only the jalapeño.

TIP: Serve with fried corn tortilla chips.

Chapter **10**

Going Bold with Bowls

RECIPES IN THIS CHAPTER

Crunchy Southwestern Bowls

Texas-Style Chopped House Bowls

Zesty Thai Steak Bowls

Fiesta Bowls

Mediterranean Farro Bowls

Creamy Coconut Chicken Bowls

Chinese Chicken Slaw Bowls

Moroccan Spiced Veggie Bowls

Asian Ground Beef and Rice Bowls

Tangy Barbecue Chicken Bowls

Grilled Chicken Shawarma Bowls

Nutty Chinese Noodle Bowls

Cold Ramen Noodle Bowls

Big, bold, flavorful salad bowls are all the rage, and they aren't going away! Salad bowls generally have a starchy base, a protein, and loads of vegetables all arranged in a visually creative way. Bowls can be simple when you use canned goods or more elaborate with extensive ingredients. In this chapter, I offer a little of both.

Bowls are great for the whole family. Building your own bowls is an empowering act for kids of all ages. You don't need to prepare bowls for people; instead, you can allow each person autonomy to craft their own dish. My daughter gets creative with her bowls and helps me choose toppings to put out on the table before mealtime. This simple act is setting her up to be skilled in the kitchen in the future.

Get your taste buds ready! This chapter includes spicy bowls, such as Zesty Thai Steak Bowls and Moroccan Spiced Veggie Bowls. If you're looking for main meals, check out the Crispy Chicken Shawarma and Asian Ground Beef and Rice Bowls. Our family favorites include Fiesta Bowls, Mediterranean Farro Bowls, and Tangy Barbecue Chicken Bowls. If you have a picnic or potluck coming up, consider the Cold Ramen Noodle Bowls and the Nutty Chinese Noodle Bowls — both pair well with barbecue!

Crunchy Southwestern Bowls

PREP TIME: ABOUT 10 MIN	COOK TIME: 25 MIN	YIELD: 4 SERVINGS

INGREDIENTS

2 tablespoons vegetable oil

1 cup basmati rice or long-grain white rice

1 cup chicken stock

One 8-ounce can tomato sauce

1 teaspoon chili powder

1 teaspoon paprika

1 teaspoon garlic powder

1 teaspoon cumin

1 teaspoon sea salt

½ cup plain Greek yogurt or sour cream

3 tablespoons lime juice

2 tablespoons Cholula hot sauce (optional)

¼ teaspoon salt

One 14.5-ounce can black beans, drained and rinsed

2 cups diced cooked chicken or shredded rotisserie chicken

3 cups shredded romaine lettuce

1 cup shredded purple cabbage

1 cup pico de gallo (chopped salsa)

1 cup prepared guacamole or 1 avocado, chopped

½ cup shredded Mexican-style cheese

1 cup crushed corn chips

DIRECTIONS

1 In medium saucepan, heat the oil over medium-high heat until it begins to pop. Add the rice, stirring to toast until it becomes translucent, about 2 to 3 minutes. Add the chicken stock, tomato sauce, chili powder, paprika, garlic powder, cumin, and sea salt. Stir, cover with a lid, and reduce the heat to a low simmer until the liquid is gone and the rice is tender, about 20 minutes.

2 Next, prepare the dressing. In a small bowl, whisk together the Greek yogurt, lime juice, and hot sauce. Season with salt, to taste.

3 To assemble the bowls, either serve family-style or divide the rice among 4 bowls. Divide the beans, chicken, lettuce, cabbage, pico de gallo, and guacamole or avocado among the 4 bowls. Top each bowl with 2 tablespoons shredded cheese and crushed tortilla chips. Drizzle the creamy yogurt sauce over the top and serve.

PER SERVING: *Calories 733 (From Fat 276); Fat 31g (Saturated 9g); Cholesterol 91mg; Sodium 1,664mg; Carbohydrate 75g (Dietary Fiber 15g); Protein 41g.*

NOTE: You can save time with this dish by using a rotisserie chicken or canned cooked chicken, using a premade rice, using prechopped lettuce and cabbage, or buying convenient store-bought items like guacamole and salsa.

Texas-Style Chopped House Bowls

PREP TIME: ABOUT 10 MIN | **COOK TIME: 20 MIN** | **YIELD: 4 SERVINGS**

INGREDIENTS

1½ pounds sirloin steaks, trimmed and cut into 1-inch cubes

One 8-ounce package button or cremini mushrooms

1 tablespoon Worcestershire sauce

¼ cup extra-virgin olive oil, divided

½ teaspoon black pepper

1 tablespoon plus ½ teaspoon salt, divided

1 pound new potatoes, quartered

1 cup sour cream

½ cup milk, or more for thinning mashed potatoes

4 cups shredded iceberg or romaine lettuce

1 carrot, grated

1 cup grape tomatoes, halved

½ cup fried onions

½ cup Blue Cheese Dressing (see Chapter 6)

DIRECTIONS

1 Heat the grill to 450 degrees. Rub the cubed steak and mushrooms with Worcestershire sauce, olive oil, pepper, and the ½ teaspoon of the salt. Skewer the mushrooms and steak. Grill for 6 to 8 minutes (depending on desired doneness), turning halfway.

2 Meanwhile, place the quartered potatoes in a pot, cover with water, and add the remaining 1 tablespoon of salt. Bring to a boil, reduce the heat, cover, and simmer until fork tender, about 15 minutes. Drain. Using a potato masher, mash the potatoes with the sour cream and milk until your desired texture is reached.

3 To assemble the bowls, place the mashed potatoes as the base of the salad. Top the potatoes with the lettuce, carrot, tomatoes, onions, cubed steak, and mushrooms. Drizzle the Blue Cheese Dressing over the top and serve.

PER SERVING: *Calories 834 (From Fat 511); Fat 57g (Saturated 22g); Cholesterol 90mg; Sodium 807mg; Carbohydrate 39g (Dietary Fiber 5g); Protein 42g.*

NOTE: Mashed potatoes in a salad bowl? Yes, trust me! This is a go-to salad bowl in our house because my daughter loves mashed potatoes, and my husband loves steak. Each family member gets to pick their favorite toppings, making it a winning family meal option.

VARY IT! Try different topping options for this salad, from Ranch Dressing (see Chapter 6) to canned corn, diced bell peppers, and shredded cheese.

TIP: Save time with preshredded lettuce and grated carrots.

Zesty Thai Steak Bowls

INGREDIENTS

¼ cup creamy, all-natural peanut butter

¼ teaspoon ground ginger powder

1 tablespoon fish sauce

1 lime, zested and juiced

1 tablespoon rice wine vinegar or white wine vinegar

2 to 3 tablespoons water, to thin dressing as needed

1 tablespoon extra-virgin olive oil

2 bird's-eye chili peppers, sliced in half lengthwise

1½ pounds sirloin steaks, thinly sliced

½ teaspoon salt

2 cups shredded red cabbage

3 cups shredded romaine lettuce

1 cup grated carrot

1 cup julienned red bell pepper

½ cup Thai basil leaves

½ cup chopped cilantro

½ red onion thinly sliced

1 cup roasted and salted peanuts, chopped

Sriracha sauce (optional)

DIRECTIONS

1 In a small bowl, whisk together the peanut butter, ginger, fish sauce, lime zest, lime juice, and vinegar. Let the dressing sit while preparing the salad. Then, thin the dressing with water as desired before dressing the salad bowls. (The dressing should be as thin as most creamy dressings.)

2 In a large skillet, heat the olive oil and chilies over medium-high heat. Season the steak with salt. Add the steak to the pan and stir-fry until browned and fully cooked, about 6 minutes. Remove from the heat.

3 The bowls can be served family-style or prepared. To prepare, layer the cabbage and lettuce at the base of a salad bowl. Add the carrots, bell pepper, basil, cilantro, onion, and peanuts. Top with the stir-fried steak and chilies. To serve, drizzle the peanut sauce over the top and drizzle with Sriracha for an added kick.

PER SERVING: *Calories 761 (From Fat 462); Fat 51g (Saturated 13g); Cholesterol 93mg; Sodium 826mg; Carbohydrate 21g (Dietary Fiber 8g); Protein 57g.*

NOTE: Grilled steak can be substituted for stir-fried steak. Sirloin is an inexpensive and lean cut of beef, perfect for weeknight meals when you crave beefy protein in a hurry.

VARY IT! For your next Meatless Monday, try 2 cups of cooked edamame or fried tofu instead of steak.

TIP: Save time with preshredded lettuce, cabbage, and carrots.

Fiesta Bowls

PREP TIME: ABOUT 10 MIN	COOK TIME: 10 MIN	YIELD: 4 SERVINGS

INGREDIENTS

1 pound ground beef

1 teaspoon cumin powder

1 teaspoon garlic powder

1 teaspoon onion powder

2 tablespoon chili powder

1 teaspoon salt

One 14.5-ounce can pinto beans, drained and rinsed

6 cups chopped or torn romaine lettuce

2 cups tortilla or corn chips, slightly crushed

2 cups shredded red cabbage

1 Haas avocado, diced

1 cup grape tomatoes, halved

½ red onion, finely diced

1 cup salsa

2 cups shredded cheddar cheese or Monterey Jack cheese

2 limes, juiced

½ cup Greek yogurt or sour cream

2 tablespoons hot sauce

DIRECTIONS

1 In a large skillet, cook the ground beef over medium-high heat for 5 minutes, crumbling the meat as it cooks. Meanwhile, in a small bowl, mix together the cumin powder, garlic powder, onion powder, chili powder, and salt. Add the spice mixture and the pinto beans to the ground meat and continue to cook for 5 minutes.

2 This dish can be served as a layered salad or family-style, allowing family members to serve themselves and create their own. To serve as a layered salad, place the lettuce at the base of a salad bowl. Top with the chips, shredded cabbage, avocado, tomatoes, onion, salsa, and cheese. Place the cooked meat on top of the salad.

3 Next, in a small bowl, make the dressing. Whisk together the lime juice, Greek yogurt or sour cream, and hot sauce. Drizzle the dressing over the top or allow people to dress their own salad as desired.

PER SERVING: *Calories 706 (From Fat 360); Fat 40g (Saturated 19g); Cholesterol 145mg; Sodium 1,842mg; Carbohydrate 42g (Dietary Fiber 12g); Protein 48g.*

NOTE: This taco-style salad is one of our favorites. I often make it while camping.

NOTE: Use the type of ground beef you prefer. If it has a higher fat content, drain off the excess liquid so the salad isn't too juicy.

TIP: You can make the beef in an Instant Pot by browning it with the spices. Add 1 can of diced tomatoes and ½ cup water and beans. Secure the lid and cook under high pressure for 4 minutes. Naturally release or do a quick release after 10 minutes. I make this in an Instant Pot and hold it warm until it's dinnertime.

Mediterranean Farro Bowls

PREP TIME: ABOUT 10 MIN	COOK TIME: 25 MIN	YIELD: 4 SERVINGS

INGREDIENTS

4 cups chicken or vegetable stock

1 cup farro, rinsed

1 lemon, zested and juiced

½ cup extra-virgin olive oil, divided

½ teaspoon sea salt

4 cups arugula or baby spinach leaves or shredded kale leaves

2 Roma tomatoes, diced

½ cup diced canned roasted red bell peppers

1 small red onion or 2 shallots, thinly sliced

½ cup chopped black olives

1 cup hummus

1 lemon, cut into wedges

¼ cup chopped parsley or basil leaves

¼ cup crumbled feta or goat cheese

DIRECTIONS

1 In a medium saucepan, bring the stock to a boil over high heat. Stir in the farro, cover, and reduce to a simmer for 25 to 35 minutes or per package instructions. Remove from the heat and drain off any excess liquid. Dress with lemon juice, lemon zest, and ¼ cup of the olive oil. Season with salt, to taste.

2 To assemble the bowls, either serve family-style or divide the dressed farro among 4 bowls. Divide the arugula, spinach, or kale; tomatoes; bell peppers; onion or shallots; olives; and hummus among the 4 bowls.

3 Squeeze 1 lemon wedge over each of the bowls and drizzle 1 tablespoon olive oil over each bowl. Top with the herbs and cheese.

PER SERVING: *Calories 682 (From Fat 357); Fat 40g (Saturated 7g); Cholesterol 16mg; Sodium 1,013mg; Carbohydrate 67g (Dietary Fiber 13g); Protein 17g.*

NOTE: Farro is an old-world grain that looks similar to barley. It has a nutty flavor and chewy texture.

VARY IT! If you feel like you're missing meat, add shredded rotisserie chicken or serve with grilled salmon.

TIP: If you can't find farro, try pearled barley for a quicker grain option.

Creamy Coconut Chicken Bowls

PREP TIME: 30 MIN	COOK TIME: 30 MIN	YIELD: 4 SERVINGS

INGREDIENTS

1¼ cups full-fat coconut milk, divided

1 tablespoon curry powder

1 teaspoon ground cumin

1 lemon, zested and juiced

1 pound boneless, skinless chicken thighs

1¾ cups water

½ teaspoon salt

1 cup jasmine or basmati rice, rinsed

3 tablespoons tahini (ground sesame butter)

1 clove garlic, minced

¼ teaspoon paprika

8 cups baby spinach

1 cup chopped cashews

DIRECTIONS

1 In a shallow baking dish, mix 1 cup of the coconut milk, the curry powder, the cumin, and the lemon zest. Add the chicken thighs and marinate at room temperature for at least 30 minutes. Preheat the grill to 425 degrees.

2 In a medium saucepan, add the water and salt and bring to a boil over high heat. Stir in the rice, cover, and reduce to a simmer until cooked, about 15 to 20 minutes. Remove from the heat. Fluff the rice with a fork, cover, and set aside.

3 Remove the chicken from the marinade and grill until fully cooked to an internal temperature of 165 degrees, about 12 to 15 minutes, turning the chicken after 8 minutes of cooking.

4 Meanwhile, make the coconut tahini dressing. In a small bowl, whisk together the lemon juice, tahini, garlic, paprika, and coconut milk (adding more coconut milk as needed to make a thin dressing).

5 Either serve as family-style at the table or, to assemble bowls, place the spinach at the base of 4 bowls; then add the rice, grilled chicken, and cashews. Drizzle with the dressing, as desired.

PER SERVING: Calories 663 (From Fat 275); Fat 31g (Saturated 9g); Cholesterol 71mg; Sodium 627mg; Carbohydrate 60g (Dietary Fiber 5g); Protein 32g.

NOTE: Coconut adds a sweetness to this dish and pairs well with the tahini.

TIP: Look for precooked rice in the freezer section or bulk-cook and freeze your own!

VARY IT! Add grilled sweet potatoes or roasted butternut squash, or replace the spinach with thinly sliced Swiss chard or baby arugula.

Chinese Chicken Slaw Bowls

PREP TIME: ABOUT 15 MIN	COOK TIME: NONE	YIELD: 4 SERVINGS

INGREDIENTS

3 tablespoons rice wine vinegar

1 teaspoon sesame oil

¼ cup canola oil or vegetable oil

2 tablespoons low-sodium soy sauce

½ teaspoon ground ginger

1 teaspoon garlic powder

1 tablespoon black sesame seeds

6 cups shredded napa cabbage

2 cups shredded rotisserie chicken or canned chicken

1 red bell pepper, julienned

1 medium carrot, grated

4 green onions, finely sliced on the bias

½ cup chopped peanuts, almonds, or cashews

1 cup crunchy wontons or fried noodles

8 ounces canned mandarin oranges (in water or juice), drained

DIRECTIONS

1 In a small bowl, whisk together the vinegar, sesame oil, canola or vegetable oil, soy sauce, ginger, garlic powder, and black sesame seeds.

2 In a large salad bowl, mix the cabbage, chicken, bell pepper, carrots, onions, nuts, wontons or fried noodles, and mandarin wedges. Drizzle over the dressing and toss to serve.

PER SERVING: Calories 488 (From Fat 287); Fat 32g (Saturated 4g); Cholesterol 60mg; Sodium 460mg; Carbohydrate 23g (Dietary Fiber 5g); Protein 30g.

NOTE: Black sesame seeds add a pop of color to this salad; try not to skip them.

NOTE: The salad will wilt over time, so be sure not to dress it until just before serving. The salad can be stored in the refrigerator for later — just be aware that the texture will change to more like a coleslaw.

TIP: Although a rotisserie chicken is my favorite, don't frown at canned chicken. It can help you out when you're in a bind! Costco brand has won taste tests for the best canned chicken, and one can is 12.5 ounces.

Moroccan Spiced Veggie Bowls

PREP TIME: ABOUT 15 MIN	COOK TIME: 25 MIN	YIELD: 4 SERVINGS

INGREDIENTS

1 teaspoon curry powder

1 teaspoon cumin

¼ teaspoon cinnamon

2 tablespoons apple cider vinegar

¼ cup extra-virgin olive oil, divided

3 orange sweet potatoes, scrubbed and ½-inch cubed

2 cups cauliflower florets

1 tablespoon white wine vinegar

2 teaspoons harissa

1 tablespoon pomegranate syrup

One 14.5-ounce can garbanzo beans, drained and rinsed

2 tomatoes, seeded and diced

1 cucumber, seeded and diced

¼ cup chopped parsley

1 cup chopped walnuts

½ cup crumbled feta

DIRECTIONS

1 Preheat the oven to 425 degrees. Line a baking sheet with parchment paper.

2 In a medium bowl, stir together the curry powder, cumin, cinnamon, apple cider vinegar, and 1 tablespoon of the olive oil. Mix in the sweet potatoes and cauliflower florets, stirring to coat. Pour onto the baking sheet and bake until the vegetables are golden and tender, about 20 to 25 minutes.

3 Next, mix the dressing. In a small bowl, whisk together the remaining 3 tablespoons of olive oil, the white wine vinegar, the harissa, and the pomegranate syrup.

4 To assemble the salad, place the roasted vegetables as the base. Top the vegetables with garbanzo beans, tomatoes, cucumbers, parsley, and walnuts. Pour the dressing over the top and toss the salad. Serve with crumbled feta over the top.

PER SERVING: *Calories 539 (From Fat 353); Fat 39g (Saturated 7g); Cholesterol 17mg; Sodium 555mg; Carbohydrate 39g (Dietary Fiber 9g); Protein 13g.*

NOTE: Harissa is a spicy, red chili paste hailing from Africa. If you want to make the salad without the spice, use ½ teaspoon of paprika instead.

VARY IT! Add grated carrots, diced zucchini, sesame seeds, pumpkin seeds, or chopped peanuts.

TIP: This is a hearty and filling vegetarian salad. If you want meat, add grilled chicken or pan-fried rockfish. Serve with flatbread.

Asian Ground Beef and Rice Bowls

PREP TIME: ABOUT 10 MIN	COOK TIME: 20 MIN	YIELD: 4 SERVINGS

INGREDIENTS

2 cups water

1 cup basmati rice, rinsed

1½ pounds ground beef

1 tablespoon brown sugar

3 tablespoons low-sodium soy sauce

1 teaspoon garlic powder

½ teaspoon ground ginger

¼ teaspoon crushed red peppers

2 tablespoons sesame seeds

1 tablespoon butter

1 tablespoon vegetable oil

4 eggs

2 carrots, julienned or grated

1 English cucumber, thinly sliced

2 green onions, thinly sliced

Sriracha sauce, to taste (optional)

DIRECTIONS

1 In a medium saucepan, bring the water to a boil over high heat. Stir in the rice, cover, and reduce the heat to a simmer until cooked, about 15 to 20 minutes.

2 Meanwhile, in a large skillet, add the ground beef and cook over medium heat until browned, about 10 minutes. Add the brown sugar, soy sauce, garlic powder, ginger, and crushed red peppers and cook over low heat for 5 minutes. Stir in the sesame seeds and remove from the heat.

3 In a medium skillet, heat the butter and oil over medium heat. Add the eggs, and fry over medium or over easy.

4 To assemble, divide the rice among 4 bowls, and divide the ground meat and sauce on top of the rice. Top with the carrots, cucumbers, and onions. Place a fried egg over the top and drizzle Sriracha over the top, if desired. Serve immediately.

PER SERVING: *Calories 612 (From Fat 201); Fat 22g (Saturated 8g); Cholesterol 325mg; Sodium 633mg; Carbohydrate 52g (Dietary Fiber 4g); Protein 48g.*

NOTE: This salad is inspired by Korean bibimbap bowls.

NOTE: Use the type of ground beef you prefer. If it has a higher fat content, drain off the excess liquid so the salad isn't too juicy.

TIP: Look for precooked rice in the freezer section or bulk-cook and freeze your own!

VARY IT! Add bean sprouts, *kimchi* (Korean fermented cabbage), or shredded cabbage to spruce up the salad bowl.

Tangy Barbecue Chicken Bowls

PREP TIME: ABOUT 5 MIN	COOK TIME: 20 MIN	YIELD: 6 SERVINGS

INGREDIENTS

1½ pounds chicken breasts or thighs

1 teaspoon salt

½ teaspoon pepper

1 cup barbecue sauce

½ cup Ranch Dressing (see Chapter 6)

1 can green chilies, drained

½ cup chopped cilantro, divided

4 cups potato salad or roasted potatoes

4 cups chopped romaine lettuce

1 cup shredded purple cabbage

½ cup canned corn, drained

1 red, yellow, or orange bell pepper, julienned

½ cup canned black beans, drained and rinsed

1 small red onion, chopped

DIRECTIONS

1 Heat the grill to 425 degrees. Season the chicken with salt and pepper. Grill until fully cooked and the chicken reaches an internal temperature of 165 degrees, about 8 to 10 minutes per side. Brush chicken with barbecue sauce the last minute of cooking and more after removing it from the grill. Let the meat rest for 5 minutes; then slice it into bite-size pieces.

2 In a food processor or blender, blend the Ranch Dressing, green chilies, and ¼ cup of the cilantro.

3 To assemble, place the potato salad or roasted potatoes as the base of the bowl. Top with romaine, cabbage, corn, bell pepper, black beans, and red onion. Drizzle the dressing over the top. Place the grilled barbecue chicken on top and sprinkle with the remaining cilantro for garnish. Serve immediately.

PER SERVING: *Calories 534 (From Fat 246); Fat 27g (Saturated 5g); Cholesterol 78mg; Sodium 890mg; Carbohydrate 44g (Dietary Fiber 6g); Protein 28g.*

NOTE: Using Ranch Dressing as a base for the dressing allows you to work with a convenient food and make it your own. Green chilies can be found in mild or spicy varieties, so pick your preferred heat level.

NOTE: Potato salad really makes this bowl delicious. Pick up your favorite prepared potato salad or make your own.

VARY IT! If potato salad isn't your thing, opt for macaroni salad or roasted potatoes. Sticking with the barbecue theme, add pickled jalapeños or chopped dill pickles, or try it with smoked brisket or ranch-style pinto beans.

TIP: Serve this salad with corn bread or cheesy garlic bread.

Grilled Chicken Shawarma Bowls

PREP TIME: 35 MIN	COOK TIME: 20 MIN	YIELD: 4 SERVINGS

INGREDIENTS

1 cup whole-fat Greek yogurt, divided

¼ cup lemon juice, divided

1 tablespoon ground cumin

2 teaspoons ground coriander

2 teaspoons paprika

4 cloves garlic, chopped, divided

1 pound skinless, boneless chicken thighs

1 cucumber, seeded

1 tablespoon dried dillweed

½ teaspoon sea salt

4 flatbreads

¼ cup extra-virgin olive oil

4 cups Lebanese Tabbouleh Salad (see Chapter 9)

1 cup hummus

12 kalamata olives, pitted and halved

½ cup crumbled feta

DIRECTIONS

1 Preheat the grill to 425 degrees.

2 In a large bowl, mix together ½ cup of the Greek yogurt, 3 tablespoons of the lemon juice, the cumin, the coriander, the paprika, and ½ of the chopped garlic. Add the chicken and marinate for at least 30 minutes or overnight.

3 Next, grate the cucumber over a tea towel. Squeeze out the liquid from the cucumber by wrapping up the tea towel and twisting to release the water from the cucumbers. Place the squeezed cucumber into a bowl. Stir in the remaining ½ cup of Greek yogurt, the remaining 1 tablespoon of lemon juice, and the remaining garlic. Add in the dillweed and salt, stir, and taste to adjust for seasonings.

4 Grill the chicken thighs until the internal temperature reaches 165 degrees, about 6 to 8 minutes per side. Remove from the grill and let the meat rest for 5 minutes before slicing. Place the flatbreads on the grill, brush with olive oil, and cook until slightly toasted, about 1 to 2 minutes per side.

5 To assemble the bowls, place the Lebanese Tabbouleh Salad at the base of the bowl. Top with the grilled chicken, hummus, cucumber mixture, olives, and feta. Serve with the toasted flatbread.

PER SERVING: *Calories 921 (From Fat 537); Fat 59g (Saturated 15g); Cholesterol 111mg; Sodium 1,599mg; Carbohydrate 61g (Dietary Fiber 11g); Protein 41g.*

NOTE: Shawarma is a popular Middle Eastern street food, often served with salad and french fries depending on where you're traveling. The meats (whether lamb, beef, or chicken) are seasoned, grilled, and thinly sliced. As you'll soon find out, it's delicious!

VARY IT! A side salad or a bed of lettuce can be swapped in for the tabbouleh. Try using radishes, cucumber slices, and raw onion on the meat.

Nutty Chinese Noodle Bowls

PREP TIME: ABOUT 15 MIN | COOK TIME: 20 MIN | YIELD: 8 SERVINGS

INGREDIENTS

16 ounces Asian egg noodles, such as Melissa's Fresh Chinese Noodles

½ cup all-natural peanut butter

¼ cup lime juice

2 tablespoons soy sauce

½ teaspoon grated fresh ginger

1 garlic clove, minced or grated

1 cup shelled edamame, cooked per package instructions and rinsed with cold water

1 cup julienned red bell pepper

1 cup grated carrots

4 green onions, thinly sliced

1 cup green beans, cut into 1-inch pieces and cooked

2 cups shredded napa cabbage

½ cup chopped peanuts

½ teaspoon crushed red peppers (optional)

DIRECTIONS

1 Cook the noodles according to package instructions. Drain and set aside.

2 Next, in a small bowl whisk together the peanut butter, lime juice, soy sauce, ginger, and garlic. Pour the dressing over the noodles, tossing to coat.

3 Add the edamame, bell peppers, carrots, green onions, green beans, cabbage, peanuts, and crushed red peppers to the pasta and toss to mix. Serve immediately or refrigerate in an air-tight container.

PER SERVING: *Calories 418 (From Fat 146); Fat 16g (Saturated 3g); Cholesterol 48mg; Sodium 295mg; Carbohydrate 53g (Dietary Fiber 6g); Protein 17g.*

NOTE: If you can't find Chinese egg noodles, don't fret! You can substitute spaghetti noodles instead — you just need to add 2 tablespoons baking soda to 8 cups boiling water. Cook the noodles in this pH-adjusted bath for egg noodle taste and texture. Don't skip this step!

VARY IT! Bok choy, radishes, purple cabbage, cilantro, or chicken all would work in this salad. If you want to kick up the heat even more, whisk Sriracha sauce into the dressing before tossing the noodles.

TIP: Serve this salad at your next potluck or with your favorite barbecue.

Cold Ramen Noodle Bowls

PREP TIME: ABOUT 15 MIN	COOK TIME: 10 MIN	YIELD: 4 SERVINGS

INGREDIENTS

2 packets ramen noodles

¼ cup sesame seeds

¼ cup mayonnaise

1 tablespoon rice vinegar

2 teaspoons soy sauce

1 teaspoon sugar

2 teaspoons sesame oil

2 ounces ham, thinly sliced and diced

1 cup shelled edamame, cooked according to package instructions and rinsed with cold water

2 cups thinly sliced romaine or iceberg lettuce

2 Persian cucumbers, thinly sliced

2 carrots, julienned

2 green onions, thinly sliced

2 hard-boiled eggs, cut in half

DIRECTIONS

1 In a medium saucepan, cook the ramen noodles according to package instructions and without the seasoning packet. Drain and place the noodles in the refrigerator for 10 minutes.

2 Meanwhile, in a small bowl, whisk together the sesame seeds, mayonnaise, vinegar, soy sauce, sugar, and sesame oil.

3 Next, toss the chilled noodles with the ham, edamame, lettuce, and dressing. Divide the dressed noodle salad among 4 individual bowls. Top each salad with cucumbers, carrots, onions, and eggs.

PER SERVING: *Calories 408 (From Fat 165); Fat 18g (Saturated 3g); Cholesterol 118mg; Sodium 980mg; Carbohydrate 45g (Dietary Fiber 6g); Protein 18g.*

NOTE: Cold ramen salads are popular in the Philippines, Guam, and Hawaii. My intern, Shai, shared this recipe with me.

VARY IT! Toppings make bowls more fun! Add julienned daikon radish, pickled ginger, sesame sticks, crispy fried chow mein noodles, corn, broccoli, and cherry tomatoes.

TIP: Serve this salad as a main dish or side salad. It's a perfect salad to share at picnics but wait to dress the salad until just before serving.

Chapter **11**

Plant-Forward Protein Salads

RECIPES IN THIS CHAPTER

- ☙ Vegetarian Cobb Salad
- ☙ Grilled Tofu with Soy and Ginger Salad
- ☙ Crunchy Peanut Zoodle Salad
- ☙ Shaved Brussels Sprouts and White Bean Salad
- ☙ Orange-Glazed Tempeh with Noodles Salad
- ☙ Lemon Miso Quinoa Crunch Salad
- ☙ Roasted Veggie Bowls with Peanut Dressing
- ☙ Roasted Butternut Squash, Pumpkin Seed, and Feta Salad
- ☙ Protein-Packed Pasta Salad
- ☙ Bean Fritters with Pesto Couscous Salad
- ☙ Turmeric-Spiced Cauliflower Salad with Tahini Dressing
- ☙ Shaved Asparagus and Walnuts Salad
- ☙ Edamame, Crispy Onions, and Farro Salad

Plant-forward or plant-based recipes have been trending, but there's still a lot of confusion behind the terms. *Plant-forward* means placing a focus on plant-based foods; it doesn't mean strictly vegetarian or vegan foods. In this chapter, I focus on clever ways to serve up protein-rich plant sources, from fun marinades to vibrant dressings. Although all of these recipes are vegetarian or vegan-friendly, the concept isn't about abstaining from meat sources — it's about filling a plate with a focus on plants first, from grains to vegetables. So, if you find yourself missing out on meat, there's no need to feel guilty if you pair these salads with your favorite meat-based proteins. You choose what you chew!

Over the years, I've heard many people say they hate tofu, but when I ask, I find they haven't even had it. A couple of salads in this chapter have protein-rich tofu or tempeh in them. Both soybean products soak up the flavors of whatever they're paired with, so if you like the flavors in the salad, there's a good chance you'll enjoy them, as well. Try it — you may like it!

Keep this chapter ready for Meatless Mondays! Our family favorites include the Roasted Veggie Bowls with Peanut Dressing and the Bean Fritters with Pesto Couscous.

Vegetarian Cobb Salad

PREP TIME: ABOUT 15 MIN	COOK TIME: 8 MIN	YIELD: 4 SERVINGS

INGREDIENTS

One 14.5-ounce can garbanzo beans, drained and rinsed

½ teaspoon sea salt

1 teaspoon paprika

¼ cup extra-virgin olive oil, for frying beans

8 cups chopped romaine lettuce

4 hard-boiled eggs, chopped

1 cup diced tomatoes

1 cup diced avocado

3 tablespoons chopped chives

¼ cup crumbled blue cheese

½ cup red wine vinaigrette

DIRECTIONS

1 With a towel, pat the garbanzo beans dry. In a medium bowl, mix the salt and paprika. In a heavy skillet, heat the olive oil over medium heat. When the oil begins to form small bubbles, add the garbanzo beans to the pan. Let the beans fry for 6 to 8 minutes, occasionally stirring the beans to fry on all sides. After the garbanzo beans are golden in color, remove them from the pan with a slotted spoon and put them into the bowl with seasonings. Toss the hot garbanzo beans with the seasonings. Set aside to cool.

2 To assemble the salad, place the lettuce at the base of a platter or serving bowl. Make lines on the lettuce with the eggs, tomatoes, avocado, and garbanzo beans. Top the salad with the chives and blue cheese. Dress the salad with the vinaigrette just before serving.

PER SERVING: *Calories 377 (From Fat 233); Fat 26g (Saturated 6g); Cholesterol 218mg; Sodium 1,091mg; Carbohydrate 25g (Dietary Fiber 8g); Protein 14g.*

NOTE: If you're missing bacon in this vegetarian version of the classic Cobb, try some of the newer meat-alternative bacons on the market.

TIP: Serve with crusty olive bread or sun-dried tomato bread.

Grilled Tofu with Soy and Ginger Salad

| PREP TIME: ABOUT 20 MIN | COOK TIME: 10 MIN | YIELD: 6 SERVINGS |

INGREDIENTS

14 ounces extra-firm tofu, drained

2 tablespoons cornstarch

1 tablespoon sesame seeds

6 tablespoons vegetable oil (for frying)

3 tablespoons light soy sauce

2 green onions, thinly sliced

½ teaspoon minced fresh ginger

2 teaspoons sesame oil

1 teaspoon sugar

3 tablespoons rice vinegar

4 cups shredded cabbage

1 cup grated carrots

½ cup thinly sliced celery

½ cup diced cucumber

1 cup julienned red, orange, or yellow bell peppers

½ cup chopped cilantro

DIRECTIONS

1 Place the drained tofu block between 2 tea towels. Place a heavy pan or plate on top to press the liquid from the tofu; press for 20 minutes. Cube the pressed tofu and toss with the cornstarch and sesame seeds.

2 Heat a skillet with vegetable oil over medium-high heat. When the oil begins to form little bubbles, add the tofu in a single layer. Fry the tofu for 2 to 3 minutes on each side or until golden brown in color. Remove from the pan and place the tofu on paper towels to drain. Repeat with the remaining tofu until all the tofu is cooked.

3 While the tofu is cooking, in a small bowl, whisk together the soy sauce, onions, ginger, sesame oil, sugar, and vinegar.

4 After the tofu is removed from the pan, turn off the heat and pour the soy mixture into the pan, stirring to deglaze the pan. Return the tofu to the pan, gently tossing the sauce over the top to coat; then set aside to cool.

5 In a large bowl, toss together the cabbage, carrots, celery, cucumber, bell peppers, and cilantro. Pour the tofu with the glaze over the salad and toss to coat. Serve immediately or chill until ready to serve. The salad will be less crunchy the longer it chills but the flavors will still be delicious.

PER SERVING: Calories 167 (From Fat 94); Fat 10g (Saturated 1g); Cholesterol 0mg; Sodium 339mg; Carbohydrate 12g (Dietary Fiber 3g); Protein 7g.

NOTE: If you've never tried pan-fried tofu, this recipe is a great place to start! It has a meat-like texture and takes on the flavors of whatever you're cooking.

VARY IT! Crush up a bag of ramen noodles (without the seasoning packet) for a crunchy addition. Add black sesame seeds for garnish to give the salad a bold pop of color and flavor.

TIP: Serve with crispy spring rolls.

Crunchy Peanut Zoodle Salad

PREP TIME: ABOUT 10 MIN	COOK TIME: NONE	YIELD: 6 SERVINGS

INGREDIENTS

½ cup chopped salted roasted peanuts

½ cup chopped cilantro

1 cup shredded carrots

1 cup julienned red bell pepper

6 cups zucchini noodles or zoodles (spiral-cut zucchini)

½ cup Spicy Peanut Dressing (see Chapter 6)

DIRECTIONS

In a large bowl, place all the ingredients. Toss and serve immediately.

PER SERVING: *Calories 186 (From Fat 124); Fat 13g (Saturated 2g); Cholesterol 1mg; Sodium 138mg; Carbohydrate 12g (Dietary Fiber 4g); Protein 6g.*

NOTE: This salad is best consumed immediately. If you want to mix and serve later, keep the dressing on the side and toss just before eating.

NOTE: During hot summer days when zucchini is in season, this salad makes a zesty side dish. The fun shape of the zucchini may even tempt a picky eater to give it a try. If you don't have a zoodle maker, look for pre-spiraled zucchini at your favorite grocery store.

VARY IT! Swap out the peanut butter in the dressing for any other favorite creamy nut butter. If nut allergies are a concern, opt for sunflower butter!

TIP: Serve with your favorite grilled meat or meat alternative.

Shaved Brussels Sprouts and White Bean Salad

PREP TIME: ABOUT 10 MIN	COOK TIME: NONE	YIELD: 6 SERVINGS

INGREDIENTS

1 tablespoon lemon juice

1 garlic clove, minced

1 tablespoon white wine vinegar

¼ cup extra-virgin olive oil

1 teaspoon Dijon mustard

½ teaspoon sea salt

½ teaspoon cracked pepper

¼ cup grated Parmesan cheese

One 14.5-ounce can cannellini beans (white kidney beans), drained and rinsed

6 cups shaved or thinly sliced Brussels sprouts

¼ cup chopped fresh parsley

DIRECTIONS

In a large bowl, whisk together the lemon juice, garlic, vinegar, olive oil, mustard, salt, and pepper. Add the Parmesan, beans, Brussels sprouts, and parsley, tossing to coat with the dressing. Serve immediately.

PER SERVING: *Calories 175 (From Fat 95); Fat 11g (Saturated 2g); Cholesterol 4mg; Sodium 283mg; Carbohydrate 15g (Dietary Fiber 6g); Protein 7g.*

NOTE: A food processor can help you whip up this salad in no time, but if you don't have one, use your best knife skills to finely slice the little cabbages.

NOTE: If Brussels sprouts are too bitter for your liking, try slicing them and then soak in salted water for 10 minutes, drain, and pat dry. This helps remove a lot of the bitter flavor.

VARY IT! Craving a crunchy addition? Add croutons or toasted sunflower seeds.

Orange–Glazed Tempeh with Noodles Salad

PREP TIME: 40 MIN	COOK TIME: 15 MIN	YIELD: 6 SERVINGS

INGREDIENTS

1 mandarin orange, zested and juiced

1 inch ginger

⅓ cup rice vinegar

1 tablespoon sesame oil

2 teaspoons light soy sauce

2 carrots

One 8-ounce block tempeh

2 tablespoons vegetable oil or coconut oil

8 ounces rice noodles, cooked to package instructions

1 cup shredded purple cabbage

4 cups baby spinach leaves

½ cup chopped fresh cilantro

½ cup chopped fresh mint

½ cup chopped cashews

DIRECTIONS

1 In a blender, place the mandarin zest, mandarin juice, ginger, vinegar, sesame oil, soy sauce, and carrots and process until smooth, about 2 minutes. Add water, a little at a time if needed to create a thin dressing consistency.

2 Next, cut the tempeh block into bite-size cubes and place in a medium bowl. Pour half of the dressing over the tempeh and marinate for 30 minutes.

3 Heat a skillet with oil over medium heat. Remove the tempeh from the marinade and pan-fry in batches for 2 to 3 minutes on each side or until a slightly crunchy exterior is formed.

4 In a large bowl, toss the remaining dressing with the noodles, cabbage, spinach, cilantro, mint, and cashews. Add the pan-fried tempeh and serve.

PER SERVING: *Calories 362 (From Fat 148); Fat 16g (Saturated 3g); Cholesterol 0mg; Sodium 240mg; Carbohydrate 44g (Dietary Fiber 3g); Protein 11g.*

NOTE: Hailing from Indonesia, tempeh is a fermented soybean patty. It has a nuttier flavor profile than tofu. Some people prefer to steam tempeh prior to marinating but there is no need to. Tempeh is precooked and ready to eat straight from the package.

VARY IT! Add thinly sliced red onions, chopped bell peppers, or grated carrots if you have them on hand!

Lemon Miso Quinoa Crunch Salad

PREP TIME: ABOUT 10 MIN	COOK TIME: 15 MIN	YIELD: 6 SERVINGS

INGREDIENTS

1¼ cups water

½ teaspoon sea salt

1 cup quinoa, rinsed

½ lemon, juiced (about 2 tablespoons)

1 tablespoon rice vinegar

3 tablespoons extra-virgin olive oil

2 teaspoons sesame oil

1 tablespoon yellow miso

6 cups baby arugula or baby kale

1 carrot, finely grated

1 cup shelled edamame, cooked

2 green onions, thinly sliced

1 tablespoon black sesame seeds

DIRECTIONS

1 In a saucepan, bring the water to a boil over high heat. Add the salt and quinoa, stir, reduce the heat to low, and cover. Cook the quinoa until the water is absorbed, about 15 to 20 minutes.

2 Meanwhile, in a small bowl, whisk together the lemon juice, vinegar, olive oil, sesame oil, and miso.

3 In a large bowl, place the arugula or kale, carrot, edamame, onions, and sesame seeds, tossing to mix.

4 Add the quinoa to the greens and toss with the miso vinaigrette. Serve immediately.

PER SERVING: *Calories 233 (From Fat 110); Fat 12g (Saturated 2g); Cholesterol 0mg; Sodium 213mg; Carbohydrate 24g (Dietary Fiber 4g); Protein 8g.*

NOTE: Yellow miso is mild fermented soybean paste, salty in flavor. It gives a salad a boost of nutrition with the fermentation and a boost of umami (meaty flavors). Use this dressing on any of your favorite greens.

VARY IT! Add in daikon radish, bell peppers, or sesame crackers, or try a different grain, like bulgur or farro.

TIP: Serve this salad with a tall glass of lemonade or sparkling orange juice. Did you know that the vitamin C found in citrus helps with iron absorption from greens? It's true, and if you stick with a plant-centric eating pattern, it's important to help boost iron absorption.

Roasted Veggie Bowls with Peanut Dressing

PREP TIME: ABOUT 15 MIN	COOK TIME: 20 MIN	YIELD: 6 SERVINGS

INGREDIENTS

2 cups cubed sweet potato

One 14.5-ounce can garbanzo beans, drained and rinsed

1 cup cubed zucchini or summer squash

½ cup cooked quinoa

1 tablespoon sesame oil

1 tablespoon vegetable oil

½ teaspoon sea salt

4 cups, thinly sliced Swiss chard

1 cup shredded red cabbage

¼ cup diced radish

½ cup grated carrot

1 avocado, thinly sliced

½ cup Spicy Peanut Dressing or Vegan Nutty Dressing (see Chapter 6)

DIRECTIONS

1 Preheat the oven to 425 degrees. Line a baking sheet with parchment paper.

2 Place the sweet potatoes in a microwave-safe bowl and cover with water. Microwave for 5 minutes; then drain. This pre-cooks the sweet potato so that the vegetables can bake and be done at the same time.

3 In a large bowl, mix the sweet potato, beans, zucchini or squash, quinoa, sesame oil, vegetable oil, and salt. Stir to combine. Pour the mixture onto a baking sheet. Roast the vegetables for 15 to 20 minutes. The vegetables and beans should be golden in color and the quinoa toasted. Vegetables can be used warm in the salad or chilled and used cold.

4 To assemble the salad, toss the Swiss chard, cabbage, radish, and carrot together. Top with the roasted veggie mix and avocado. Drizzle the dressing over the top and serve immediately.

PER SERVING: Calories 307 (From Fat 161); Fat 17g (Saturated 3g); Cholesterol 0mg; Sodium 394mg; Carbohydrate 32g (Dietary Fiber 8g); Protein 8g.

NOTE: Roasted vegetables are delicious both warm and cold in this salad. They add a caramelized flavor that pairs well with the Spicy Peanut Dressing. This bowl is jam-packed with nutrient-dense vegetables. Keep it undressed and pack it in containers for the week — it's the perfect way to meal prep!

TIP: Swiss chard is mild in flavor. If you can't find any, try a butter leaf or red leaf lettuce instead.

VARY IT! If you're using the Vegan Nutty Dressing, consider adding dried cranberries and chopped apples to this salad for a fun twist.

Roasted Butternut Squash, Pumpkin Seed, and Feta Salad

PREP TIME: ABOUT 5 MIN	COOK TIME: 30 MIN	YIELD: 6 SERVINGS

INGREDIENTS

3 cups cubed butternut squash

1 teaspoon minced fresh rosemary

2 tablespoons extra-virgin olive oil

1 teaspoon salt

8 large kale leaves, stems removed and thinly sliced (chiffonade)

2 teaspoons lemon juice

¼ cup dried cranberries

1 cup green pumpkin seeds

½ cup Balsamic Vinaigrette (see Chapter 6)

¼ cup crumbled feta

DIRECTIONS

1 Preheat the oven to 400 degrees. Line a baking sheet with parchment paper.

2 In a medium bowl, mix together the squash, rosemary, olive oil, and salt. Stir to combine. Pour the mixture onto a baking sheet and roast the vegetables for 25 to 30 minutes. The butternut squash should be tender and golden brown in color.

3 While the squash is roasting, place the kale leaves in a serving bowl. Add the lemon juice and massage the kale to tenderize the leaves — you may even find your leaves look brighter in color. Next, add the roasted squash, cranberries, pumpkin seeds, and Balsamic Vinaigrette. Toss to mix the salad. Top with crumbled feta cheese and serve immediately.

PER SERVING: *Calories 186 (From Fat 84); Fat 9g (Saturated 2g); Cholesterol 6mg; Sodium 920mg; Carbohydrate 26g (Dietary Fiber 5g); Protein 5g.*

NOTE: Massaging kale with lemon juice mellows the bitters and tenderizes the texture of the leaves. Any green kale can work in this recipe, but my favorite is Tuscan or Lacinato kale. It has a flatter leaf and is naturally more tender than regular kale.

VARY IT! Dried or fresh blueberries, pears, or apples work in this salad. Swap out the butternut squash with roasted sweet potatoes or acorn squash.

TIP: This salad makes a beautiful addition to a holiday meal!

Protein-Packed Pasta Salad

PREP TIME: 1 HR 10 MIN | COOK TIME: 10 MIN | YIELD: 8 SERVINGS

INGREDIENTS

16 ounces rotini pasta

2 cups broccoli florets

1 cup Classic Italian Vinaigrette (see Chapter 6)

One 8-ounce jar marinated artichoke hearts, drained

1 cup cannellini beans, drained and rinsed

1 cup halved cherry tomatoes

½ cup cubed mozzarella cheese

¼ cup toasted pine nuts

¼ cup thinly sliced basil

DIRECTIONS

1 Cook the pasta in salted water according to the package directions.

2 In a large serving bowl, place the broccoli florets. Add the drained, hot pasta over the broccoli. Add the vinaigrette, stirring to coat. Let the mixture cool for 10 minutes before adding the remaining ingredients. Stir and chill for at least 1 hour prior to serving.

PER SERVING: *Calories 388 (From Fat 104); Fat 12g (Saturated 2g); Cholesterol 6mg; Sodium 482mg; Carbohydrate 57g (Dietary Fiber 6g); Protein 14g.*

NOTE: Adding the hot pasta over the raw broccoli slightly cooks and tenderizes the tougher vegetable. If people need a more tender broccoli texture, add the broccoli the last 3 minutes of cooking the pasta; then drain and toss with the vinaigrette.

VARY IT! Add bell peppers, onions, celery, cauliflower, or Brussels sprouts to this salad.

TIP: Serve with cheesy garlic bread.

Crispy Bacon Wedge Salad (Chapter 7) with Blue Cheese Dressing (Chapter 6)

Lemony Kale and Parmesan Salad (Chapter 8)

GRACE GERI GOODALE AND WENDY JO PETERSON

GRACE GERI GOODALE AND WENDY JO PETERSON

GRACE GERI GOODALE AND WENDY JO PETERSON

Lemony Orzo Pasta Salad (Chapter 8)

GRACE GERI GOODALE AND WENDY JO PETERSON

Japanese Seaweed Salad (Chapter 9)

Korean Bun Noodle Salad (Chapter 9)

Creamy Coconut Chicken Bowls (Chapter 10)

GRACE GERI GOODALE AND WENDY JO PETERSON

GRACE GERI GOODALE AND WENDY JO PETERSON

GRACE GERI GOODALE AND WENDY JO PETERSON

Asian Ground Beef and Rice Bowls (Chapter 10)

GRACE GERI GOODALE AND WENDY JO PETERSON

Grilled Tofu with Soy and Ginger Salad (Chapter 11)

Arugula Parmesan Crisps and Bacon-Wrapped Date Salad (Chapter 12)

GRACE GERI GOODALE AND WENDY JO PETERSON

Pantry Pasta Salad (Chapter 13)

GRACE GERI GOODALE AND WENDY JO PETERSON

GRACE GERI GOODALE AND WENDY JO PETERSON

Spring Pea, Bulgur, and Goat Cheese Salad (Chapter 14)

GRACE GERI GOODALE AND WENDY JO PETERSON

Fennel and Orange Beet Farro Salad (Chapter 14)

GRACE GERI GOODALE AND WENDY JO PETERSON

Mediterranean Watermelon Salad (Chapter 15)

GRACE GERI GOODALE AND WENDY JO PETERSON

Roasted Grape and Barley Salad (Chapter 15)

GRACE GERI GOODALE AND WENDY JO PETERSON

Grape and Melon Mojito Salad (Chapter 16)

GRACE GERI GOODALE AND WENDY JO PETERSON

Cherry Waldorf Salad (Chapter 16)

Bean Fritters with Pesto Couscous Salad

PREP TIME: ABOUT 15 MIN | COOK TIME: 20 MIN | YIELD: 6 SERVINGS

INGREDIENTS

5 tablespoons extra-virgin olive oil, divided

1 cup Israeli couscous

1¼ cups water

One 14.5-ounce can cannellini beans, drained and rinsed

¾ cup panko bread crumbs, divided

1 egg

¼ cup finely diced onion

½ cup prepared pesto, divided

1 teaspoon salt, divided

¼ cup sour cream or Greek yogurt

2 tablespoons mayonnaise

1½ lemons, zested and juiced (about 6 tablespoons juice)

6 cups baby arugula

½ cup sliced black or green olives

½ cup chopped walnuts

DIRECTIONS

1   In a medium saucepan, heat 1 tablespoon of the oil with the couscous over medium-high heat, stirring frequently until the couscous begins to become golden in color, about 5 minutes. Add the water, stir, reduce the heat to low, and cover the couscous, cooking for 12 minutes or until all the liquid is absorbed.

2   Meanwhile, in a medium bowl, stir the beans, ½ cup of the panko, the egg, the onion, 1 tablespoon of the pesto, and ½ teaspoon of the salt. Form the bean mixture into 12 patties, each about 1-inch thick. Dip the patties on both sides in the remaining ¼ cup of panko. Heat a skillet with the remaining 4 tablespoons of olive oil over medium-high heat. When bubbles start to form, place the bean patties into the oil. Cook the patties for 2 to 3 minutes per side, until golden in color. Cook in batches, if needed. It's important not to crowd the pan while cooking in oil because or the oil will cool and the fritters will absorb more oil.

3   In a small bowl, whisk together the remaining 3 tablespoons of pesto, the sour cream or Greek yogurt, the mayonnaise, the lemon zest and juice, and the remaining ½ teaspoon of salt. Mix ¼ cup of the dressing into the couscous, tossing to coat.

4   To assemble the salad, place the couscous and arugula into a serving bowl. Toss to mix. Top the salad with the olives, walnuts, and bean fritters. Drizzle the remaining dressing over the top or serve on the side. Serve immediately.

PER SERVING: *Calories 458 (From Fat 261); Fat 29g (Saturated 5g); Cholesterol 45mg; Sodium 719mg; Carbohydrate 40g (Dietary Fiber 6g); Protein 12g.*

(continued)

NOTE: Bean fritters are fun for the whole family. If you're serving these to a baby, make them into fingers for easy holding. This has long been one of my daughter's favorite meals, and now she helps me make it.

VARY IT! Most any bean can be used to make fritters, from garbanzo to pinto. Add your favorite Mediterranean toppings, from artichoke hearts to roasted red bell peppers.

TIP: This makes for a stunning main dish. Serve with crusty French bread or focaccia.

Turmeric–Spiced Cauliflower Salad with Tahini Dressing

PREP TIME: ABOUT 10 MIN	COOK TIME: 25 MIN	YIELD: 6 SERVINGS

INGREDIENTS

1 teaspoon turmeric

½ teaspoon cracked pepper

1 teaspoon cumin

1 teaspoon paprika

½ teaspoon ground coriander

½ teaspoon sea salt

1 tablespoon apple cider vinegar

2 tablespoons extra-virgin olive oil

4 cups cauliflower florets

6 cups thinly sliced kale leaves, stems removed

½ cup toasted and salted cashews

½ cup Creamy Tahini Dressing (see Chapter 6)

DIRECTIONS

1 Preheat the oven to 425 degrees. Line a baking sheet with parchment paper.

2 In a medium bowl, stir together the turmeric, pepper, cumin, paprika, coriander, salt, vinegar, and olive oil. Add the cauliflower to the spiced slurry, stirring to coat. Pour the cauliflower onto the baking sheet, scraping out the sauce with a rubber spatula. Bake until the cauliflower becomes tender and starts to brown slightly, about 20 to 25 minutes.

3 To assemble the salad, place the kale on the base, top with roasted cauliflower and cashews, and then drizzle with Creamy Tahini Dressing. Serve immediately.

PER SERVING: *Calories 272 (From Fat 200); Fat 22g (Saturated 4g); Cholesterol 0mg; Sodium 486mg; Carbohydrate 17g (Dietary Fiber 4g); Protein 6g.*

NOTE: Turmeric is a powerful spice, in both flavor and nutrition. Combining pepper with turmeric helps our bodies better use the phytochemical curcumin, which may aid digestion, have anti-arthritic properties, and reduce inflammation. If seeing all these spices overwhelms you, opt for curry powder instead but still add the salt and pepper.

VARY IT! You can use arugula or Swiss chard in place of the kale.

TIP: Serve this salad with warm flatbread or pita chips.

Shaved Asparagus and Walnuts Salad

PREP TIME: ABOUT 15 MIN	COOK TIME: 20 MIN	YIELD: 6 SERVINGS

INGREDIENTS

1½ pounds asparagus, ends trimmed

1 avocado, pitted and thinly sliced

One 8-ounce jar marinated quartered artichoke hearts, drained

1 cup chopped walnuts, toasted

2 hard-boiled eggs, grated or finely chopped

¼ cup shaved Parmesan cheese

¼ cup chopped parsley or basil

½ cup Classic Italian Vinaigrette (see Chapter 6)

DIRECTIONS

1 Using a vegetable peeler, peel off long strands of asparagus. Place the asparagus on a serving platter.

2 Arrange the avocado, artichoke hearts, walnuts, and grated or chopped hard-boiled eggs over the top of the asparagus. Finish with the fresh herbs and shaved Parmesan. Then drizzle the salad with the vinaigrette. Serve immediately.

PER SERVING: *Calories 364 (From Fat 291); Fat 32g (Saturated 5g); Cholesterol 74mg; Sodium 474mg; Carbohydrate 13g (Dietary Fiber 6g); Protein 10g.*

VARY IT! Zucchini works well in this dish, too! Thinly slice the zucchini on a mandoline or with a vegetable peeler.

TIP: Serve this salad in spring when asparagus are at their peak. This salad is a favorite of ours at Easter. Serve with crusty French bread.

Edamame, Crispy Onions, and Farro Salad

PREP TIME: ABOUT 15 MIN	COOK TIME: 25 MIN	YIELD: 4 SERVINGS

INGREDIENTS

1 cup chicken or vegetable stock

¼ cup farro, rinsed

1 cup cooked and shelled edamame

2 cups watercress

1 cup sugar snap peas

¼ cup sunflower seeds or pumpkin seeds

1 cup diced cucumbers

1 cup halved cherry tomatoes

½ cup Creamy Green Herb Dressing or Ranch Dressing (see Chapter 6)

1 cup crispy fried onions

DIRECTIONS

1 In a small saucepan, add the stock and bring to a boil over high heat. Stir in the farro, cover, and reduce to a simmer until tender, about 25 to 35 minutes or per package instructions. Remove from the heat and drain off any excess liquid. Cool the farro for at least 10 minutes in the refrigerator while you prepare the remaining ingredients.

2 In a serving bowl, stir together the edamame, watercress, snap peas, sunflower seeds, cucumbers, and tomatoes. Add in the cooled farro, stirring to mix. Drizzle the dressing over the top, stirring to mix. Top with the fried onions and serve immediately.

PER SERVING: *Calories 427 (From Fat 274); Fat 30g (Saturated 6g); Cholesterol 10mg; Sodium 601mg; Carbohydrate 29g (Dietary Fiber 7g); Protein 12g.*

NOTE: Farro is an old-world grain that looks similar to barley. It has a nutty flavor and chewy texture. This salad only uses a small amount. You can cook 1 cup farro to 4 cups liquid and freeze the remaining farro for another salad. It'll keep in the freezer up to 3 months.

VARY IT! If you can't find watercress, use torn butter lettuce instead.

TIP: Serve with warm flatbread or a crusty French bread.

Chapter **12**

Crowd Pleasers

RECIPES IN THIS CHAPTER

- Mayo and Mustard Potato Salad
- Classic Macaroni Salad

    Sunflower Seed and Broccoli Salad
- Layered Bean Salad

    Antipasto Salad

    Crunchy Chicken Salad with Orange Ginger Dressing
- Chickpea and Cucumber Dill Salad
- Spinach and Orzo Salad
- Avocado and Crunchy Corn Salad

    Arugula Parmesan Crisps and Bacon-Wrapped Date Salad

    Grilled Romaine Salad with Warm Bacon Vinaigrette
- Fiesta Grilled Sweet Potato and Cilantro Salad

t's time for a picnic or barbecue and you don't know what to bring. This is your chapter! Instead of hopping on the web, discover the right salad for all occasions right here.

Everyone brings their favorite dish to a potluck or picnic — be bold and bring a salad to your next gathering. In this chapter, I included some family favorites, like my mom's Classic Macaroni Salad, Layered Bean Salad, and my Fiesta Grilled Sweet Potato and Cilantro Salad. If you need something on the elegant side, make the Arugula Parmesan Crisps and Bacon-Wrapped Date Salad or the Antipasto Salad, which serves up like a charcuterie board.

REMEMBER

Even though you may be attending a big event, you're not the only one bringing something, so you may not need to increase the servings.

WARNING

Keep your friends and family safe. If your salad stays out longer than two hours, toss it. If the temperatures are hot, be sure to keep your salad on ice to keep it at a safer temperature for serving. When in doubt, err on the side of safety.

Mayo and Mustard Potato Salad

PREP TIME: ABOUT 10 MIN	COOK TIME: 20 MIN	YIELD: 8 SERVINGS

INGREDIENTS

2 pounds red new potatoes (boiling potatoes)

1 tablespoon salt (for boiling potatoes)

4 hard-boiled eggs, divided

1 tablespoon white wine vinegar

½ cup mayonnaise

¼ cup Greek yogurt or sour cream

2 tablespoons mustard

1 teaspoon sugar

½ teaspoon cracked pepper

½ teaspoon sea salt

½ cup finely diced onion

½ cup thinly sliced celery

2 tablespoons chopped parsley

DIRECTIONS

1 In a large stock pot, place the potatoes and 1 tablespoon of salt. Cover the potatoes with water and bring to a boil over high heat. Cover and reduce the heat to low; simmer until tender, about 15 to 25 minutes, depending on the size of the potatoes. (At 15 minutes, begin checking the potatoes with a fork; fork tender means done.) Drain the potatoes and cut into bite-size pieces.

2 While the potatoes are cooking, in a large bowl, whisk the boiled egg yolks, vinegar, mayonnaise, Greek yogurt or sour cream, mustard, sugar, pepper, and sea salt until creamy and smooth.

3 Place the warm potatoes into the dressing, stirring to coat. Stir in the onion, celery, crumbled or chopped hard-boiled egg whites, and parsley. Cover and refrigerate for at least 2 hours before serving. The salad will taste even better the next day!

PER SERVING: *Calories 226 (From Fat 83); Fat 9g (Saturated 2g); Cholesterol 114mg; Sodium 276mg; Carbohydrate 30g (Dietary Fiber 2g); Protein 6g.*

NOTE: Potato salads can start fights at a barbecue! Well, maybe not that extreme, but I've witnessed decent arguments over what should go into a potato salad. This one has both mayonnaise and mustard, but if you prefer no mustard, feel free to skip it. I like the balancing of flavors by adding in Greek yogurt — it's a tanginess that's mellowed by the creaminess of mayo.

NOTE: Store in an airtight container in the refrigerator for up to 5 days. If you pull the potato salad out for a barbecue, be sure to keep it on ice or discard after the barbecue.

VARY IT! Add olives, pickles, peas, cubed cheese, radishes, dill, bacon, ham, celery seed, garlic, paprika, and/or chives — whatever you like best!

TIP: This salad is the perfect addition to any barbecue. Any time I smoke a brisket, this salad is on the menu, too. Pair it with pulled pork, ribs, or your favorite sandwiches.

Classic Macaroni Salad

INGREDIENTS

1 tablespoon salt (for boiling pasta)

16 ounces macaroni noodles

6 hard-boiled eggs, divided

1 cup mayonnaise

½ teaspoon cracked pepper

½ teaspoon sea salt

1 cup finely diced onion

1 cup thinly sliced celery

1 cup chopped cucumber, peeled and seeded

2 tablespoons finely chopped parsley

DIRECTIONS

1 Bring a large stock pot of water to a boil with 1 tablespoon salt. Add the pasta and cook according to package directions. Drain and run under cold water for 3 minutes or immerse in ice water for 1 minute to chill the pasta. Drain and set aside.

2 In a serving bowl, mix together the hard-boiled egg yolks, mayonnaise, pepper, salt, onion, celery, cucumber, and parsley. Chop up the egg whites and add to the mixture. Add the chilled pasta, stir to coat, and refrigerate until ready to serve.

PER SERVING: *Calories 401 (From Fat 133); Fat 15g (Saturated 3g); Cholesterol 167mg; Sodium 392mg; Carbohydrate 54g (Dietary Fiber 3g); Protein 13g.*

NOTE: This recipe is my mom's — she always reminds me to taste and add more mayonnaise if you need it. If you have kids who despise onions, blend the onion into the mayonnaise. (I was that kid when I was little!)

VARY IT! Much like with potato salad, many people have their favorite additions to a macaroni salad. Try adding cubed cheese, pickles, bell peppers, sun-dried tomatoes, radishes, peas, mustard, pickle juice, or diced ham.

TIP: After visiting Hawaii, I realized macaroni salad can go with just about any dish you serve, from grilled fish to pulled pork or barbecue.

Sunflower Seed and Broccoli Salad

PREP TIME: ABOUT 10 MIN	COOK TIME: 20 MIN	YIELD: 6 SERVINGS

INGREDIENTS

4 slices bacon

½ cup mayonnaise

1 tablespoon apple cider vinegar

½ teaspoon salt

1 tablespoon sugar

½ cup sunflower seeds

½ cup crunchy fried onions

4 cups broccoli florets

½ cup dried cranberries or raisins

DIRECTIONS

1 Preheat the oven to 400 degrees. Line a baking sheet with parchment paper.

2 Lay the bacon on the parchment paper and bake for 20 - 25 minutes or until crispy. (Alternatively, you can cook the bacon in the microwave or on the stovetop, if you prefer.) Crumble or chop the bacon after it's cooked.

3 In a serving bowl, stir together the mayonnaise, vinegar, salt, and sugar. Add in the bacon and remaining ingredients, stirring to coat with the dressing. Serve immediately or refrigerate until ready to serve. Stir before serving.

PER SERVING: *Calories 260 (From Fat 156); Fat 17g (Saturated 4g); Cholesterol 11mg; Sodium 474mg; Carbohydrate 23g (Dietary Fiber 3g); Protein 6g.*

NOTE: The broccoli will become more tender as the salad sits.

VARY IT! Add crushed ramen noodles, chopped red bell pepper, or grated carrots for pops of color and crunch.

TIP: Serve this salad at a picnic, potluck, or barbecue.

Layered Bean Salad

PREP TIME: ABOUT PLUS 30 MIN FOR CHILLING	COOK TIME: NONE	YIELD: 10 SERVINGS

INGREDIENTS

One 14.5-ounce can refried beans

2 avocados, pitted and peeled

1 lime, juiced

1 teaspoon salt, divided

2 cups sour cream, divided

½ teaspoon cumin

2 teaspoons chili powder

½ teaspoon garlic powder

½ teaspoon onion powder

1 cup pico de gallo, salsa, or chopped tomatoes

2 cups shredded cheddar or Monterey Jack cheese

3 cups shredded lettuce

1 cup sliced black olives

½ cup chopped cilantro

DIRECTIONS

1   In a medium bowl, stir the refried beans to make them smooth. Pour the beans into the bottom of a glass trifle bowl or a clear serving bowl.

2   In another medium bowl, using a fork, mash the avocados with the lime juice, ½ teaspoon of the salt, and ¼ cup of the sour cream. Pour the avocado layer onto the bean layer.

3   Next, in another medium bowl, stir together the remaining 1¾ cups sour cream, cumin, chili powder, garlic powder, onion powder, and the remaining ½ teaspoon of salt. Pour the sour cream layer onto the avocado layer. Top the sour cream layer with pico de gallo, salsa, or chopped tomatoes. Then add a layer of shredded cheese, followed by the shredded lettuce, and finish with the olives and cilantro. Chill the layered salad for at least 30 minutes before serving.

PER SERVING: *Calories 303 (From Fat 211); Fat 23g (Saturated 14g); Cholesterol 20mg; Sodium 776mg; Carbohydrate 15g (Dietary Fiber 6g); Protein 10g.*

NOTE: Store tightly covered with plastic wrap in the refrigerator up to 3 days.

NOTE: Adding the lime juice and sour cream to the avocado layer helps keep the avocado from browning.

VARY IT! Add a layer of canned corn, ground beef seasoned with taco seasoning, or chopped bell peppers.

TIP: Though this salad is often served as a dip, it's very much a layered salad. Serve with corn chips or warm tortillas.

Antipasto Salad

INGREDIENTS

2 ounces prosciutto ham

2 ounces soppressata

2 ounces salami or pepperoni

4 ounces fresh mozzarella or cubed mozzarella

2 ounces cubed Grana Padano or Parmigiano-Reggiano

1 cup cured mixed olives

1 cup steamed green beans

1 cup cherry tomatoes

1 cup basil leaves

1 cup jarred roasted red bell peppers, drained

One 8-ounce jar marinated artichoke hearts, drained and reserved

1 pound baguette

DIRECTIONS

1 On a large platter, arrange a line of each ingredient (except the bread) or follow a charcuterie-board style for serving. Keep the meats together, the vegetables together, and the cheeses together. Pour the reserved marinade from the artichoke hearts over the vegetables. Serve immediately with the baguette.

PER SERVING: *Calories 370 (From Fat 150); Fat 17g (Saturated 5g); Cholesterol 32mg; Sodium 1,414mg; Carbohydrate 37g (Dietary Fiber 2g); Protein 19g.*

NOTE: Antipasto is an Italian family-style board salad, which is traditionally served as a first course. The ingredients included can vary based on season and location in Italy.

VARY IT! Add steamed asparagus, provolone cheese, stuffed peppers, marinated mushrooms, sardines, or fried calamari.

TIP: This salad serves 8 but can easily be doubled or tripled based on guests. I've been known to serve it as a main dish, too.

Crunchy Chicken Salad with Orange Ginger Dressing

PREP TIME: ABOUT 20 MIN	COOK TIME: NONE	YIELD: 10 SERVINGS

INGREDIENTS

¼ cup peanut oil

1 tablespoon sesame oil

1 teaspoon grated fresh ginger root

1 tablespoon soy sauce

3 tablespoons rice wine vinegar

1 tablespoon sugar

2 cups shredded cooked chicken

4 cups shredded Napa cabbage

1 cup shredded purple cabbage

1 cup grated carrot

1 cup shelled and cooked edamame

3 green onions, thinly sliced

1 cup fried chow mein noodles

One 8-ounce can mandarin oranges (canned in water or juice)

½ cup chopped peanuts

1 tablespoon black sesame seeds

DIRECTIONS

1 In a small bowl, whisk together the peanut oil, sesame oil, ginger, soy sauce, vinegar, and sugar.

2 In a large serving bowl, mix the chicken, Napa cabbage, purple cabbage, carrot, edamame, onions, and noodles. Pour the dressing over the salad and toss. Top with remaining ingredients and serve, or chill until ready to serve.

PER SERVING: *Calories 223 (From Fat 127); Fat 14g (Saturated 2g); Cholesterol 24mg; Sodium 149mg; Carbohydrate 12g (Dietary Fiber 2g); Protein 14g.*

NOTE: Store in an airtight container in the refrigerator up to 24 hours. If you want to make it in advance, don't add the dressing or oranges until you're ready to serve.

VARY IT! Mango, cilantro, peanuts, cashews, bell peppers, kale, green beans, and peas can all be added to this recipe.

TIP: If you can't find Napa cabbage, green cabbage will work. This salad is fun for the whole family. Serve with egg rolls.

Chickpea and Cucumber Dill Salad

PREP TIME: ABOUT 5 MIN	COOK TIME: NONE	YIELD: 8 SERVINGS

INGREDIENTS

1 tablespoon lemon juice

2 tablespoons red wine vinegar

2 cloves garlic

1 tablespoon capers or olives

½ teaspoon sea salt

⅛ teaspoon red pepper flakes

2 tablespoons fresh parsley

⅓ cup extra-virgin olive oil

Two 14.5-ounce cans garbanzo beans, drained and rinsed

4 Persian cucumbers, diced

1 cup halved cherry or grape tomatoes

½ cup chopped dill

DIRECTIONS

1 Place the lemon juice, vinegar, garlic, capers or olives, salt, red pepper flakes, and parsley into a blender or food processor, and pulse for 1 minute. Then, while the machine is running, drizzle in the olive oil.

2 Place the remaining ingredients into a serving bowl, toss with the dressing, and serve.

PER SERVING: *Calories 204 (From Fat 91); Fat 10g (Saturated 1g); Cholesterol 0mg; Sodium 422mg; Carbohydrate 24g (Dietary Fiber 5g); Protein 5g.*

NOTE: Store in an airtight container in the refrigerator up to 2 days.

NOTE: Even in winter, this salad can come together and make you feel like you're in the heart of summer. If you don't have a blender, finely chop the dressing ingredients and muddle the ingredients together with the back of a spoon.

VARY IT! Zucchini, olives, croutons, and artichoke hearts can be added to the salad, too.

TIP: Serve this salad with any grilled meat or fish and crusty bread or flatbread.

Spinach and Orzo Salad

PREP TIME: ABOUT 10 MIN	COOK TIME: 10 MIN	YIELD: 8 SERVINGS

INGREDIENTS

1 cup dried orzo pasta

1 tablespoon lemon juice

2 tablespoons white wine vinegar

2 cloves garlic, minced

½ teaspoon sea salt

⅛ teaspoon cracked pepper

2 teaspoons dried oregano

⅓ cup extra-virgin olive oil

8 cups chopped baby spinach leaves

½ cup halved kalamata olives

½ cup julienned red bell pepper

1 cup finely grated Parmesan cheese

DIRECTIONS

1 Cook the orzo pasta according to package instructions. Drain and rinse with cool water.

2 In a small bowl, whisk the lemon juice, vinegar, garlic, salt, pepper, oregano, and olive oil.

3 In a serving bowl, place the spinach, olives, bell pepper, and Parmesan cheese. Add the pasta and dressing, tossing to mix. Serve immediately.

PER SERVING: *Calories 222 (From Fat 125); Fat 14g (Saturated 4g); Cholesterol 11mg; Sodium 510mg; Carbohydrate 16g (Dietary Fiber 2g); Protein 8g.*

NOTE: Any small-shaped pasta can work in this recipe, from macaroni to ditalini.

VARY IT! Add any of your favorite Mediterranean additions, including raw zucchini, peas, asparagus tips, artichoke hearts, or cucumbers.

TIP: Serve this salad any time of the year with grilled or baked fish and meats.

Avocado and Crunchy Corn Salad

PREP TIME: ABOUT 5 MIN	COOK TIME: 20 MIN	YIELD: 8 SERVINGS

INGREDIENTS

4 ears of corn on the cob

1 tablespoon sugar (for boiling corn)

1 red bell pepper, diced

2 jalapeño peppers, seeded and finely diced

1 medium red onion, diced

1 cup crushed corn tortilla chips (blue corn if you can find it)

1 cup chopped cilantro

2 tablespoons mayonnaise

2 tablespoons sour cream or Greek yogurt

1 teaspoon chili powder

½ teaspoon cumin

½ teaspoon dried oregano

1 lime, juiced and zested

2 slightly firm avocados, seeded, peeled, and diced

½ cup crumbled cotija cheese

DIRECTIONS

1 In a large stock pot, place the corn and sugar and cover with water. Bring to a boil over medium-high heat. Cover, remove from the heat, and let the corn sit in the hot water for 15 minutes. Remove from the water, and cut the kernels away from the cobs.

2 In a serving bowl, stir together the bell pepper, jalapeño, onion, tortilla chips, cilantro, mayonnaise, sour cream or Greek yogurt, chili powder, cumin, oregano, lime zest, and lime juice. Add the corn, stirring to combine. Add the avocado and gently stir. Top with the cotija and serve, or cover and refrigerate.

PER SERVING: Calories 205 (From Fat 107); Fat 12g (Saturated 3g); Cholesterol 10mg; Sodium 182mg; Carbohydrate 23g (Dietary Fiber 5g); Protein 5g.

NOTE: This salad is best consumed within 2 days. If you want it to keep longer, add the chips, cheese, and avocado just before serving.

NOTE: Imagine Mexican street corn but in a bowl! Street corn is one of my favorites. One year I decided to make it into a salad. Canned corn can work in this recipe, but I get the best results with corn at the peak of season — in the summer! The tortilla chips add a fun crunch to the salad.

VARY IT! Black beans, olives, pumpkin seeds, and diced tomatoes would make great additions to this salad.

TIP: Serve with tomato soup or hot dogs or at a taco party.

Arugula Parmesan Crisps and Bacon-Wrapped Date Salad

| PREP TIME: ABOUT 15 MIN | COOK TIME: 20 MIN | YIELD: 8 SERVINGS |

INGREDIENTS

1 cup grated Parmesan cheese

½ teaspoon minced rosemary

1 teaspoon cracked pepper, divided

16 dates

8 slices center-cut bacon, cut in half to make 16 short slices

½ cup balsamic vinegar

1 tablespoon honey

8 cups arugula

½ cup toasted walnuts or almonds

½ teaspoon sea salt

¼ cup extra-virgin olive oil

DIRECTIONS

1 Preheat the oven to 400 degrees. Line a baking sheet with parchment paper.

2 In a small bowl, stir together the Parmesan, rosemary, and ½ teaspoon of the pepper. Place 16 tablespoon mounds of cheese onto the baking sheet. Bake until golden in color, about 5 minutes. Let the cheese cool before removing it from the parchment paper.

3 Next, wrap each date with ½ slice of bacon. Place onto the same parchment paper you used for the cheese. Place into the hot oven and bake until the bacon is browned, about 15 minutes.

4 Meanwhile, make the balsamic reduction. In a small saucepan, heat the vinegar and honey on medium to medium-low heat to a low simmer, stirring occasionally. Cook until the vinegar reduces by half, about 10 minutes. It should be slightly thickened.

5 On a serving platter, arrange the arugula across the bottom. Top with the bacon-wrapped dates. Break up the crisps and sprinkle onto the salad. Top with the nuts, salt, and the remaining ½ teaspoon of pepper. Drizzle with the balsamic glaze and olive oil. Serve immediately.

PER SERVING: *Calories 366 (From Fat 168); Fat 19g (Saturated 5g); Cholesterol 20mg; Sodium 503mg; Carbohydrate 43g (Dietary Fiber 4g); Protein 10g.*

NOTE: This salad has a lot of moving parts but it's elegant for entertaining. Whip up extra bacon-wrapped dates for appetizers.

VARY IT! This salad works beautiful with goat cheese or burrata mozzarella (soft mozzarella). Also try pistachios or candied pecans in this salad.

TIP: Serve with steak and crusty French bread or croissants.

Grilled Romaine Salad with Warm Bacon Vinaigrette

PREP TIME: ABOUT 5 MIN	COOK TIME: 20 MIN	YIELD: 4 SERVINGS

INGREDIENTS

4 slices center-cut bacon

3 tablespoons apple cider vinegar

1 teaspoon Dijon mustard

½ teaspoon salt

½ teaspoon cracked pepper

4 hard-boiled eggs, divided

1 head romaine lettuce, quartered lengthwise

2 tablespoons extra-virgin olive oil

DIRECTIONS

1 Preheat the grill to 400 degrees.

2 In a skillet, fry the bacon over medium to medium–high heat until crispy, about 8 to 10 minutes. Place the cooked bacon on paper towels to remove the excess oil. When all the bacon has been cooked, remove all but ¼ cup of the bacon drippings from the pan. To the pan, whisk in the vinegar, mustard, salt, and pepper. Add the egg yolks to make a creamy dressing. Remove from the heat and set aside.

3 Brush the cut side of the lettuce with the olive oil. Place the lettuce cut side down on the grill, and grill long enough to get grill lines, about 2 minutes. Plate the lettuce and pour the warm vinaigrette over the lettuce. Top with crumbled egg whites and the chopped bacon.

PER SERVING: *Calories 209 (From Fat 143); Fat 16g (Saturated 4g); Cholesterol 221mg; Sodium 494mg; Carbohydrate 6g (Dietary Fiber 3g); Protein 11g.*

NOTE: Grilled romaine just looks cool. If you happen to be grilling, it's a perfect excuse to make this salad.

VARY IT! Add chopped chives, crumbled blue cheese, and diced tomatoes to further dress up this salad.

Fiesta Grilled Sweet Potato and Cilantro Salad

PREP TIME: ABOUT 10 MIN | COOK TIME: 20 MIN | YIELD: 6 SERVINGS

INGREDIENTS

2 pounds sweet potatoes

½ teaspoon paprika

½ teaspoon cumin

½ teaspoon ground coriander

2 limes, juiced

¼ cup extra-virgin olive oil or avocado oil

1 avocado, pitted, peeled, and thinly sliced

2 green onions, thinly sliced

¼ cup green pumpkin seeds

½ cup chopped cilantro

DIRECTIONS

1 Preheat the grill to 425 degrees.

2 Slice the sweet potatoes into ½-inch-thick rounds. Grill the sweet potatoes for 10 minutes on each side; they should be fork tender after 20 minutes.

3 Meanwhile, in a small bowl, whisk together the paprika, cumin, coriander, lime juice, and oil.

4 Place the cooked sweet potatoes onto a serving platter. Drizzle with the vinaigrette. Top with avocado, onions, pumpkin seeds, and cilantro. Serve immediately.

PER SERVING: *Calories 269 (From Fat 118); Fat 13g (Saturated 2g); Cholesterol 0mg; Sodium 58mg; Carbohydrate 36g (Dietary Fiber 7g); Protein 4g.*

TIP: If you want to speed up the cooking time, pierce the sweet potatoes with a fork and microwave them for 3 minutes. Then slice and grill.

VARY IT! This recipe can work with zucchini, potatoes, bell peppers, or a combination of all of these.

NOTE: I've served this salad with grilled steaks, ribs, hot dogs, and blackened fish. It's a nice-looking salad that holds up well for parties.

4

Getting Creative with Salads

Discover ways to use up pantry staples to craft a quick and delicious salad.

Boost your diet with whole grains with unique grain-based salads.

Break out the fruit bowl for fruity salads.

Craft something sweet with blast-from-the-past salads.

Chapter **13**

Pantry Stars

RECIPES IN THIS CHAPTER

🍳 **Lentil Salad**

🍳 **Three Bean Salad**

🍳 **Antipasto Pantry Salad**

🍳 **Pantry Pasta Salad**

🍳 **Chickpea and Sunflower Smashed Salad**

🍳 **Southwestern Black Bean Salad**

We've all heard that foods around the perimeter of a grocery store are the best to buy but that's plain hogwash. Before you turn up your nose to canned salad recipes, hear me out! Canned goods are packed at the peak of freshness, whereas fresh goods are picked, placed on a truck, and driven across the country or flown in from other countries. I grew up with canned goods — my great-grandmother and mom were both avid gardeners and canners.

Here are three reasons to keep pantry goods on hand:

» **They're less expensive than fresh goods.** Dried beans can cost around $1 for a bag versus $1.59 for a single can.

» **They're sustainable.** Canned goods go from the field to being processed in less than five hours, whereas fresh produce requires longer transports and risks being wasted due to spoilage. For more sustainable reasons why I love canned goods, check out https://lovecannedfood.com/8-environment-friendly-facts-about-canned-food.

» **They're packed with nutrition.** Canning foods can increase the nutrient load. For instance, canned pumpkin contains 540 percent Recommended Dietary Allowance (RDA) of the vitamin A content but fresh pumpkin only has 26 percent.

It's time to head to the pantry! If you're looking for a nutrition star, dig into the Lentil Salad. Planning a party? Antipasto Pantry Salad is certain to please a crowd. My all-time favorite is the Three Bean Salad, because it's incredibly easy, nutrient dense, and lasts in the refrigerator all week! Finally, although this chapter highlights the versatility of pantry goods, I also include optional fresh additions, which can elevate these pantry favorites.

Lentil Salad

PREP TIME: 40 MIN | COOK TIME: 20 MIN | YIELD: 8 SERVINGS

INGREDIENTS

1½ cups dried brown lentils

4 cups water

⅓ cup extra-virgin olive oil

1 teaspoon cumin seeds

2 tablespoons dried parsley, crushed

1 teaspoon dried oregano

½ teaspoon garlic powder

½ teaspoon onion powder

½ cup pine nuts

½ cup canned roasted red bell peppers, drained and chopped

1 cup canned hearts of palm, drained and sliced into ½-inch slices

3 tablespoons lemon juice

Salt, to taste

½ cup thinly sliced green onions (optional)

¼ cup crumbled feta cheese (optional)

DIRECTIONS

1 Rinse the lentils, and then place them in a saucepan with the water. Bring to a boil; then cover and reduce the heat to low. Simmer until tender, but not mushy, about 15 to 20 minutes. Drain and set aside.

2 Meanwhile, in a small saucepan, heat the olive oil and cumin seeds over medium-low heat for 2 minutes. Remove from the heat and whisk in the parsley, oregano, garlic powder, and onion powder.

3 In a small skillet, toast the pine nuts over medium-low heat until fragrant but not brown, about 3 minutes. (If the pine nuts begin to darken, remove them from the skillet immediately and place on a cool plate.)

4 In a medium bowl, stir together the cooked lentils, olive oil mixture, toasted pine nuts, bell peppers, hearts of palm, and lemon juice. Season with salt. Refrigerate for 30 minutes and then add the onions and feta, if desired, and serve or store in the refrigerator until ready to serve.

PER SERVING: *Calories 274 (From Fat 137); Fat 15g (Saturated 2g); Cholesterol 0mg; Sodium 172mg; Carbohydrate 25g (Dietary Fiber 12g); Protein 11g.*

NOTE: Store in an airtight container in the refrigerator for up to 5 days, making it a perfect addition to meal planning and prepping for the week!

NOTE: Avoid salting beans while cooking because the salt can prevent them from getting tender.

VARY IT! You can use red wine vinegar or white wine vinegar in place of the lemon juice.

TIP: Heating spices in olive oil can heighten their flavors.

Three Bean Salad

PREP TIME: ABOUT 12 MIN | COOK TIME: NONE | YIELD: 4 SERVINGS

INGREDIENTS

¼ cup apple cider vinegar

3 tablespoons sugar

¼ cup extra-virgin olive oil

1 tablespoon dried parsley

½ teaspoon garlic powder

½ teaspoon salt

One 15-ounce can pinto beans, drained and rinsed

One 15-ounce can kidney beans, drained and rinsed

One 15-ounce can garbanzo beans, drained and rinsed

½ cup thinly sliced red onion, soaked in ice water for 5 minutes, drained (optional)

¼ cup thinly sliced celery (optional)

½ cup grated carrot (optional)

DIRECTIONS

In a medium bowl, whisk together the apple cider vinegar, sugar, olive oil, parsley, garlic powder, and salt. Stir in the pinto beans, kidney beans, and garbanzo beans. Add the onion, celery, and carrot, if desired. Refrigerate for at least 1 hour before serving.

PER SERVING: *Calories 442 (From Fat 122); Fat 14g (Saturated 2g); Cholesterol 0mg; Sodium 628mg; Carbohydrate 59g (Dietary Fiber 22g); Protein 22g.*

NOTE: Store in an airtight container the refrigerator for up to 5 days, making it a perfect addition to meal planning and prepping for the week!

VARY IT! Fresh or canned green beans are also great to add into this mix.

TIP: Soaking onions in vinegar or water can help cut the sharpness of their flavor. If you enjoy that sharp bite, feel free to skip the soaking.

Antipasto Pantry Salad

PREP TIME: 40 MIN	COOK TIME: 15 MIN	YIELD: 6 SERVINGS

INGREDIENTS

One 14.5-ounce can diced tomatoes, drained

½ cup extra-virgin olive oil

4 cloves garlic, chopped

5 ounces dried salami, diced

One 15-ounce can or jar marinated artichoke hearts, drained and quartered

One 16-ounce jar giardiniera (pickled Italian vegetables), drained

One 14.5-ounce can garbanzo beans, drained and rinsed

¼ cup sliced oil-cured black olives

¼ cup red wine vinegar

2 teaspoons sugar

Salt, to taste

½ cup thinly sliced white onion (optional)

¼ cup chopped fresh parsley (optional)

¼ cup thinly sliced basil (optional)

6 ounces fresh mozzarella, drained and cubed (optional)

DIRECTIONS

1 Preheat the oven to 425 degrees.

2 In an oven-safe baking dish, mix the tomatoes with the olive oil and garlic. Roast for 15 minutes.

3 Meanwhile, in a medium bowl, mix the salami, artichoke hearts, giardiniera, garbanzo beans, olives, red wine vinegar, and sugar. Stir in the tomatoes, garlic, and olive oil. Stir in the onion, parsley, and basil (if using). Stir to mix and season with salt, to taste. Chill until ready to serve, about 30 minutes. When the salad is chilled, you can stir in the diced mozzarella (if using).

PER SERVING: *Calories 344 (From Fat 241); Fat 27g (Saturated 5g); Cholesterol 19mg; Sodium 910mg; Carbohydrate 17g (Dietary Fiber 5g); Protein 10g.*

NOTE: Store in an airtight container in the refrigerator for up to 5 days without the cheese. Adding the cheese will shorten the life span of your salad to 3 days.

NOTE: Generally, giardiniera consists of cauliflower, carrots, garlic, peppers, and hot peppers.

VARY IT! If you can't find giardiniera, you can replace it with canned green beans, canned red bell peppers, and/or canned pepperoncini, all drained.

TIP: Roasting canned tomatoes elevates the flavor, and roasting with garlic and olive oil infuses the olive oil, further enhancing the overall flavor profile of the dish.

Pantry Pasta Salad

PREP TIME: ABOUT 10 MIN	COOK TIME: 9 MIN	YIELD: 8 SERVINGS

INGREDIENTS

8 ounces rotini pasta

½ cup diced pepperoni

One 6-ounce jar quartered and marinated artichoke hearts, undrained

One 14.5-ounce can diced tomatoes with basil, garlic, and oregano, drained

One 14.5-ounce can green beans, drained

1 cup canned kidney beans, drained and rinsed

3 tablespoons red wine vinegar

3 green onions, thinly sliced (optional)

2 ounces mozzarella, cubed (optional)

¼ cup chopped fresh parsley (optional)

DIRECTIONS

1 Cook the pasta according to package directions.

2 Meanwhile, place the pepperoni, artichoke hearts (with oil), tomatoes, green beans, kidney beans, and vinegar in a medium bowl and stir to mix.

3 When the pasta is done cooking, drain and add the hot pasta to the mixture. Stir and allow the pasta to cool, occasionally stirring to mix the ingredients. Stir in the onions, mozzarella, and parsley (if using). Serve or cover and refrigerate.

PER SERVING: *Calories 248 (From Fat 75); Fat 8g (Saturated 2g); Cholesterol 7mg; Sodium 559mg; Carbohydrate 34g (Dietary Fiber 5g); Protein 9g.*

NOTE: Store in an airtight container in the refrigerator for up to 5 days, making it a perfect addition to meal planning and prepping for the week!

VARY IT! Baby corn, canned mushrooms, and canned roasted red bell peppers are great additions.

TIP: Buying preflavored tomatoes and marinated artichoke hearts is a great way to add flavor without needing to keep extra spices on hand.

Chickpea and Sunflower Smashed Salad

PREP TIME: 40 MIN | COOK TIME: NONE | YIELD: 4 SERVINGS

INGREDIENTS

⅓ cup raw sunflower seeds

1 cup warm water (for soaking)

One 15-ounce can garbanzo beans, drained and rinsed

¼ cup mayonnaise

2 teaspoons Dijon mustard

¼ teaspoon garlic powder

¼ teaspoon onion powder

½ teaspoon dried dill (or 1 tablespoon fresh dill)

½ teaspoon salt

¼ teaspoon cracked pepper

2 green onions, thinly sliced (optional)

¼ cup thinly sliced celery (optional)

DIRECTIONS

1 In a small bowl, soak the sunflower seeds in the warm water for 15 minutes to soften. Drain the water from the sunflower seeds.

2 Place the sunflower seeds and garbanzo beans in a medium bowl. Using a fork, pastry blender, or food processor, mash until slightly chunky. Stir in the mayonnaise, mustard, garlic powder, onion powder, dill, salt, and pepper. Stir in the onions and celery, if desired. Cover and refrigerate for at least 30 minutes before serving. Adjust the seasonings, as desired.

PER SERVING: *Calories 178 (From Fat 96); Fat 11g (Saturated 2g); Cholesterol 4mg; Sodium 417mg; Carbohydrate 16g (Dietary Fiber 5g); Protein 7g.*

NOTE: Imagine the texture of egg salad with the flavors of hummus and sunflower seeds for this salad. I was traveling in Hawaii when I was first introduced to this idea of a salad. At a quaint vegan restaurant, I was served a mock tuna sunflower salad on toast with avocado and sunflower sprouts. I was hooked!

NOTE: Store in an airtight container in the refrigerator for up to 5 days.

VARY IT! Walnuts, peanuts, and cashews are great substitutes for sunflower seeds to continue the plant-based salad theme. Soak the nuts for 20 minutes to soften, and use a food processor to pulse them with the beans. If you prefer to keep this salad vegan-friendly, use vegan mayo.

TIP: Serve this salad on toasted bread, your favorite crackers, or wrapped up in lettuce leaves, or use it as a dip for vegetables.

Southwestern Black Bean Salad

PREP TIME: ABOUT 10 MIN	COOK TIME: NONE	YIELD: 6 SERVINGS

INGREDIENTS

Two 15-ounce cans black beans, drained and rinsed

One 8.75-ounce can corn, drained

¼ cup chopped canned roasted red bell pepper

½ cup drained, fire-roasted diced canned tomatoes

¼ teaspoon ground cumin

¼ teaspoon ground coriander

¼ teaspoon garlic powder

¼ teaspoon onion powder or 3 tablespoons finely diced fresh red onion

2 teaspoons dried cilantro or 3 tablespoons fresh cilantro

1 tablespoon lime juice

3 tablespoons extra-virgin olive oil or avocado oil

½ teaspoon salt

1 medium avocado, diced (optional)

2 tablespoons crumbled cotija cheese (optional)

DIRECTIONS

In a medium bowl, mix all the ingredients. Store in the refrigerator until ready to serve or serve immediately.

PER SERVING: *Calories 180 (From Fat 63); Fat 7g (Saturated 1g); Cholesterol 0mg; Sodium 477mg; Carbohydrate 22g (Dietary Fiber 8g); Protein 8g.*

NOTE: Store in an airtight container in the refrigerator for up to 5 days.

NOTE: This salad is quick, easy, and packed with flavor. My daughter takes this to school in her lunchbox with chips.

VARY IT! Swap out the black beans with pinto beans or green beans.

TIP: Serve with tortilla chips or as a side dish.

Chapter **14**

Starchy Salads

RECIPES IN THIS CHAPTER

Mediterranean Potato Salad

Quinoa, Herbed Bean, and Olive Salad

Southwestern Quinoa Salad

Fennel and Orange Beet Farro Salad

Creamy Green Macaroni Salad

Italian Tortellini and Bean Salad

Cold Soba and Edamame Salad

Cali BLT Panzanella Salad

Roasted Mushroom, Arugula, and Buckwheat Salad

Smoky Sumac and Freekeh Salad

Barley and Lemon Chive Salad

Spring Pea, Bulgur, and Goat Cheese Salad

Loaded Roasted Potato and Kale Salad

ost dinner plans start with a protein, pair it with a starch, and then add a vegetable. Why not combine the starch and vegetable instead? These salads take the guesswork out of your side dishes and make the side dish the star of the plate. Bulgur, farro, barley, quinoa, and pasta pair up with bold, colorful vegetables and herbs to brighten any dinner plate or lunch box.

Grains extend your basic salad. If you use a hardy green, such as arugula, kale, spinach, or cabbage, you can keep your salad for five days — making it a perfect match for those who want to meal-prep for the week. In this chapter, I used a wide variety of grains and added a touch of cultural flair, such as Fennel and Orange Beet Farro Salad and Cold Soba Edamame Salad.

Our family favorites include the Cali BLT Panzanella Salad and the Spring Pea, Bulgur, and Goat Cheese Salad. My daughter's favorite is the Southwestern Quinoa Salad.

Mediterranean Potato Salad

PREP TIME: ABOUT 10 MIN | **COOK TIME: 30 MIN** | **YIELD: 10 SERVINGS**

INGREDIENTS

1½ pounds new potatoes (boiling potatoes)

1 tablespoon salt (for boiling)

⅓ cup extra-virgin olive oil

3 cloves garlic

4 cups baby spinach

½ cup thinly sliced pepperoni

1 small yellow onion, thinly sliced

½ cup thinly sliced red bell pepper

½ cup black or green olives

2 tablespoons lemon juice

1 teaspoon paprika

1 teaspoon dried oregano

¼ cup chopped parsley

2 tablespoons red wine vinegar

½ teaspoon sea salt

½ teaspoon cracked pepper

DIRECTIONS

1 Place the potatoes in a large pot of water with 1 tablespoon salt. Bring to a boil, then cover and reduce the temperature to a low simmer until fork tender, about 15 to 20 minutes.

2 While the potatoes are cooking, place the olive oil and garlic in a small saucepan. Heat the garlic over medium-low heat for 3 minutes to infuse the oil. Remove from the heat and set aside to cool.

3 In a large serving bowl, place the spinach, pepperoni, onion, bell pepper, and olives, tossing to mix.

4 Drain the potatoes and run under cold water to cool the potatoes. Cube the boiled potatoes.

5 Next, in a small bowl, whisk together the lemon juice, paprika, oregano, parsley, vinegar, sea salt, pepper, and garlic-infused olive oil. Add the potatoes to the spinach then drizzle the dressing over the top. Toss the salad gently to mix.

PER SERVING: *Calories 176 (From Fat 95); Fat 11g (Saturated 2g); Cholesterol 5mg; Sodium 304mg; Carbohydrate 17g (Dietary Fiber 2g); Protein 4g.*

NOTE: This salad can keep for up to 5 days in the refrigerator.

VARY IT! Add crumbled feta, artichoke hearts, canned corn, steamed green beans, or asparagus to the salad.

TIP: Serve with grilled or baked meats any season.

TIP: Not all potatoes are created equal. Be sure to use the right potato for the right job. When boiling potatoes, use new potatoes or small, waxy varieties. Russets won't hold up for boiling and are best for roasting.

Quinoa, Herbed Bean, and Olive Salad

PREP TIME: ABOUT 12 MIN | **COOK TIME: 15 MIN** | **YIELD: 6 SERVINGS**

INGREDIENTS

½ cup quinoa, rinsed

1 cup water

One 14.5-ounce can garbanzo beans, drained and rinsed

½ cup chopped parsley

½ cup sliced olives

1 lemon, zested and juiced

1 tablespoon red wine vinegar

¼ cup extra-virgin olive oil

2 green onions, thinly sliced

1 cup cherry tomatoes, halved

DIRECTIONS

1 In a medium saucepan, bring the quinoa and water to a boil. Cover and reduce the heat to a low simmer until the liquid is absorbed, about 15 minutes. Set aside to cool, about 5 minutes.

2 In a serving bowl, stir together the beans, parsley, olives, lemon zest, lemon juice, vinegar, and olive oil. Add the quinoa, stirring to mix. Top with the green onions and tomatoes, stirring gently to mix. Serve immediately or refrigerate.

PER SERVING: *Calories 191 (From Fat 101); Fat 11g (Saturated 2g); Cholesterol 0mg; Sodium 178mg; Carbohydrate 18g (Dietary Fiber 5g); Protein 5g.*

NOTE: This salad will keep for up to 5 days in the refrigerator.

VARY IT! Add artichoke hearts, diced bell pepper, or fresh basil. Replace the garbanzo beans with kidney beans.

TIP: Serve with your favorite sandwiches, roasted chicken, or grilled salmon.

Southwestern Quinoa Salad

PREP TIME: ABOUT 10 MIN	COOK TIME: 15 MIN	YIELD: 8 SERVINGS

INGREDIENTS

½ cup quinoa, rinsed

1 cup water

One 14.5-ounce can black beans, drained and rinsed

One 8-ounce can corn, drained

1 red bell pepper, diced

1 small red onion, diced

½ cup chopped cilantro

2 green onions, thinly sliced

1 cup cherry tomatoes, halved

2 limes, zested and juiced

1 teaspoon ground cumin

½ teaspoon chipotle powder

1 teaspoon dried oregano

¼ cup extra-virgin olive oil

DIRECTIONS

1 In a medium saucepan, bring the quinoa and water to a boil. Cover and reduce the heat to a low simmer until the liquid is absorbed, about 15 minutes. Set aside to cool, about 5 minutes.

2 In a serving bowl, stir together the beans, corn, bell pepper, red onion, cilantro, green onions, and tomatoes. Add the quinoa and stir. Add the lime zest and lime juice, cumin, chipotle powder, and oregano, stirring to combine. Drizzle the olive oil over the top, stir, and serve or refrigerate until ready to serve.

PER SERVING: *Calories 160 (From Fat 70); Fat 8g (Saturated 1g); Cholesterol 0mg; Sodium 109mg; Carbohydrate 19g (Dietary Fiber 4g); Protein 5g.*

NOTE: This salad will keep for up to 5 days in the refrigerator.

VARY IT! Add pumpkin seeds, diced zucchini, steamed green beans, or pickled jalapeños.

TIP: Serve with tacos, grilled meats, quesadillas, or tostadas.

Fennel and Orange Beet Farro Salad

PREP TIME: ABOUT 15 MIN	COOK TIME: 25 MIN	YIELD: 6 SERVINGS

INGREDIENTS

1 cup whole-grain farro

2 cups chicken or vegetable stock

1 bay leaf

½ teaspoon cinnamon

1 cup finely sliced fennel

1 cup grated raw beets

3 tablespoons red wine vinegar

½ cup extra-virgin olive oil

1 tablespoon chopped mint

¼ cup chopped parsley

2 segmented oranges

½ cup chopped and toasted walnuts

DIRECTIONS

1 In a medium saucepan, bring the farro, stock, bay leaf, and cinnamon to a boil. Cover and reduce the heat to a low simmer for 25 to 30 minutes, stirring occasionally. Set aside to cool.

2 In a serving bowl, stir together the fennel, beets, vinegar, olive oil, mint, and parsley. Add the cooked farro, stirring to mix. Top with the orange segments and chopped walnuts and serve.

PER SERVING: *Calories 412 (From Fat 238); Fat 26g (Saturated 4g); Cholesterol 2mg; Sodium 147mg; Carbohydrate 38g (Dietary Fiber 10g); Protein 9g.*

NOTE: Oil a cutting board and wear an apron when grating beets. The oil will protect your board from staining and the apron will guard your clothes.

TIP: When slicing fennel, trim off the top fronds and thinly slice with a mandoline or sharp knife. Much like an onion, you can slice in any direction. Remove the woodsy end where the root attaches.

NOTE: To toast the walnuts, add them to a skillet and heat over medium heat, stirring frequently until they become fragrant. Watch closely so the nuts don't burn. When you can smell them, immediately remove them from the heat and from the pan.

VARY IT! Add crumbled goat cheese or feta.

TIP: Serve with poached fish or grilled chicken.

Creamy Green Macaroni Salad

PREP TIME: ABOUT 30 MIN	COOK TIME: 10 MIN	YIELD: 8 SERVINGS

INGREDIENTS

1 pound macaroni

1 tablespoon salt (for boiling pasta)

1 cup Creamy Green Herb Dressing (see Chapter 6)

½ cup finely diced onion

½ cup thinly sliced celery

2 cups chopped raw spinach

1 cup chopped sugar snap peas or sweet peas

DIRECTIONS

1 Place the pasta and salt in a large pot and cook according to package instructions. Drain and run cold water over the pasta for 1 minute. Place the pasta in the refrigerator to chill while you prepare the remaining ingredients.

2 In a serving bowl, stir the chilled pasta, dressing, onion, celery, spinach, and peas. Chill for 30 minutes or serve immediately.

PER SERVING: *Calories 264 (From Fat 29); Fat 21g (Saturated 2g); Cholesterol 1mg; Sodium 87mg; Carbohydrate 49g (Dietary Fiber 3g); Protein 10g.*

NOTE: The flavors of the pasta salad will be better if chilled for at least 30 minutes prior to serving.

VARY IT! Add olives, diced zucchini, broccoli florets, or shredded cabbage.

TIP: This pasta dish is as green as they get! Serve in place of both a starch and a vegetable at a meal.

Italian Tortellini and Bean Salad

PREP TIME: ABOUT 10 MIN PLUS 1 HR FOR CHILLING	COOK TIME: 30 MIN	YIELD: 8 SERVINGS

INGREDIENTS

20 ounces cheese tortellini

1 cucumber, peeled, seeded, and diced

1 cup halved cherry or grape tomatoes

½ cup sliced pepperoncini, drained

½ cup sliced black olives, drained

4 ounces salami, thinly sliced

½ cup sliced basil leaves

8 ounces fresh mozzarella, drained and cut into bite-size pieces

1½ cups Classic Italian Vinaigrette (see Chapter 6)

DIRECTIONS

1 Cook the pasta according to package instructions. Drain and run cold water over the pasta. Chill in the refrigerator while you prepare the remaining ingredients.

2 In a large serving bowl, stir the cucumber, tomato, pepperoncini, olives, salami, basil, mozzarella, and vinaigrette. Add the chilled pasta, stirring to mix. Refrigerate for at least 1 hour prior to serving.

PER SERVING: *Calories 461 (From Fat 227); Fat 25g (Saturated 9g); Cholesterol 65mg; Sodium 903mg; Carbohydrate 39g (Dietary Fiber 3g); Protein 20g.*

VARY IT! Replace the Italian dressing with a balsamic vinaigrette. Add diced bell peppers, artichoke hearts, parsley, and broccoli florets.

TIP: Serve with your favorite sandwich or soup or as the main dish.

Cold Soba and Edamame Salad

PREP TIME: ABOUT 10 MIN	COOK TIME: 4 MIN	YIELD: 8 SERVINGS

INGREDIENTS

4 ounces Soba noodles

3 tablespoons apple cider vinegar

¼ cup orange marmalade

2 tablespoons vegetable oil

1 tablespoon sesame oil

1 teaspoon grated ginger

1 teaspoon grated garlic

2 tablespoons lime juice

2 tablespoons soy sauce

2 Persian cucumbers, thinly sliced on the bias

½ cup grated carrots

1 cup shelled edamame

1 cup thinly sliced purple cabbage

1 cup canned-in-water mandarin oranges, drained

2 cups fried wonton noodles

1 tablespoon black sesame seeds

DIRECTIONS

1 In a large pot, bring water to a boil. Add the soba noodles, stirring to submerge. Cook according to package instructions, about 2 to 4 minutes. While the soba noodles are cooking, ready an ice bath. Strain the cooked soba noodles and immediately submerge them into the ice bath, stirring to quickly cool the noodles.

2 Next, in a serving bowl whisk together the vinegar, marmalade, vegetable oil, sesame oil, ginger, garlic, lime juice, and soy sauce. Add the cucumbers, carrots, edamame, cabbage, and mandarin oranges, stirring to combine. Strain the cold soba noodles. Add the soda noodles to the vegetables, tossing to coat. Add the fried wonton noodles and sesame seeds, tossing to mix the salad. Serve immediately.

PER SERVING: *Calories 231 (From Fat 93); Fat 10g (Saturated 1g); Cholesterol 0mg; Sodium 404mg; Carbohydrate 32g (Dietary Fiber 3g); Protein 6g.*

NOTE: Soba noodles are gluten-free because they're made from buckwheat. They must be cooled quickly or the noodles will clump together. If you're preparing these for someone who must eat gluten-free, be sure to check the label. Sometimes food manufacturers cut costs by adding wheat to the noodles.

VARY IT! Try thinly sliced red or orange bell peppers, green onions, chopped peanuts or cashews, and roasted sweet potatoes.

TIP: Serve with teriyaki chicken, ribs, or barbecue chicken.

Cali BLT Panzanella Salad

PREP TIME: ABOUT 5 MIN	COOK TIME: 20 MIN	YIELD: 8 SERVINGS

INGREDIENTS

8 slices center-cut bacon

4 cups chopped tomatoes, cut into bite-size wedges or diced

1 teaspoon sea salt

3 tablespoons red wine vinegar

1 shallot, minced

3 cloves garlic, minced

½ cup extra-virgin olive oil

2 Haas avocados, peeled, seeded, and diced

4 cups chopped romaine or iceberg lettuce

One 5-ounce bag croutons

DIRECTIONS

1 Preheat the oven to 400 degrees. Line a baking sheet with parchment paper, and lay out the bacon in a single layer. Bake until crispy, about 12 to 20 minutes. Remove the bacon from the baking sheet and place on paper towels to absorb the oil.

2 While the bacon is cooking, place the tomatoes in a bowl and stir in the salt. Let the tomatoes sit while the bacon is cooking. After the bacon is done, drain the juice from the tomatoes.

3 Next, in a serving bowl, whisk the vinegar, shallot, and garlic. Drizzle in the olive oil while whisking the dressing. Add the strained tomatoes, avocados, and lettuce to the dressing, tossing gently to mix.

4 Chop the bacon into crumbles. Add bacon and croutons to the salad, stirring to combine, and serve.

PER SERVING: *Calories 339 (From Fat 231); Fat 26g (Saturated 4g); Cholesterol 9mg; Sodium 553mg; Carbohydrate 22g (Dietary Fiber 6g); Protein 7g.*

NOTE: Panzanella is a classic Italian salad, and this twist of ingredients won't disappoint. If you want to keep the salad for 2 days, keep the lettuce and avocados separated from the tomato salad. Add just when serving.

VARY IT! Add in thinly sliced fennel, fresh mozzarella balls, and olives.

TIP: Serve in the peak of summer when tomatoes are ripe and bursting with flavors. Pair the salad with barbecue, corn on the cob, and crusty bread.

Roasted Mushroom, Arugula, and Buckwheat Salad

PREP TIME: ABOUT 5 MIN	COOK TIME: 20 MIN	YIELD: 8 SERVINGS

INGREDIENTS

12 ounces button mushrooms (cremini or baby bells), washed and patted dry

½ cup extra-virgin olive oil

4 cloves garlic

¼ cup balsamic vinegar

¾ cup water

½ cup toasted buckwheat groats

1 tablespoon salted butter

1 teaspoon sea salt, divided

8 cups baby arugula

1 cup cherry tomato halves

½ cup finely grated Pecorino Romano

DIRECTIONS

1 Preheat the oven to 400 degrees. Place the mushrooms in an oven-safe Dutch oven. Add the olive oil and garlic. Roast the mushrooms for 10 minutes. Pour in the vinegar, stir, and continue roasting for 10 more minutes.

2 Meanwhile, in a saucepan, bring the water to a boil. Stir in the buckwheat groats, butter, and ½ teaspoon of the salt. Cover and simmer until the liquid is mostly absorbed, about 12 minutes. Remove from the heat and let the groats sit for 10 minutes with the lid on.

3 Arrange the arugula on a serving platter. Top the arugula with the buckwheat; then pour the roasted mushrooms and sauce over the top. Top the salad with the tomatoes, the remaining ½ teaspoon of salt, and the cheese. Serve immediately.

PER SERVING: *Calories 211 (From Fat 156); Fat 17g (Saturated 4g); Cholesterol 9mg; Sodium 351mg; Carbohydrate 10g (Dietary Fiber 2g); Protein 5g.*

NOTE: Arugula holds up well for warm salads. This is a perfect fall or winter salad.

VARY IT! Add roasted red bell pepper and roasted asparagus.

TIP: Serve with pork, roasted chicken, or stew and crusty bread.

Smoky Sumac and Freekeh Salad

PREP TIME: ABOUT 10 MIN | COOK TIME: 20 MIN | YIELD: 6 SERVINGS

INGREDIENTS

½ cup cracked freekeh

1¼ cups water

1 teaspoon sea salt, divided

¼ cup extra-virgin olive oil

½ teaspoon cumin seeds

1 teaspoon sumac

1 lemon, zested and juiced (about 5 tablespoons juice)

1 cup halved grape tomatoes

1 cup diced cucumber

½ cup chopped parsley

¼ cup chopped mint

1 tablespoon toasted sesame seeds

DIRECTIONS

1 Place the freekeh in a saucepan and toast over medium heat for 2 to 3 minutes. Add the water and ½ teaspoon of the salt and bring to a boil over high heat. Cover and reduce the heat to a simmer for 15 minutes. Remove from the heat and let the freekeh rest for 5 minutes. Drain off the excess liquid and fluff the freekeh with a fork.

2 While the freekeh cooks, heat the olive oil and cumin seeds in a skillet over medium heat until fragrant, about 2 minutes. Remove from the heat so as not to burn the cumin.

3 After the freekeh is cooled (about 10 minutes), in a serving bowl, stir together the freekeh, sumac, lemon juice, lemon zest, and cumin-infused olive oil. Add in the tomatoes, cucumber, parsley, mint, and sesame seeds. Season with the remaining ½ teaspoon of salt and serve.

PER SERVING: *Calories 117 (From Fat 89); Fat 10g (Saturated 1g); Cholesterol 0mg; Sodium 320mg; Carbohydrate 7g (Dietary Fiber 2g); Protein 1g.*

NOTE: Freekeh is made from green durum wheat and is an ancient grain from Africa. It's popular throughout Africa and the Middle East. If you use whole-grain freekeh, the cooking time can almost double.

NOTE: You can buy toasted sesame seeds or toast your own. To toast sesame seeds, add them to a small skillet and heat over medium-high heat, stirring frequently, until the sesame seeds become slightly golden in color. Remove immediately from the heat and from the skillet.

NOTE: Sumac is a popular Middle Eastern and Mediterranean spice. Red berries are harvested and dried, creating a beautiful red spice that has citrus flavors.

VARY IT! Swing this salad to the Southwest by using lime juice instead of lemon, use cilantro instead of parsley and mint, and add corn and minced jalapeño.

TIP: Serve with kabobs or falafel.

Barley and Lemon Chive Salad

PREP TIME: ABOUT 25 MIN	COOK TIME: 45 MIN	YIELD: 8 SERVINGS

INGREDIENTS

½ cup hulled barley, rinsed

1½ cups water

1 teaspoon sea salt, divided

1 lemon, juiced and zested (about 5 tablespoons)

⅓ cup extra-virgin olive oil

2 tablespoons finely chopped chives

¼ cup chopped parsley

¾ teaspoon ground cumin

½ cup dried cherries or cranberries

½ cup chopped pistachios

4 cups baby kale, thinly sliced

DIRECTIONS

1 Place the barley, water, and ½ teaspoon of the salt in a medium saucepan. Bring to a boil over medium–high heat; then partially cover and lower the heat to a low simmer on low heat. Cook until the barley is fully cooked and tender, about 35 to 45 minutes. Drain off the excess liquid and pour the barley onto a plate to cool, about 15 minutes.

2 In a serving bowl, mix the remaining ½ teaspoon of salt, lemon juice, lemon zest, olive oil, chives, parsley, and cumin. Add the barley to a serving bowl and pour the dressing over the top. Stir in the dried cherries or cranberries, pistachios, and baby kale. Serve immediately.

PER SERVING: *Calories 203 (From Fat 117); Fat 13g (Saturated 2g); Cholesterol 0mg; Sodium 252mg; Carbohydrate 20g (Dietary Fiber 4g); Protein 4g.*

NOTE: Hulled barley is a more nutrient-dense barley than pearl barley. If you're short on time, opt for pearl barley instead. This salad can keep for up to 3 days in the refrigerator.

VARY IT! Use cherries instead of raisins and use mint in place of the parsley. Add any chopped lettuce or cabbage in place of the kale, but just keep in mind that it may not hold up as well in the refrigerator.

TIP: Serve with roasted turkey or a prime rib roast.

Spring Pea, Bulgur, and Goat Cheese Salad

PREP TIME: ABOUT 10 MIN	COOK TIME: 20 MIN	YIELD: 8 SERVINGS

INGREDIENTS

½ cup fine bulgur

1 cup boiling water

2 shallots, finely diced

¼ cup champagne or white wine vinegar

1 teaspoon Dijon mustard

1 teaspoon salt

1 teaspoon sugar

⅓ cup extra-virgin olive oil

3 cups fresh or frozen and defrosted sweet peas

½ cup chopped fresh dill

¼ cup chopped parsley

½ cup crumbled goat cheese

DIRECTIONS

1 Place bulgur into a heat-safe bowl and add the boiling water. Cover and let the bulgur reconstitute for 20 minutes; then drain off any excess water. Fluff and set aside.

2 In a serving bowl, whisk together the shallots, champagne or white wine vinegar, mustard, salt, and sugar. While whisking, drizzle in the olive oil until combined. Add the bulgur, peas, dill, and parsley. Top with crumbled goat cheese and serve immediately.

PER SERVING: *Calories 197 (From Fat 107); Fat 12g (Saturated 3g); Cholesterol 7mg; Sodium 329mg; Carbohydrate 17g (Dietary Fiber 4g); Protein 6g.*

NOTE: This salad can be kept for up to 3 days in the refrigerator; if you want to keep it for 5 days, keep the goat cheese separate.

NOTE: Bulgur can come in many different sizes, including fine, medium fine, and coarse ground. If you use a coarser-ground bulgur, check for tenderness after reconstituting. The longer the salad sits mixed, the more tender a coarser-ground bulgur will become.

VARY IT! Add chopped red bell pepper and toasted walnut pieces.

TIP: Serve in spring, when sweet peas are in season. Serve with lamb chops or pork tenderloin.

Loaded Roasted Potato and Kale Salad

PREP TIME: ABOUT 15 MIN	COOK TIME: 20 MIN	YIELD: 6 SERVINGS

INGREDIENTS

1½ pounds baby Yukon gold potatoes, quartered

½ teaspoon smoked paprika

½ teaspoon garlic powder

½ teaspoon onion powder

1½ teaspoons sea salt, divided

2 tablespoons extra-virgin olive oil or avocado oil

4 slices center-cut bacon

¼ cup mayonnaise

1 teaspoon Dijon mustard

2 tablespoons white wine vinegar

1 teaspoon dried dill weed or 1 tablespoon fresh dill

¼ cup chopped fresh parsley

6 cups thinly sliced kale leaves, stems removed

2 green onions, thinly sliced

DIRECTIONS

1 Preheat the oven to 400 degrees. Line a baking sheet with parchment paper or foil.

2 In a medium bowl, place the potatoes and season with paprika, garlic powder, onion powder, and ½ teaspoon of the salt. Toss with the oil and pour onto the baking sheet. Add the bacon to baking sheet and bake until the potatoes are golden and tender and the bacon is crispy, about 20 minutes. Allow to cool slightly, and then crumble or chop the bacon.

3 Meanwhile, in a small bowl, whisk together the mayonnaise, mustard, vinegar, the remaining 1 teaspoon of salt, dill, and parsley.

4 In a large bowl, toss the dressing with the kale. Plate the kale on a serving platter. Top the kale with the roasted potatoes, crumbled bacon, and green onions. Serve immediately.

PER SERVING: Calories 253 (From Fat 96); Fat 11g (Saturated 2g); Cholesterol 8mg; Sodium 708mg; Carbohydrate 34g (Dietary Fiber 4g); Protein 7g.

NOTE: If you love loaded baked potatoes try this salad.

VARY IT! Grated cheddar cheese makes for a delicious addition. If you want to boost the nutrition, use Greek yogurt in place of mayonnaise.

TIP: Serve with steak.

Chapter **15**

Fruity Concoctions

RECIPES IN THIS CHAPTER

🍃 Bold Berry Salad

🍃 Apple and Walnut Salad

🍃 Apple, Candied Pecan, and Orange Salad

🍃 Balsamic Berry and Mozzarella Salad

🍃 Blood Orange, Avocado, and Pistachio Salad

🍃 Citrus Salad

🍃 Roasted Grape and Barley Salad

🍃 Tropical Fruit Salad

🍃 Minty Melon Salad

🍃 Mediterranean Watermelon Salad

🍃 Orange Pomegranate Salad

🍃 Pear Gorgonzola Salad

🍃 Delicata Squash and Apple Salad

🍃 Lime, Jicama, and Mango Salad

🍃 Spicy Pineapple and Mango Salad

🍃 Grilled Fig and Pistachio-Crusted Goat Cheese Salad

🍃 Orange Arugula Salad with Pistachio-Crusted Date Croutons

Fruit salads are fun, but have you tried adding fruit to your green salads? In this chapter, I use common fruits, such as berries, pears, apples, and oranges, as well as more exotic fruits, such as figs, pomegranate arils, and roasted grapes. I also dive into seasonality with fruit and vegetable seasonal salads.

When eating out, I tend to get excited when I see fruits served in a more savory dish. We often pigeonhole a fruit as being served one way, and I'm hoping to shed light on new ways to serve some of your favorite fruits. For instance, grapes taste wonderful when roasted, as do figs when they're grilled. This chapter is stout, with 17 recipes, and I hope you try them all!

My family asks for a couple of these salads again and again, from the Apple Candied Pecan and Orange Salad to the Spicy Pineapple and Mango Salad. My daughter's favorite is the Minty Melon Salad, and my favorite is the Delicata Squash and Apple Salad. You can't go wrong with the Bold Berry Salad — it's perfect for breakfast, lunch, and dinner!

Bold Berry Salad

PREP TIME: ABOUT 10 MIN | COOK TIME: NONE | YIELD: 6 SERVINGS

INGREDIENTS

2 cups strawberries, hulled and sliced

1 cup blackberries

1 cup raspberries

1 cup blueberries

1 tablespoon sugar

2 teaspoons lemon juice

1 tablespoon thinly sliced mint leaves

DIRECTIONS

1 Place the strawberries, blackberries, raspberries, and blueberries in a serving bowl.

2 In a small bowl, stir together the sugar, lemon juice, and mint leaves. Pour the sauce over the berries and gently stir. Serve immediately or refrigerate until ready to eat.

PER SERVING: *Calories 60 (From Fat 4); Fat 0g (Saturated 0g); Cholesterol 0mg; Sodium 1mg; Carbohydrate 14g (Dietary Fiber 4g); Protein 1g.*

NOTE: Adding a little bit of lemon juice can help protect the integrity of the fruit as it refrigerates. This salad can be stored up to 3 days in the refrigerator.

VARY IT! Grapes, pineapple, orange wedges, mango, or kiwi make for easy additions to this salad. For every 2 cups of fruit added, double the sauce.

TIP: Berries are a great source of fiber, with raspberries and blackberries boasting 8 grams of fiber per cup. We serve this salad all throughout the day. For breakfast, we serve it over yogurt; for dessert, my daughter loves it with ice cream or a dollop of whipped cream.

Apple and Walnut Salad

PREP TIME: ABOUT 10 MIN	COOK TIME: NONE	YIELD: 6 SERVINGS

INGREDIENTS

1 large Granny Smith apple, thinly sliced

1 teaspoon lemon juice

¼ teaspoon cinnamon

2 shallots, minced

3 tablespoons red wine vinegar

1 tablespoon honey

1 teaspoon Dijon mustard

½ teaspoon sea salt

½ teaspoon cracked pepper

¼ cup extra-virgin olive oil

8 cups baby arugula or spinach

½ cup chopped walnuts, toasted

½ cup canned hearts of palm, drained and sliced

½ cup dried cranberries

½ cup blue cheese crumbles

DIRECTIONS

1 In a small bowl, stir together the apple, lemon juice, and cinnamon.

2 In a small bowl, whisk together the shallots, vinegar, honey, mustard, salt, pepper, and olive oil until combined.

3 In a large serving bowl, place the greens on the bottom and top with the walnuts, hearts of palm, cranberries, and apples. Drizzle with the dressing and toss the salad. Top with the blue cheese and serve immediately.

PER SERVING: *Calories 258 (From Fat 173); Fat 19g (Saturated 4g); Cholesterol 8mg; Sodium 399mg; Carbohydrate 20g (Dietary Fiber 3g); Protein 6g.*

NOTE: Adding lemon juice to the apples helps decrease the browning that can occur when an apple sits out. Adding the cinnamon helps further mask the browning. Don't skip it!

NOTE: To toast the nuts, gently heat them over medium-high heat in a skillet, stirring frequently. When the nuts become fragrant, remove them from the heat and from the skillet.

VARY IT! If you prefer a sweeter apple than the tart Granny Smith, try a Honeycrisp or Pink Lady apple instead. You can also use goat cheese or feta in place of the blue cheese. Dried blueberries, cherries, or raisins can be used in place of the cranberries.

TIP: This salad is great for fall or the holidays. It's simple to pull together yet elegantly spruces up any meal. Serve with pork chops or oven-roasted turkey.

Apple, Candied Pecan, and Orange Salad

PREP TIME: ABOUT 10 MIN	COOK TIME: NONE	YIELD: 6 SERVINGS

INGREDIENTS

1 large Honeycrisp apple, thinly sliced and julienned

1 large navel orange, segmented

1 teaspoon lemon juice

8 cups torn butter lettuce

1 cup candied pecans, chopped

½ cup crumbled goat cheese

2 tablespoons champagne vinegar

1 tablespoon maple syrup or honey

½ teaspoon salt

½ teaspoon cracked pepper

¼ cup avocado or sunflower oil

DIRECTIONS

1 In a medium bowl, toss the apples, oranges, and lemon juice.

2 In a serving bowl, place the greens on the bottom. Top with the pecans, apples, oranges, and goat cheese.

3 In a small bowl, whisk together the vinegar, maple syrup or honey, salt, pepper, and oil. Pour the dressing over the salad, tossing to combine, and serve immediately.

PER SERVING: *Calories 249 (From Fat 172); Fat 19g (Saturated 4g); Cholesterol 9mg; Sodium 211mg; Carbohydrate 17g (Dietary Fiber 3g); Protein 5g.*

NOTE: To make candied pecans, whisk 1 egg white with ½ cup sugar, 2 teaspoons cinnamon, 1 teaspoon salt, and 4 cups pecans. Spread onto a baking sheet and bake at 250 degrees for 1 hour, stirring every 15 minutes.

VARY IT! You can also use grapefruit, mango, or pears in this salad.

TIP: Serve in the fall or winter, when citrus and apples are in season.

Balsamic Berry and Mozzarella Salad

PREP TIME: ABOUT 30 MIN	COOK TIME: 10 MIN	YIELD: 6 SERVINGS

INGREDIENTS

½ cup balsamic vinegar

½ cup blueberries

1 tablespoon sugar

4 cups strawberries, hulled and sliced

1 cup blackberries

4 ounces fresh mozzarella, ciliegine or pearls (small balls)

¼ cup thinly sliced basil

1 tablespoon thinly sliced fresh mint

DIRECTIONS

1 In a small saucepan, heat the vinegar, blueberries, and sugar over medium-low heat for 10 minutes. Mash the berries and stir every couple of minutes. The sauce should reduce by ⅓ or ½. Strain through a sieve to remove the skins, if desired. Set aside to cool for 20 minutes.

2 In a serving bowl, place the strawberries, blackberries, mozzarella, basil, and mint. Drizzle the blueberry balsamic reduction over the fruit, gently stirring to combine. Serve immediately or refrigerate.

PER SERVING: *Calories 132 (From Fat 42); Fat 5g (Saturated 3g); Cholesterol 15mg; Sodium 125mg; Carbohydrate 18g (Dietary Fiber 4g); Protein 5g.*

NOTE: This recipe may shock your tastebuds. The smooth acidity of a balsamic reduction pairs beautifully with berries and fresh mozzarella. Cheeses often pair nicely with fruit.

VARY IT! Serve this as an appetizer by skewering the fruit and mozzarella, drizzling with the sauce, and topping with fresh herbs. It plates well for parties.

TIP: Don't buy a bottled version of balsamic reduction. Often, they have a lot of unnecessary ingredients, from food coloring to excess sugar.

Blood Orange, Avocado, and Pistachio Salad

PREP TIME: ABOUT 15 MIN	COOK TIME: NONE	YIELD: 6 SERVINGS

INGREDIENTS

4 blood oranges, skin and white pith removed and thinly sliced

2 navel oranges, skin and white pith removed and thinly sliced

2 Haas avocados, peeled, pitted, and thinly sliced

½ cup shelled pistachios, chopped

2 tablespoons champagne vinegar

1 tablespoon lime juice

1 tablespoon honey

½ teaspoon sea salt

¼ cup extra-virgin olive oil

DIRECTIONS

1 Arrange the orange slices on a platter. Top with the avocados and pistachios.

2 In a small bowl, whisk together the vinegar, lime juice, honey, salt, and olive oil. Drizzle over the salad and serve immediately.

PER SERVING: *Calories 312 (From Fat 187); Fat 21g (Saturated 3g); Cholesterol 0mg; Sodium 192mg; Carbohydrate 32g (Dietary Fiber 9g); Protein 5g.*

NOTE: Avocado season starts in February in San Diego — the major producer of U.S. avocados. Citrus is in peak season then, too.

VARY IT! Use grapefruit, jicama, or thinly sliced fennel, or serve over a bed of butter lettuce leaves.

TIP: This salad is gorgeous. The blood orange makes this salad pop with color and flavor. Serve with chicken kabobs or grilled flank steak.

Citrus Salad

INGREDIENTS

1 tablespoon white balsamic vinegar

1 tablespoon lemon juice

2 tablespoons honey

¼ cup extra-virgin olive oil

½ teaspoon sea salt

½ teaspoon cracked pepper

½ cup thinly sliced red onion

2 Cara Cara oranges, skin and white pith removed and thinly sliced

1 grapefruit, skin and white pith removed and thinly sliced

1 navel orange, skin and white pith removed and thinly sliced

2 tablespoons thinly sliced fresh mint

DIRECTIONS

1 In a small bowl, whisk together the vinegar, lemon juice, honey, olive oil, salt, and pepper. Add the onions and let the mixture sit for 5 minutes.

2 Arrange the citrus on a serving platter. Remove the onion from the vinaigrette and add on top of the salad. Drizzle the dressing over the salad and top with the mint leaves. Serve immediately.

PER SERVING: *Calories 255 (From Fat 124); Fat 14g (Saturated 2g); Cholesterol 0mg; Sodium 237mg; Carbohydrate 34g (Dietary Fiber 5g); Protein 2g.*

VARY IT! Add fennel, jicama, watercress, or sprouts. If you're craving a crunch, add chopped macadamia nuts, pistachios, or hazelnuts.

TIP: Feel like summer all winter long with this salad. You can even use canned orange wedges in this salad as well.

Roasted Grape and Barley Salad

PREP TIME: ABOUT 15 MIN	COOK TIME: 30 MIN	YIELD: 6 SERVINGS

INGREDIENTS

1 cup red grapes

1 teaspoon sea salt, divided

¼ cup extra-virgin olive oil

1 cup water

½ cup quick cooking barley

¼ cup balsamic vinegar

1 cup chopped walnuts

6 cups thinly sliced Lacinato or Italian kale (flat leaf)

1 tablespoon lemon juice

DIRECTIONS

1 Preheat the oven to 400 degrees.

2 In an oven-safe baking dish, mix the grapes, ¼ teaspoon of the salt, and olive oil. After the grapes have been roasting for 15 minutes, remove from the oven and add the vinegar and walnuts, stirring to mix. Return to the oven for 5 minutes. Roast the grapes for a total time of 20 minutes or until their skins begin to burst.

3 Meanwhile, in a small saucepan, bring 1 cup of water to a boil and add the barley. Cover and reduce the heat to a simmer for 10 minutes. Drain off any excess liquid and set aside to cool.

4 Place the kale in a serving bowl. Add the lemon juice and massage the kale. Add the barley to the kale, tossing to mix. Pour the oven-roasted grapes and walnuts over the kale and barley, tossing to mix. Sprinkle with the remaining ¾ teaspoon salt and serve immediately.

PER SERVING: *Calories 325 (From Fat 206); Fat 23g (Saturated 3g); Cholesterol 0mg; Sodium 347mg; Carbohydrate 27g (Dietary Fiber 6g); Protein 7g.*

NOTE: The roasted grapes create almost a jam-like intensity in flavor. Combined with the balsamic vinegar and nuts, the flavor melds into a well-balanced dressing. Guests are always surprised at the idea of roasting grapes. Serve them on toasted bread with cream cheese.

VARY IT! Add feta or goat cheese, use pecans in place of walnuts, or add caramelized onions by roasting the onions with the grapes.

Tropical Fruit Salad

PREP TIME: ABOUT 10 MIN	COOK TIME: NONE	YIELD: 6 SERVINGS

INGREDIENTS

2 cups fresh diced pineapple

1 cup diced mango

1 cup diced papaya

1 banana, sliced

½ cup unsweetened coconut flakes

2 tablespoons lime juice

2 tablespoons honey

½ cup chopped macadamia nuts

DIRECTIONS

1 Place the pineapple, mango, papaya, banana, and coconut flakes in a large serving bowl, stirring gently to combine.

2 In a microwave-safe bowl, heat the lime and honey for 10 seconds. Stir the sauce and pour over the tropical fruits. Top with the nuts and serve immediately.

PER SERVING: *Calories 198 (From Fat 98); Fat 11g (Saturated 3g); Cholesterol 0mg; Sodium 4mg; Carbohydrate 27g (Dietary Fiber 4g); Protein 2g.*

NOTE: Tropical fruits naturally go well together. I held back adding in fruits that aren't from the tropics but feel free to add in your favorite fruits.

VARY IT! Pitaya or dragon fruit, lychee, rambutan, or carambola (star fruit) are great tropical additions. If you want to veer from the tropics, try adding sliced kiwi and strawberries for pops of color.

Minty Melon Salad

PREP TIME: ABOUT 10 MIN | COOK TIME: NONE | YIELD: 6 SERVINGS

INGREDIENTS

2 cups honeydew melon, cubed or in balls

2 cups cantaloupe, cubed or in balls

3 cups watermelon, cubed or in balls

1 tablespoon lime juice

2 tablespoons honey

½ teaspoon salt

2 tablespoons thinly sliced mint

DIRECTIONS

1 In a serving bowl, mix the melons.

2 In a microwave-safe dish, heat the lime juice, honey, and salt for 10 seconds. Pour over the melons and top with the mint. Toss before serving.

PER SERVING: *Calories 86 (From Fat 3); Fat 0g (Saturated 0g); Cholesterol 0mg; Sodium 178mg; Carbohydrate 22g (Dietary Fiber 1g); Protein 1g.*

NOTE: Melons are best in summer when their flavors are the sweetest.

VARY IT! Add sliced peaches, kiwi, pineapple, or strawberries. Cucumbers and avocados also make great additions to this salad.

Mediterranean Watermelon Salad

PREP TIME: ABOUT 15 MIN	COOK TIME: NONE	YIELD: 8 SERVINGS

INGREDIENTS

½ cup thinly sliced red onion

3 tablespoons red wine vinegar

1 teaspoon sugar

½ teaspoon sea salt

1 teaspoon dried oregano

6 cups cubed watermelon

1 cup diced Persian cucumbers

¼ cup sliced black olives

¼ cup thinly sliced or torn basil leaves

¼ cup extra-virgin olive oil

½ cup crumbled feta

DIRECTIONS

1 In a small bowl, stir together the onion, vinegar, sugar, salt, and oregano. Let the mixture rest for 5 minutes.

2 In a serving bowl, add the watermelon, cucumbers, olives, and basil and stir gently to combine. Drizzle the onion mixture over the top and stir. Add the olive oil and stir. Top with the feta and serve immediately.

PER SERVING: *Calories 131 (From Fat 84); Fat 9g (Saturated 2g); Cholesterol 8mg; Sodium 261mg; Carbohydrate 11g (Dietary Fiber 1g); Protein 2g.*

VARY IT! If I have pine nuts or walnuts on hand, I'll add them to this salad. You can swing the salad flavors more Southwestern by adding diced jalapeños, mangos, and avocados. Use cumin and lime juice in place of the red wine vinegar.

Orange Pomegranate Salad

PREP TIME: ABOUT 10 MIN	COOK TIME: NONE	YIELD: 6 SERVINGS

INGREDIENTS

½ cup thinly sliced red onions

½ teaspoon sea salt

½ teaspoon cracked pepper

¼ teaspoon ground cumin

1 tablespoon fresh lemon juice

3 tablespoons extra-virgin olive oil

6 cups baby arugula or spinach

1 navel orange, skin and white pith removed and thinly sliced

½ cup pomegranate arils

½ cup shelled and chopped pistachios

¼ cup crumbled feta or goat cheese

DIRECTIONS

1 In a small bowl, stir together the onions, salt, pepper, cumin, lemon juice, and olive oil. Set aside for 5 minutes while you prepare the salad.

2 Place the greens on a serving platter. Arrange the oranges around the perimeter of the salad. Sprinkle the pomegranate arils on the greens and top with the pistachios. Drizzle the dressing on the salad and top with crumbled cheese before serving. Serve immediately.

PER SERVING: *Calories 179 (From Fat 123); Fat 14g (Saturated 3g); Cholesterol 4mg; Sodium 238mg; Carbohydrate 11g (Dietary Fiber 3g); Protein 5g.*

NOTE: Pomegranate arils can be found in the refrigerated section of a grocery store or in the freezer.

VARY IT! Sliced dried dates, avocados, or olives can be added to this salad.

Pear Gorgonzola Salad

PREP TIME: ABOUT 10 MIN	COOK TIME: NONE	YIELD: 4 SERVINGS

INGREDIENTS

6 cups torn romaine lettuce

1 Bosc or Bartlett pear, thinly sliced

½ cup dried cranberries or cherries

¼ cup Balsamic Vinaigrette (see Chapter 6)

½ cup chopped, toasted walnuts

⅓ cup crumbled gorgonzola

DIRECTIONS

Place the lettuce in a serving bowl. Top with the pear, cranberries, and Balsamic Vinaigrette. Toss to mix and coat the salad. Finish the salad by topping with the walnuts and gorgonzola. Serve immediately.

PER SERVING: *Calories 343 (From Fat 228); Fat 26g (Saturated 5g); Cholesterol 8mg; Sodium 303mg; Carbohydrate 28g (Dietary Fiber 5g); Protein 5g.*

NOTE: Gorgonzola is an Italian blue cheese and is salty and earthy in flavor. If you can't find it, try using a blue cheese instead.

VARY IT! Apples can be use in place of the pears; hazelnuts or pecans can be used in place of the walnuts; and raisins, dried cherries, or dried blueberries can be used in place of the cranberries. If balsamic vinaigrette isn't your favorite, try a nice Champagne vinaigrette instead.

Delicata Squash and Apple Salad

PREP TIME: ABOUT 15 MIN	COOK TIME: 30 MIN	YIELD: 8 SERVINGS

INGREDIENTS

1 delicata squash (less than 1 pound in size)

½ teaspoon sea salt

¼ teaspoon black pepper

¼ cup plus 1 tablespoon olive oil, divided

¼ cup plus 3 tablespoons pepitas (green pumpkin seeds), divided

1 clove garlic

¼ cup fresh parsley

1 tablespoon lemon juice

8 cups baby arugula or thinly sliced Swiss chard or baby spinach

2 Honeycrisp apples, thinly sliced

8 ounces crumbled goat cheese

DIRECTIONS

1 Preheat the oven to 425 degrees. Line a baking sheet with parchment paper.

2 Slice the squash down the center. Remove the seeds. Leaving the skin on, slice the squash in ¼-inch-thick half-moon slices. Sprinkle the squash with salt, pepper, and 1 tablespoon of the olive oil, tossing to coat. Spread the squash out on the baking sheet and bake for 15 minutes; then flip over and continue baking until they start to become golden in color, about 10 to 15 minutes.

3 Meanwhile, in a blender or food processor, blend ¼ cup of the pepitas, the garlic, parsley, lemon juice, and the remaining ¼ cup of olive oil together until smooth, about 2 minutes.

4 Next, toss the greens with the dressing (reserving any dressing that doesn't coat the greens) and plate on a serving platter. Top with the apple, cooked squash, goat cheese, and remaining 3 tablespoons of pepitas. Drizzle with any remaining dressing over the top and serve immediately.

PER SERVING: *Calories 278 (From Fat 188); Fat 21g (Saturated 8g); Cholesterol 22mg; Sodium 243mg; Carbohydrate 16g (Dietary Fiber 3g); Protein 10g.*

NOTE: If you've never roasted a delicata squash before, get ready to fall in love! Perfect for fall, pumpkin seeds and delicata squash meld well with apples. This salad will be on repeat all winter long!

VARY IT! If making the dressing seems taxing, try a honey mustard vinaigrette instead (see Chapter 6 for a recipe or use a store-bought dressing). Pine nuts or pistachios can be used in place of pumpkin seeds, and roasted sweet potatoes or peeled acorn squash can be used in place of the delicata squash.

Lime, Jicama, and Mango Salad

PREP TIME: ABOUT 15 MIN	COOK TIME: NONE	YIELD: 6 SERVINGS

INGREDIENTS

1 jicama, peeled and julienned

1 mango, peeled, pitted, and diced

1 jalapeño, seeds removed and finely diced

1 cup halved cherry or grape tomatoes

2 tablespoons red wine vinegar

3 tablespoons lime juice

1 teaspoon sugar

3 tablespoons avocado or extra-virgin olive oil

¼ cup chopped cilantro

DIRECTIONS

In a large serving bowl, add the jicama, mango, jalapeño, and tomatoes. Drizzle with vinegar and lime juice, stirring to coat the vegetables and fruit. Sprinkle with sugar and add the oil, tossing to coat. Stir in the cilantro and serve immediately or refrigerate until ready to serve.

PER SERVING: *Calories 136 (From Fat 63); Fat 7g (Saturated 1g); Cholesterol 0mg; Sodium 9mg; Carbohydrate 18g (Dietary Fiber 6g); Protein 1g.*

NOTE: Jicama looks like a starchy potato, but it has a crisp and refreshing bite. It also has a slightly sweet flavor, and the texture is a cross between an apple and a potato.

VARY IT! Add diced avocado and orange segments.

Spicy Pineapple and Mango Salad

PREP TIME: ABOUT 15 MIN | COOK TIME: NONE | YIELD: 8 SERVINGS

INGREDIENTS

1 tablespoon rice wine vinegar

1 tablespoon sweet chili sauce

1 tablespoon lime juice

2 tablespoons peanut oil or avocado oil

3 cups diced pineapple

3 cups diced mango

½ cup diced red bell pepper

½ cup diced English cucumber

2 green onions, finely sliced

1 serrano pepper, seeded and finely diced

½ cup chopped cilantro

¼ cup chopped peanuts

DIRECTIONS

1 In a small bowl, whisk together the vinegar, sweet chili sauce, lime juice, and oil.

2 In a serving bowl, stir together the pineapple, mango, bell pepper, cucumber, onions, serrano pepper, and cilantro. Pour the dressing over the salad and stir to combine. Top with the peanuts and serve immediately or refrigerate.

PER SERVING: *Calories 132 (From Fat 53); Fat 6g (Saturated 1g); Cholesterol 0mg; Sodium 17mg; Carbohydrate 20g (Dietary Fiber 3g); Protein 2g.*

NOTE: This fruit and vegetable salad can keep for up to 5 days in the refrigerator.

VARY IT! Tomatoes, green bell pepper, jicama, and radish make great additions to this salad.

Grilled Fig and Pistachio-Crusted Goat Cheese Salad

PREP TIME: ABOUT 15 MIN	COOK TIME: 20 MIN	YIELD: 6 SERVINGS

INGREDIENTS

½ cup balsamic vinegar

1 tablespoon honey

8 ounces goat cheese in a tube (not crumbles)

½ cup finely crushed pistachio

8 large fresh mission figs, cut in half

8 cups baby arugula or baby spinach

½ teaspoon sea salt

½ teaspoon cracked pepper

¼ cup extra-virgin olive oil

DIRECTIONS

1 In a small saucepan, heat the balsamic vinegar and honey over medium-low heat until it reduces in half, about 10 to 20 minutes, stirring occasionally. Remove from the heat and set aside to cool.

2 Meanwhile, remove the goat cheese from the packaging. Place the crushed pistachios on a plate. Gently roll the goat cheese into the crushed nuts, coating all sides. Wrap in plastic wrap and chill until ready to serve the salad.

3 Heat a grill or grill pan over medium-high heat. Grill the figs cut side down for 3 minutes.

4 Next, plate the greens on a serving platter. Top with the grilled figs, cut side up. Top with salt and pepper. Slice the pistachio-crusted goat cheese and place on the salad. Drizzle with the balsamic reduction and finish with olive oil. Top with any remaining pistachios, and serve immediately.

PER SERVING: *Calories 352 (From Fat 226); Fat 25g (Saturated 9g); Cholesterol 29mg; Sodium 357mg; Carbohydrate 21g (Dietary Fiber 3g); Protein 12g.*

NOTE: Figs are a Mediterranean favorite. If you're using the grill, it's the perfect time to make this salad. Look for figs that are firm to the touch.

VARY IT! If someone has a nut allergy, sesame seeds, sunflower seeds, or pumpkin seeds can be used instead. If you'd like to add meat, add prosciutto.

Orange Arugula Salad with Pistachio–Crusted Date Croutons

PREP TIME: ABOUT 15 MIN	COOK TIME: NONE	YIELD: 6 SERVINGS

INGREDIENTS

8 Medjool dates

½ cup finely crushed pistachios

2 oranges, divided

2 tablespoons red wine vinegar

1 teaspoon dried oregano or 1 tablespoon fresh oregano

1 shallot, finely chopped

½ teaspoon sea salt

¼ teaspoon cracked pepper

¼ teaspoon paprika

¼ teaspoon ground cumin

¼ cup extra-virgin olive oil

8 cups arugula or torn spinach

½ cup crumbled feta

DIRECTIONS

1 Pit the dates. Place the pistachio crumbs on a plate. Roll the dates in the pistachio crumbs, opening the dates to coat the inside as well. Reshape the dates and refrigerate until ready to serve the salad.

2 Next, juice ½ of an orange. With the remaining 1½ oranges, remove the peel and pith and thinly slice; set aside.

3 To make the dressing, whisk the orange juice, vinegar, oregano, shallot, salt, pepper, paprika, cumin, and olive oil.

4 Place the greens on a serving platter. Top with the orange slices. Take the dates from the refrigerator and cut each date into 3 pieces. Sprinkle the date croutons onto the salad. Drizzle the salad with the vinaigrette. Sprinkle the crumbled feta over the top and serve immediately.

PER SERVING: *Calories 268 (From Fat 128); Fat 14g (Saturated 3g); Cholesterol 11mg; Sodium 319mg; Carbohydrate 35g (Dietary Fiber 5g); Protein 5g.*

NOTE: Cara Cara or navel oranges are my favorites for this salad.

VARY IT! Dates are sweet and often used as sugar throughout the Middle East. You can roll them in crushed walnuts or almonds as well. Most any greens can be used in this dish.

Chapter **16**

Sweet Salads

RECIPES IN THIS CHAPTER

- Pineapple and Carrot Sweet Slaw
- Cherry Waldorf Salad
- Ambrosia
- Grape and Melon Mojito Salad
- Pear and Amaretti Cookie Salad
- Grilled Pineapple and Macadamia Nut Salad
- Nutty Strawberry Jell-O Salad
- Creamy Filipino Coconut Salad
- Fruity Cottage Cheese and Jell-O Salad

Yes, even *salads* can be served for desserts. This chapter may cause you to have flashbacks to the '70s, but don't worry: I've added modern twists to some classic recipes.

I'll be honest, I had to do some digging to find out why fluffy fruity concoctions are called salads. It seems that the answer lies in the fact that the dishes contain a mixture of fruits and nutty elements, creating a salad. I'm all for it! This chapter was fun to create and test with my daughter's help.

Serve these sweet salads at your favorite holiday meal or picnic or with dinner. I tend to make a batch for the week, and my daughter enjoys it after school.

If you have a party coming up, dive into the Grape and Melon Mojito Salad — it's fun and festive for a summer splash! Our family favorites include the Grilled Pineapple and Macadamia Nut Salad and the Cherry Waldorf Salad. And, if I were heading out to a picnic or a potluck I'd take the Nutty Strawberry Jell-O Salad! I hope you enjoy this blast to the past when making these salads — they're making a comeback!

Pineapple and Carrot Sweet Slaw

PREP TIME: ABOUT 20 MIN	COOK TIME: NONE	YIELD: 6 SERVINGS

INGREDIENTS

½ cup golden raisins

1 tablespoon lime juice

¼ cup vanilla Greek yogurt

¼ cup mayonnaise

2 tablespoons sugar

1 pound carrots, grated or spiralized (about 3½ cups)

½ teaspoon salt

1 cup finely diced pineapple

DIRECTIONS

1 Bring 1 cup water to a boil in the microwave (approximately 2 minutes on high), add the raisins, and let them sit for 5 minutes in the hot water.

2 Meanwhile, in a small bowl, stir together the lime juice, yogurt, mayonnaise, and sugar.

3 Drain the water from the raisins.

4 Place the carrots and salt into a bowl, tossing to mix. Let the carrots sit for 10 minutes. Rinse the carrots in ice water and drain. Pat the carrots dry (no need for perfection — you're just removing some of the excess liquid).

5 In a serving bowl, place the carrots, raisins, pineapple, and dressing, stirring to mix completely. Serve immediately or refrigerate until ready to serve.

PER SERVING: *Calories 143 (From Fat 32); Fat 4g (Saturated 1g); Cholesterol 3mg; Sodium 284mg; Carbohydrate 28g (Dietary Fiber 3g); Protein 2g.*

NOTE: Salting the carrots helps them stay crisper in the salad and removes excess water so that the dressing doesn't get watery as it sits over time. This salad can be stored in the refrigerator for up to 5 days.

TIP: You can use canned pineapple if you don't have fresh.

VARY IT! Try other dried fruits, from cranberries to apricots.

Cherry Waldorf Salad

PREP TIME: 40 MIN | COOK TIME: NONE | YIELD: 6 SERVINGS

INGREDIENTS

2 ounces softened cream cheese, at room temperature

¼ cup sour cream

¼ cup mayonnaise

3 tablespoons sugar

1 tablespoon lemon juice

1 cup Honeycrisp apple, diced

1 cup Granny Smith apple, diced

1 cup fresh cherries, pitted and halved

½ cup diced jicama or celery

½ cup toasted chopped pecans or walnuts

DIRECTIONS

1 In a mixer or food processor, blend the cream cheese, sour cream, mayonnaise, sugar, and lemon juice until blended and fluffy, about 2 to 3 minutes.

2 In a serving bowl, place the apples, cherries, jicama or celery, and nuts; stir. Pour the sauce over the fruit and stir to combine. Refrigerate at least 30 minutes before serving.

PER SERVING: *Calories 234 (From Fat 136); Fat 15g (Saturated 4g); Cholesterol 18mg; Sodium 116mg; Carbohydrate 25g (Dietary Fiber 3g); Protein 3g.*

VARY IT! Swap out the cherries with grapes or blueberries.

Ambrosia

PREP TIME: 40 MIN | **COOK TIME: NONE** | **YIELD: 10 SERVINGS**

INGREDIENTS

8 ounces frozen whipped topping, thawed

½ cup vanilla Greek yogurt

2 ounces cream cheese, at room temperature

One 11-ounce can mandarin oranges, drained

½ cup flaked, unsweetened coconut

One 8-ounce can diced pineapple, drained

1 cup Bordeaux maraschino cherries, drained, stems removed, and chopped

½ cup chopped pistachios or pecans

1 cup mini marshmallows

DIRECTIONS

1 In a mixer or food processor, blend the whipped topping, yogurt, and cream cheese until fully combined and fluffy, about 2 to 3 minutes.

2 In a serving bowl, place the mandarin oranges, coconut flakes, pineapple, cherries, nuts, and marshmallows; stir to mix. Pour the creamy sauce over the fruit, stirring to fully combine. Refrigerate at least 30 minutes prior to serving.

PER SERVING: *Calories 192 (From Fat 89); Fat 10g (Saturated 5g); Cholesterol 7mg; Sodium 46mg; Carbohydrate 25g (Dietary Fiber 2g); Protein 3g.*

NOTE: Cool Whip is a popular brand of frozen whipped topping and one I most frequently use for this salad. Bordeaux maraschino cherries are rich in color and made without artificial food dye; their flavor is rich with deep Bing cherry flavors.

VARY IT! You can use sour cream in place of the yogurt but add ¼ teaspoon of vanilla extract to the mix. I've also used a can of mixed fruit in this salad with success.

Grape and Melon Mojito Salad

PREP TIME: ABOUT 20 MIN PLUS 1 HR FOR CHILLING	COOK TIME: 18 MIN	YIELD: 8 SERVINGS

INGREDIENTS

4 cups halved green grapes

½ cup white rum

¼ cup sugar

2 cups cubed honeydew melon

2 kiwis, peeled and diced

2 tablespoons lime juice

1 tablespoon honey

¼ cup thinly sliced mint leaves

DIRECTIONS

1 In a bowl, place the grapes, rum, and sugar, stirring to mix. Let the fruit sit for 1 hour or overnight in the refrigerator. Drain off the excess liquid, reserving for another use (like a cocktail!).

2 In a serving bowl, place the booze-infused grapes, melon, kiwis, lime juice, honey, and mint, stirring to combine. Serve immediately.

PER SERVING: *Calories 147 (From Fat 3); Fat 0g (Saturated 0g); Cholesterol 0mg; Sodium 11mg; Carbohydrate 29g (Dietary Fiber 2g); Protein 1g.*

NOTE: Clearly, this salad is not for children, but it's perfect for your next adult party! Save the rum for a fun cocktail.

VARY IT! Pineapple, mango, and watermelon can be used in place of any of the fruits. If you want to kick this salad up a notch, roast the grapes for 20 minutes at 350 degrees prior to marinating; the caramelized sugars in the grapes will elevate the salad.

Peach and Amaretti Cookie Salad

PREP TIME: ABOUT 20 MIN | COOK TIME: 4 MIN | YIELD: 6 SERVINGS

INGREDIENTS

4 ripe but firm peaches, cut into ½-inch slices

1 tablespoon honey

1 tablespoon lemon juice

½ cup almond slivers

½ cup Amaretti cookies, crushed

¼ cup thinly sliced basil leaves

DIRECTIONS

1 Heat a grill or grill pan over medium-high heat. Grill the peach wedges for 1 minute on each side; then transfer to a serving bowl.

2 In a microwave-safe bowl, microwave the honey for 10 seconds; then stir in the lemon juice. Pour the sauce over the peaches, stirring to coat.

3 Add the almonds, cookies, and basil to the peaches. Serve immediately.

PER SERVING: *Calories 148 (From Fat 62); Fat 7g (Saturated 0g); Cholesterol 0mg; Sodium 7mg; Carbohydrate 21g (Dietary Fiber 3g); Protein 4g.*

NOTE: Grilled fruit makes for a sophisticated, yet simple dessert. Amaretti cookies are a light egg white and almond cookie.

NOTE: You can also heat a grill pan over medium-high heat and cook the fruit on that instead.

VARY IT! Grilled pineapple with crushed gingersnaps and mint also makes for a fun combination!

TIP: Serve this salad with a dollop of whipped cream or over ice cream.

Grilled Pineapple and Macadamia Nut Salad

PREP TIME: ABOUT 10 MIN	COOK TIME: 10 MIN	YIELD: 8 SERVINGS

INGREDIENTS

1 pineapple, peeled, cored, and sliced into 1-inch spears

1 tablespoon lime juice

1 tablespoon honey

¼ cup sour cream or Greek yogurt

Pinch cayenne pepper or chipotle powder (optional)

2 tablespoons chopped mint

½ cup chopped macadamia nuts

DIRECTIONS

1 Preheat a grill or grill pan to medium-high heat. Grill the pineapple spears for 4 minutes; then flip and grill on the other side until grill marks are visible, about 4 to 5 minutes. Remove from the grill and place on a cutting board to cool.

2 In a serving bowl, whisk together the lime juice, honey, sour cream or yogurt, and a pinch of cayenne or chipotle powder (if desired) for a little heat.

3 Chop the grilled pineapple into bite-size pieces. Add the pineapple to the sauce, stirring to coat. Add the mint and nuts, stir, and serve.

PER SERVING: *Calories 138 (From Fat 70); Fat 8g (Saturated 2g); Cholesterol 4mg; Sodium 29mg; Carbohydrate 18g (Dietary Fiber 2g); Protein 1g.*

NOTE: You can also heat a grill pan over medium-high heat and cook the fruit on that instead.

VARY IT! Apples, bananas (brushed with lemon juice and oil first), mangos, peaches, pears, and plums are all great fruits to grill! Pair your favorite fruit and nut in this simple salad dish.

Nutty Strawberry Jell-O Salad

PREP TIME: 3 HR	COOK TIME: 15 MIN	YIELD: 12 SERVINGS

INGREDIENTS

1½ cup pecans

1½ cup pretzels

3 tablespoons sugar

¼ cup unsalted butter, melted

One 8-ounce package cream cheese

One 8-ounce container frozen whipped topping, thawed

½ cup sour cream

One 6-ounce package strawberry Jell-O

2 cups boiling water

4 cups sliced fresh strawberries

DIRECTIONS

1   Preheat the oven to 350 degrees.

2   In a food processor, pulse the pecans and pretzels with the sugar until both are crushed, about 2 to 3 minutes. Add the melted butter and process for 1 minute. Pour the crumble into the bottom of a 9-x-13-inch casserole dish and press to form a crust. Bake for 10 minutes and then chill in the refrigerator for 20 minutes.

3   Next, in the food processor or with a mixer, beat the cream cheese, whipped topping, and sour cream until creamy and fully combined, about 3 minutes.

4   Pour the cream cheese mixture over the top of the cooled crust, gently smoothing it across the top. Refrigerate for at least 30 minutes to chill and set.

5   Meanwhile, whisk the strawberry Jell-O package with boiling water until dissolved. Chill the Jell-O mixture in the refrigerator for 15 minutes.

6   Stir the sliced strawberries into the slightly chilled strawberry Jell-O mixture. Take the casserole dish out of the refrigerator and pour the Jell-O mixture onto the cream cheese layer. Arrange the strawberries evenly throughout the Jell-O layer. Refrigerate for at least 2 hours before slicing and serving.

PER SERVING: Calories 348 (From Fat 215); Fat 24g (Saturated 10g); Cholesterol 36mg; Sodium 218mg; Carbohydrate 31g (Dietary Fiber 2g); Protein 5g.

NOTE: My husband's aunt always made this salad for our family gatherings. It's nostalgia in every bite!

VARY IT! If whipped topping isn't your thing, try using full-fat coconut cream instead — coconut cream solidifies beautifully when chilled. The recipe can also be made with all pretzels instead of adding nuts, but you'll need to increase the butter to ½ cup.

Creamy Filipino Coconut Salad

| PREP TIME: ABOUT 5 MIN | COOK TIME: NONE | YIELD: 10 SERVINGS |

INGREDIENTS

7 ounces canned sweetened condensed milk

½ cup heavy whipping cream

One 12-ounce jar nata de coco (coconut gel), drained and rinsed with cold water

1 cup drained, shredded young coconut meat (often packed in syrup)

One 12-ounce jar kaong (palm fruit), drained

One 15-ounce can fruit salad, drained

DIRECTIONS

In a large bowl, stir the sweetened condensed milk and whipping cream. Add the remaining ingredients, stirring to combine. Refrigerate at least 1 hour before serving.

PER SERVING: *Calories 266 (From Fat 104); Fat 12g (Saturated 8g); Cholesterol 25mg; Sodium 51mg; Carbohydrate 40g (Dietary Fiber 2g); Protein 3g.*

NOTE: Step out of your comfort zone and head to the closest Asian or Filipino market near you. This salad can also be frozen and served like ice cream on hot summer days! One of my interns shared her family's recipe with me — thanks, Shai!

NOTE: You can find these ingredients at Asian markets or on Amazon.

VARY IT! Add diced mango, pineapple bits, or grapes.

Fruity Cottage Cheese and Jell-O Salad

PREP TIME: ABOUT 5 MIN	COOK TIME: NONE	YIELD: 10 SERVINGS

INGREDIENTS

16 ounces small-curd cottage cheese

One 3-ounce package orange Jell-O

One 8-ounce container frozen whipped topping, thawed

One 11-ounce can mandarin oranges, drained

One 15-ounce can crushed pineapple, drained

1 cup halved grapes

½ cup chopped pistachios or pecans

DIRECTIONS

In a serving bowl, stir the cottage cheese, Jell-O, and whipped topping. Add the remaining ingredients, stirring to combine. Serve immediately or refrigerate.

PER SERVING: *Calories 195 (From Fat 64); Fat 7g (Saturated 4g); Cholesterol 5mg; Sodium 244mg; Carbohydrate 25g (Dietary Fiber 1g); Protein 9g.*

NOTE: Growing up, a salad like this would be served with dinner. My daughter really loves it, too. If you want to skip the Jell-O packet, you can add 1 tablespoon orange zest, 2 tablespoons orange juice concentrate, and 2 tablespoons sugar — it's different but does the trick!

VARY IT! Add chopped apples, diced mango, or dried cranberries to this fun salad.

5

The Part of Tens

IN THIS PART . . .

Build salads in a jar that won't get mushy.

Craft your own salad kits.

Discover fun salad additions that add crunch and texture.

Find the best ways to keep produce fresh longer.

Chapter **17**

Ten (or So) Tips for Building Salads in a Jar

S alads in a jar are a great way to pack lunch or dinner. Mason jars are often used to craft these beauties, and they're great space savers in the refrigerator. If you want to make a meal in a jar, opt for a 24- to 32-ounce wide-mouth jar; if you just want a side salad, a 16-ounce wide-mouth jar will be plenty.

In this chapter, I tell you the order in which to build a salad in the jar. Order really matters, because certain vegetables don't do well if they touch each other. Grab your jars, and let's get started!

TIP

I recommend keeping a few vegetables out of the jar entirely, including chopped tomatoes, diced cucumbers, and diced avocados. These items can either get mushy fast or make other vegetables spoil.

Start with the Dressing

Dressings go on the bottom because you want the salad to last in the refrigerator until you're ready to eat it. If the dressing mixes with other ingredients, it will change their texture, making them soft. If you're worried your salad will get knocked around in transit (for example, if you bike to work), consider keeping your dressing in a separate container.

TIP

Thicker dressings may take more effort to shake and mix when you're ready to eat your salad. If that annoys you, choose a thinner dressing instead.

Know Which Vegetables Can Touch the Dressing

A few key players don't mind getting their feet wet, so those are the best to place on top of the dressing. Here are some suggestions:

>> Artichokes (canned)

>> Beans (canned)

>> Bell peppers

>> Broccoli

>> Brussels sprouts (shredded)

>> Cabbage (shredded)

>> Carrots

>> Cauliflower

>> Celery

>> Corn (canned)

>> Green beans (canned)

>> Jicama

>> Kohlrabi

>> Mandarin oranges (canned)

>> Mushrooms (canned)

>> Olives

>> Peas or snap peas

>> Pineapple (canned)

>> Radishes

>> Roasted red bell peppers (canned)

>> Sun-dried tomatoes (canned)

Protect Delicate Ingredients with a Layer of Grains

Adding in whole grains helps stretch your salad and creates a nice layer to protect the more delicate salad additions from the dressing. Try the following:

>> Barley

>> Bulgur

>> Farro

>> Orzo pasta

>> Quinoa

>> Rice

Pack a Protein Punch

After adding a layer of grains, throw in your favorite protein. Here are some ideas to try:

>> Chicken (grilled and cubed)

>> Eggs (hard-boiled)

>> Ham

>> Salami

>> Turkey (from the deli — it lasts longer than fresh cooked turkey)

TIP

If you'd like to add canned tuna or salmon, keep them separate in their cans until you're ready to eat the salad.

WARNING

Protein foods are the ones that pose the greatest food safety risk, so if you add a protein layer, keep the salad in the refrigerator no more than three days before eating.

Use Nuts and Seeds to Separate the Protein Foods from the Toppings

Nuts and seeds are fun for the crunch, excellent in nutrition, and a great barrier between protein foods and the toppings. Try the following:

>> Almonds

>> Chia seeds

>> Flaxseeds

>> Hazelnuts

>> Hemp seeds (also known as hemp hearts)

>> Pecans

>> Pumpkin seeds

>> Sesame seeds

>> Sunflower seeds

>> Walnuts

Think Crunchy for Toppings

I love a good crunch in a salad! Crunch toppings can get soggy, though, so it's best to keep them toward the top of the jar. Here are some crunchy ingredients to try:

>> Chips

>> Croutons

>> Crunchy chow mein noodles

>> Fried onions

>> Fried wontons

Choose Hardy Greens

When it comes to salads in a jar, lettuce is just a layer and not the main star of the show. Opt for hardier greens that hold up better, like the following:

>> Arugula

>> Kale

>> Romaine

>> Spinach

>> Sprouts

>> Swiss chard

TIP

If you really want to use a more tender green (like butter lettuce or red leaf lettuce), just monitor the salad and try to eat it within three days.

Finish the Salad with Cheese

If you love cheese as much as I do, add a layer at the top of the jar. Use harder grating cheeses instead of fresh cheeses, though, like the following:

>> Asiago

>> Cheddar

>> Gruyere

>> Mozzarella

>> Parmesan

TIP

If you want to use a fresh cheese (such as feta, goat cheese, or fresh mozzarella), add it just before eating.

Chapter **18**

Ten Homemade Salad Kits

Premade salad kits from the grocery store are great way to get your greens in a quick and convenient way. They're easy to grab and fix, whether you're camping, needing a fast side dish, or wanting extra greens at lunch. But they come at a cost. Instead of paying $5 to $10 for a salad kit, why not make your own?

First, you need to pick the right greens. Softer green lettuces will wilt quickly, so think hardy greens — such as arugula, Brussels sprouts, cabbage, shredded broccoli, shredded kale, and spinach.

Next, you need to keep them dry. Put the greens through a salad spinner, and store them in a resealable plastic bag with a paper towel. The paper towel will collect extra moisture, helping your greens last longer.

After that, you're ready to build your salad. In this chapter, I share my favorite kits to make for the week. I include tips on what to store together and what to keep separate. If you follow this guide, your salad kit should last for at least five days in the refrigerator. When you're ready to eat it, simply toss the ingredients together with your desired dressing and serve. Come on, let's get prepping!

Cobb Salad

To make this salad kit, include the following:

>> 4 cups shredded cabbage

>> 4 cups thinly sliced kale

>> 1 cup turkey lunchmeat

>> 3 hard-boiled eggs

>> ½ cup crumbled bacon

>> ½ cup blue cheese

>> Blue Cheese Dressing (see Chapter 6)

TIP

Keep the lunchmeat, eggs, bacon, blue cheese, and dressing separate from the greens.

Caesar Salad

To make this salad kit, include the following:

>> 4 cups shredded cabbage

>> 4 cups shredded romaine

>> ½ cup Parmesan cheese

>> 1 cup croutons

>> Caesar Dressing (see the Caesar Salad recipe in Chapter 7 for the dressing)

TIP

Keep the dressing separate from the other ingredients. Because romaine is used, this salad will keep for only three to five days.

Cranberry and Pecan Salad

To make this salad kit, include the following:

- 2 cups shredded Brussels sprouts
- 3 cups shredded purple cabbage
- 3 cups shredded kale
- 1 cup dried cranberries
- 1 cup candied pecans
- Sweet Raspberry Vinaigrette (see Chapter 6)

TIP

Keep the dressing separate from the other ingredients. The cranberries and pecans can be kept in a separate container but together.

Rancher's Delight Salad

To make this salad kit, include the following:

- 3 cups shredded green cabbage
- 2 cups shredded purple cabbage
- 3 cups baby spinach
- 1 cup crumbled bacon
- 1 cup canned pinto beans
- 1 cup cherry or grape tomatoes
- ½ cup sunflower seeds
- Ranch Dressing (see Chapter 6)

Keep the bacon and beans in their own containers. The tomatoes and sunflower seeds can be added to the lettuce. Keep the dressing separate.

Southwestern Salad

To make this salad kit, include the following:

>> 3 cups shredded green cabbage

>> 2 cups shredded purple cabbage

>> 3 cups baby arugula

>> 1 cup canned corn (drained)

>> 1 cup canned black beans (drained and rinsed)

>> 1 cup cherry or grape tomatoes

>> ½ cup pumpkin seeds

>> Ranch Dressing (see Chapter 6)

TIP

Put the corn and black beans together in one container. The tomatoes and pump-kin seeds can be added to the lettuce. Keep the dressing separate.

Mediterranean Salad

To make this salad kit, include the following:

>> 8 cups baby arugula

>> ½ cup black olives

>> ½ cup sun-dried tomatoes

>> 1 cup artichoke hearts (chopped)

>> ½ cup roasted red bell peppers

>> ½ cup Parmesan cheese

>> Balsamic Vinaigrette (see Chapter 6)

TIP

Put the olives, sun-dried tomatoes, artichoke hearts, and bell peppers together, and pour the dressing over the top. Keep the arugula and Parmesan separate.

Thai Salad

To make this salad kit, include the following:

>> 6 cups shredded cabbage

>> 2 cups grated carrots

>> 1 cup cilantro

>> 1 cup peanuts

>> 2 cups grilled chicken

>> Spicy Peanut Dressing (see Chapter 6)

Don't chop the cilantro until you're about to serve. The cabbage, carrots, and peanuts can be stored together. Keep the chicken separate and the dressing separate.

Harvest Salad

To make this salad kit, include the following:

>> 2 cups shredded Brussels sprouts

>> 2 cups shredded broccoli

>> 4 cups shredded kale

>> 1 cup dried chopped apples

>> ½ cup raisins

>> 1 cup candied walnuts

>> Honey Dijon Dressing (see Chapter 6)

Keep the dressing separate from the other ingredients.

Carrot Crunch Salad

To make this salad kit, include the following:

- 2 cups shredded cabbage
- 2 cups shredded broccoli
- 2 cups baby spinach
- 2 cups grated carrot
- 1 cup sliced celery
- ½ cup almonds
- ½ cup sunflower seeds
- Roasted Carrot Vinaigrette (see Chapter 6)

TIP

Keep the dressing separate from the other ingredients. Store the carrot, celery, almonds, and sunflower seeds together.

Orange Poppyseed Salad

To make this salad kit, include the following:

- 2 cups shredded Brussels sprouts
- 3 cups shredded purple cabbage
- 4 cups shredded kale
- 3 green onions (sliced)
- 1 cup mandarin oranges (drained)
- 1 cup fried chow mein noodles
- ½ cup almonds
- Poppyseed Dressing (see Chapter 6)

TIP

Keep the dressing separate from the other ingredients. Keep the oranges separate. You can store the crunchy noodles and almonds together. Keep the green onions whole until ready to serve.

Chapter **19**

Ten Fun Ways to Add Crunch to a Salad

Texture is key to a great salad. Whether it's the crispness of greens or the crunch of a fresh carrot, we all look for that crunch! From croutons to crispy bacon and chopped nuts, each of these elements helps you build a better, more appealing, and tastier salad. This chapter explores these fun, crunchy toppings that you can either keep in your pantry or make from scratch.

Croutons

If you find yourself with a day-old baguette or bread that needs to be used, it's time to make croutons! Croutons add a savory crunch and flavor to salads. Many recipes call for a higher temperature when baking croutons, but I prefer to bake them at a lower temperature for a longer period of time. This technique ensures that the croutons will stay crispy.

Start by cutting your bread into ½-inch cubes, until you have a total of 4 cups. Toss the bread with ¼ cup olive oil, ½ teaspoon dried oregano, ½ teaspoon garlic powder, ½ teaspoon onion powder, ½ teaspoon paprika, and ½ teaspoon salt. Place the bread on a heavy baking sheet and bake at 325 degrees, stirring every

15 minutes until toasted. (The total baking time will vary based on the type of bread you're using.) When the bread is golden brown, remove it from the oven and let the croutons cool completely. Store in an airtight container at room temperature for 1 week or in the freezer for up to 6 months.

Crispy, Fried Onions

Crispy, fried onions aren't just for casseroles. Even kids tend to enjoy these crispy, crunchy salad additions. Grab a bag at the market or make your own. To make your own, thinly slice a white onion with a mandoline or a knife. Soak the sliced onion in a bowl of ice water for 5 minutes. Drain and pat dry. Toss the sliced onion with ½ cup semolina flour (or garbanzo flour for a gluten-free version), 1 teaspoon paprika, and 1 teaspoon salt. Heat a heavy pan with 2 cups peanut oil or grapeseed oil and fry until golden and crispy. Remove with a slotted spoon and let cool on paper towels or on a brown paper bag. Store in an airtight container at room temperature for 2 days or in the freezer for up to 3 months.

Sweet or Savory Nuts

Depending on the salad, you can grab any or all of your favorite nuts, from peanuts to cashews to hazelnuts. Nuts add more than just crunch — they're packed with fiber, essential fatty acids, and nutrients. I like chopping savory or candied nuts and adding them to my Simple Side Salad (Chapter 7). My favorite additions are candied pecans or rosemary almonds.

To make candied pecans, whisk 1 egg white with 4 cups pecans, 1 tablespoon cinnamon, ½ cup sugar, and ½ teaspoon salt. Bake at 300 degrees, stirring every 10 minutes, until toasted, about 30 to 40 minutes. Cool completely and store in an airtight container at room temperature for 2 weeks or in the freezer for up to 6 months.

To make rosemary almonds, heat a heavy skillet with 1 tablespoon butter and 1 tablespoon extra-virgin olive oil over medium heat. Add 3 cups of almonds and 1 tablespoon finely chopped rosemary, stirring constantly for 2 to 3 minutes. Add 1 teaspoon sea salt, ½ teaspoon cracked pepper, and ¼ teaspoon paprika. Stir until the nuts begin to toast and become fragrant, about 1 minute.

Seedy Wonders

Chia seeds, flaxseeds, hempseeds, pumpkin seeds (also known as pepita), sesame seeds, and sunflower seeds are all delicious and simple ways to add crispy, crunchy texture to your favorite salads. Much like nuts, seeds can be toasted or added in raw.

Spicy pumpkin seeds are one of my favorites to keep on hand. Start with 2 cups green pumpkin seeds. Toss with 3 tablespoons olive oil, 2 teaspoons paprika, 1 teaspoon ground cumin, 1 teaspoon sea salt, and a pinch of cayenne pepper. Bake at 325 degrees, stirring every 5 minutes until golden, about 20 to 25 minutes. Store at room temperature in an airtight container for up to 1 month or in the freezer up to 6 months.

Roasted Garbanzo Beans

Garbanzo beans (also referred to as chickpeas) toast up and become as crispy and crunchy as a nut. You can find roasted garbanzo beans at specialty markets, or you can make your own. Start with a 15-ounce can of garbanzo beans. Drain and rinse the beans and pat them dry. Toss the beans with ¼ cup extra-virgin olive oil, 1 teaspoon ground cumin, 1 teaspoon curry powder, ½ teaspoon cracked pepper, and 1 teaspoon sea salt. Bake on a baking sheet at 425 degrees, stirring every 10 minutes to ensure even cooking, until golden, about 25 to 30 minutes. Remove from the heat and cool completely. Store in an airtight container at room temperature for up to 1 week or in the freezer up to 6 months.

Parmesan Crisps

Freshly grated Parmesan cheese can be transformed into crispy, crunchy crackers in less than 5 minutes! I love adding these to many of my salads, from Lemony Kale and Parmesan Salad (Chapter 8) to Caesar Salad (Chapter 7). Toss 1½ cups finely grated Parmesan cheese with 1 teaspoon minced rosemary and ½ teaspoon cracked pepper. Place 1-tablespoon mounds onto a baking sheet lined with parchment paper. Bake at 425 degrees for 3 to 5 minutes. Cool completely and store in an airtight container in the freezer for up to 1 month.

Crunchy Noodles

Ramen noodles or crispy chow mein noodles make a fun addition to cabbage salads, Asian-inspired salads, and slaws. La Choy makes a delicious crispy chow mein noodle, and Top Ramen makes an easy and inexpensive addition to any salad (just skip the flavor packet).

Dried Fruit

Dried cranberries, currants, raisins, blueberries, finely diced mango, chopped pineapple, and dates are popular dried fruit additions that give salads a chewy and crispy texture. Did you also know that freeze-dried fruits such as strawberries and coconut are also great additions? Try the strawberries in the Blushed Strawberry and Spinach Salad in Chapter 7 instead of the fresh variety.

Crushed Chips

Wait! Before you throw out the crumbs at the bottom of your favorite chip bag, store them in the freezer for your next salad. Chips — from Doritos to potato chips to crunchy corn chips — are a great way to add a salty crunch to a salad. Try adding in cheesy Doritos to the classic Taco Salad in Chapter 7 or potato chip crumbs to the Cobb Salad in Chapter 7.

Crisped Bacon

Bacon is the ultimate salty, crunchy salad addition. Add bacon crumbles to any of your favorite savory salads. My taste testing has led me to believe that homemade bacon crumbles beat out anything you can buy on the shelf. To make super crispy (but not burned) bacon, place aluminum foil on a baking sheet and place a wire cooling rack on top. Place bacon onto the cooling rack, and bake at 350 degrees until the bacon is crispy and brown, but not burned, about 20 to 25 minutes. Cool completely — the bacon will become crispier as it cools. Transfer the cooled bacon to a cutting board and finely chop. Store the bacon crumbles in an airtight container in the freezer for up to 6 months.

Chapter **20**

Ten Common Types of Produce and How to Keep Them Fresh

When you open your refrigerator and the lettuce you bought three days ago is mushy or the berries are moldy, it can derail your meal plans. Over the years, I've explored many different techniques and tricks from around the world to keep my produce fresh. If you frequently find yourself with wilted greens or moldy berries, this chapter has the tips you need.

REMEMBER

The best way to keep produce fresh is to buy fresh produce. Make sure that the produce you're buying is at the peak of freshness. As soon as you get home from the market wash and process all produce to keep it fresh longer!

Greens

TIP

Arugula, lettuce, kale, mustard greens, spinach, and Swiss chard all require similar care and attention. To keep greens fresh, follow these tips:

>> If it's an intact head of lettuce, don't cut it until you're ready to use it.

>> Immediately remove all damaged or wilted leaves.

>> Salad-spin your greens dry after washing and refrigerate them in an airtight container with paper towels to help absorb moisture.

>> Head lettuce, such as iceberg, is best stored in a vacuum-sealed container.

>> Avoid storing greens near apples, avocados, or bananas — ethylene-producing produce can ripen other vegetables.

>> If your greens wilt, dip them into an ice bath for one minute; then spin them in a salad spinner to dry.

Tomatoes

TIP

This statement may create a fight, but tomatoes should *never* be stored in a refrigerator unless the temperature is above 68 degrees. Refrigeration affects the taste and texture of tomatoes. Here are some additional tips to get those vine ripe beauties fresh:

>> Store tomatoes stem side down in a cool, dark space away from direct sunlight.

>> If a tomato needs ripening, store it near an avocado or banana, but keep a close eye on the tomato to make sure it doesn't get overripe.

>> Monitor cherry or grape tomatoes. Remove any spoiled or pierced tomato before it spoils the others.

Cucumbers

TIP

English cucumbers always baffled me as a kid, but as a chef, I understand why the thin-skinned cuke is stored in a vacuum-sealed wrap. That's what you're going for if you need them to last longer. Here are some other tips to help keep cucumbers fresh:

>> Wrap them individually in a paper towel to reduce moisture, and then store in an airtight container on the top shelf (or the warmest part) of the refrigerator.

>> If you can vacuum-seal them, do so individually after fully drying the outside.

>> If you have Persian cucumbers, remove them from the bag, dry the outer skin, and store them on the counter or in the warmest part of the refrigerator.

Mirepoix

TIP

Celery, carrots, and onions create a mirepoix, the fancy French term for these three aromatic veggies. Here's how to keep them fresh:

>> Wash, cut, and store carrots and celery in water.

>> If you need to preslice an onion, store it in water, oil, or vinegar if you want to pickle it.

>> Whole onions or shallots should be kept in a cool, dark, and dry basket that allows for air flow.

>> Celery, carrots, and onions can be chopped and stored in an airtight container in the freezer for up to 6 months.

Herbs

TIP

Fresh herbs elevate any recipe but often you only need a small amount. Then what? They sit in a plastic bag (gasp!) in the fridge and get mushy and ruined. Here are some solutions to this conundrum:

>> Trim the tips of the herbs. Fill a cup partially with water and place the herbs, stem side down, into the water. Use a fresh bag to cover the greens of the herbs and store them on the top shelf (or the warmest part) of the refrigerator.

>> If your refrigerator lacks space, wash the herbs and spin dry or fully dry with paper towels or a tea towel. Roll up the herbs in a paper towel and store in a resealable bag, removing as much air as you can.

WARNING

Keeping vegetables in their original bags or boxes can put them at greater risk for spoilage.

Berries

TIP

They looked great at the store but now they're full of mold! What went wrong with your berries? Here's how to avoid this situation:

>> Immediately after buying your berries, soak them for 10 minutes in 3 cups of cold water with 2 tablespoons white vinegar. Then drain and pat dry. Place in a vented container with a paper towel in it (to absorb extra moisture) and store in the refrigerator.

>> Remove any berries that are smashed or beginning to mold.

>> If you can't use the berries within a week, consider freezing them. They'll keep for up to 6 months.

REMEMBER

Soaking berries in a vinegar wash will help your berries last longer!

Tubers

TIP

Potatoes and sweet potatoes will sprout eyes if kept in the wrong conditions. To keep your tubers from craving soil, follow these tips:

>> Brush off any excess dirt with a dry towel. Then store in a brown paper bag in a cool, dark spot.

>> Keep potatoes away from onions — onions promote sprouting.

>> You can freeze cooked potatoes for up to 3 months.

Green Beans

TIP

Slimy green beans will make you want to toss the whole bag. Avoid that with these simple tips:

>> Lay the green beans out on a towel. Remove any beans that are already looking bad or spoiled. Dry the beans with the towel but don't wash them. Then wrap them in a paper towel and store the bunch in an airtight container in the refrigerator.

>> You can keep blanched green beans in the freezer for up to a year.

Citrus

TIP

Living in Southern California and growing citrus, from limes and lemons to kumquats and grapefruit, I quickly became an expert in keeping them fresh longer. You may be surprised by what I discovered:

>> Citrus fruits prefer a high-moisture environment, so you can keep them in a high-moisture drawer in the refrigerator.

>> If you have a lot of fruit, consider storing it in water or freezing it. Yes, you can freeze whole citrus.

>> Avoid leaving the fruit in a bag. This can trap moisture-fostering mold.

>> Preserving citrus in salt or sugar is a common practice in the Middle East and throughout the Mediterranean. This is something I do every year for delicate citrus like Meyer lemons. I typically quarter 10 lemons and stir in 1 cup sea salt. Then I place the lemons into a glass canning jar and cover with lemon juice. Store in the refrigerator for up to a year.

Salad Toppings

TIP

Okay, nuts, seeds, and cheese aren't technically produce, but they're used frequently in salads, and you can keep these toppings fresher longer, too. Here's how:

>> Store nuts and seeds in a glass jar in the refrigerator or freezer because the oils can go rancid quickly. Avoid buying in bulk, unless you're going to use them quickly.

>> Fresh cheeses, like feta and fresh mozzarella, are best kept in a brine. Mix 2 teaspoons salt in 1 cup of water and store the cheeses in an airtight container in the salted water. Store in the refrigerator for up to three weeks.

>> Another option for fresh cheese is to store it in oil. Season with fresh herbs, salt, and spices, and then store it in the refrigerator for up to two weeks.

>> Remove block cheese from the packaging and wrap it tightly in paper towels. Then wrap it in a resealable plastic bag, removing the air. Store in the refrigerator for up to two to three weeks.

6 Appendixes

IN THIS PART . . .

Convert recipes with ease using a metric conversion guide.

Find out how to store your food to make it last.

Keep food safe with a food safety chart.

Appendix A

Metric Conversion Guide

Note: The recipes in this book weren't developed or tested using metric measurements. There may be some variation in quality when converting to metric units.

Common Abbreviations

Abbreviation(s)	What It Stands For
cm	Centimeter
C., c.	Cup
G, g	Gram
kg	Kilogram
L, l	Liter
lb.	Pound
mL, ml	Milliliter
oz.	Ounce
pt.	Pint
t., tsp.	Teaspoon
T., Tb., Tbsp.	Tablespoon

Volume

U.S. Units	Canadian Metric	Australian Metric
¼ teaspoon	1 milliliter	1 milliliter
½ teaspoon	2 milliliters	2 milliliters
1 teaspoon	5 milliliters	5 milliliters
1 tablespoon	15 milliliters	20 milliliters
¼ cup	50 milliliters	60 milliliters
⅓ cup	75 milliliters	80 milliliters
½ cup	125 milliliters	125 milliliters
⅔ cup	150 milliliters	170 milliliters
¾ cup	175 milliliters	190 milliliters
1 cup	250 milliliters	250 milliliters
1 quart	1 liter	1 liter
1½ quarts	1.5 liters	1.5 liters
2 quarts	2 liters	2 liters
2½ quarts	2.5 liters	2.5 liters
3 quarts	3 liters	3 liters
4 quarts (1 gallon)	4 liters	4 liters

Weight

U.S. Units	Canadian Metric	Australian Metric
1 ounce	30 grams	30 grams
2 ounces	55 grams	60 grams
3 ounces	85 grams	90 grams
4 ounces (¼ pound)	115 grams	125 grams
8 ounces (½ pound)	225 grams	225 grams
16 ounces (1 pound)	455 grams	500 grams (½ kilogram)

Length

Inches	Centimeters
0.5	1.5
1	2.5
2	5.0
3	7.5
4	10.0
5	12.5
6	15.0
7	17.5
8	20.5
9	23.0
10	25.5
11	28.0
12	30.5

Temperature (Degrees)

Fahrenheit	Celsius
32	0
212	100
250	120
275	140
300	150
325	160
350	180
375	190
400	200
425	220
450	230
475	240
500	260

Appendix B

Food Storage Guide

During meal prep, you need to consider the shelf stability of foods. Whether in your refrigerator, pantry, or freezer, all foods have a shelf life. Here's the information you need to help keep your foods fresh and safe.

Food Storage: Meats

Food Item	Refrigerator	Freezer
Beef, ground, or stew meat	1–2 days	3–4 months
Beef, steaks	3–5 days	4–6 months
Deli meats	3–5 days	1–2 months
Fish, cooked	3–4 days	4–6 months
Fish, raw	1–2 days	2–3 months
Ham, fully cooked	3–5 days	2–3 months
Lamb	3–5 days	4–6 months
Leftover cooked meat	3–4 days	2–3 months
Pork chops	3–5 days	1–2 months
Poultry, raw	1–2 days	9–12 months
Sausage, cooked	1 week	1–2 months
Sausage, raw	1–2 days	3–4 months
Shrimp, raw	1–2 days	3–6 months
Veal	3–5 days	4–6 months

Food Storage: Dairy

Food Item	Refrigerator	Freezer
Butter, unsalted	1 month	6–9 months
Cheese, hard	6–12 weeks	6–12 months
Cheese, soft	1–2 weeks	6 months
Ice cream	N/A	2–4 months
Milk	1 week	3 months
Sour cream	1–2 weeks	N/A
Yogurt	1–2 weeks	1–2 months

Food Storage: Produce

Food Item	Refrigerator	Freezer
Apples	4–6 weeks	8 months
Asparagus	1 week	5 months
Avocados, cut	3–4 days	6 months
Bananas	3 days	2–3 months
Beans (legumes), cooked	3–4 days	6 months
Berries	1 week	8–12 months
Broccoli	1–2 weeks	10–12 months
Cabbage	1–3 weeks	10–12 months
Carrots	3–4 weeks	10–12 months
Cauliflower	1 week	10–12 months
Celery	2–3 weeks	10–12 months
Citrus	2–3 weeks	4–6 months
Cucumbers	4–6 days	N/A
Green beans	3–4 days	10–12 months
Greens, bagged or boxed	3–5 days	N/A
Melon, cut	2–4 days	N/A
Onions	2 months	10–12 months
Spinach	1 week	10–12 months

Produce can spoil quickly if you don't store it correctly. Heed my advice when prepping and storing these popular salad stars:

>> **Berries:** After purchasing, soak berries in a water and vinegar bath to get rid of bacteria and potential mold spores, which will extend shelf life. Dry them thoroughly and place in a container lined with paper towels (use a container with ventilation or leave uncovered to prevent condensation). Strawberries and blueberries can be refrigerated for five to seven days; blackberries, raspberries, and gooseberries can last three to five days. Berries can be frozen for a year or more.

>> **Cucumbers:** Wrap them individually in paper towels to reduce moisture and store them in an airtight container in the warmest part of the refrigerator (on the top shelf near the door) for up to one week. You can also freeze them to enjoy year-round, but cut them first. Do not store cucumbers in water because it will leech out the nutrients.

>> **Green beans:** Avoid washing until use. You can store them in a plastic bag in the refrigerator for five to seven days. You can also freeze them for 10 to 12 months (blanching before freezing can help to retain color and texture). Cooked green beans can be stored in an airtight container in the refrigerator for three to five days.

>> **Green onions:** Place a bunch of green onions in a container filled with water and submerge them; leave them at room temperature, and the onions will continue to grow. Or if you prefer, wrap them in paper towels and store them in an airtight container in the refrigerator for one or two weeks or in the freezer for three to four months. Avoid washing onions prior to storing to prevent excess moisture.

>> **Lettuce**

- **Heads of lettuce:** Do not cut heads of lettuce or wash them until ready to use. When you get home from the store, remove the damaged leaves, and then wrap the lettuce in damp paper towels and store in an airtight container in the refrigerator. For iceberg lettuce, store in a vacuum-sealed container. When left intact, a head of lettuce can last one to three weeks.

- **Loose-leaf lettuce:** Wrap the lettuce in damp paper towels and store in an airtight container in the refrigerator for seven to ten days.

- **Chopped, prepared lettuce:** Wrap the lettuce in dry paper towels and store in an airtight, vacuum-sealed container in the refrigerator for seven to ten days. Replace the paper towels when needed to keep the greens dry. Storing lettuce in water can help keep leaves crisp for up to ten days but it isn't ideal because nutrients will leech out into the water. Lettuce can be revitalized by shocking it in ice-cold water before serving. Do not store lettuce near ethylene-producing foods such as apples and bananas.

- **Kale:** Dry thoroughly and wrap in paper towels to prevent moisture. Store in an airtight container in the refrigerator for up to seven days. Kale gets more bitter the longer it stays at room temperature. Keep unwashed and fully intact until ready to use. You can also freeze kale up to eight months (blanching first will help to retain quality, but some nutrients may be lost). Keep away from ethylene-producing foods such as apples and bananas. You can revitalize kale by shocking it in ice-cold water before serving.

>> **Nuts and seeds:** Store nuts and seeds in the freezer for up to two years, but make sure to keep them dry. Most seeds and nuts will retain nutritional value even when frozen. You can store nuts or seeds in a sealed container in the refrigerator for four to six months. Nuts and seeds are best stored in cooler temperatures because warm temperatures promote rancidity, but they can be stored at room temperature, away from sunlight, for a couple of months. Keep them away from foods with strong odors because the nuts or seeds will absorb the scents.

>> **Onions:** Store whole onions in a cool, dry place at room temperature; they'll last two to three months. Keep away from sunlight. Cut onions can be stored in plastic wrap or a resealable plastic bag in the refrigerator for up to ten days. Onions can also be frozen for up to three to six months; the longer they're kept in the freezer, the stronger their taste will become.

TIP

Putting onions in the freezer for 15 minutes can prevent crying when you're cutting onions.

>> **Potatoes:** Uncooked potatoes are best stored in an open bowl or paper bag at room temperature for one to two weeks. Keep away from onions because they promote sprouting. Store cooked potatoes in an airtight container in the refrigerator for up to three to five days. You can also freeze cooked potatoes in airtight freezer bags for up to three months.

>> **Spinach:** Thoroughly dry spinach prior to storing. Remove any wilted or damaged leaves. Line a container with dry paper towels to prevent moisture buildup and store in the refrigerator for up to seven days. Avoid washing spinach until use. Do not store near ethylene-producing foods such as apples and bananas.

>> **Tomatoes:** Store whole tomatoes at room temperature for up to one week. (Cold temperatures affect the taste of tomatoes.) Keep them at room temperature until they've fully ripened. You can refrigerate tomatoes for up to two weeks if necessary, in the warmest part of the fridge (on the top shelf near the door). Tomatoes are best stored with the stem side down.

Appendix C

Food Safety Guide

Note: Keeping food safe is an important part of preparing foods. Food safety includes food storage and cooking temperatures and understanding ways to stop cross-contamination. Use this as a guide to help you and your family keep foods safe.

Food Temperature

For food safety, it's always wise to have a thermometer on hand to test the inner temperature of the meats you're preparing. Here's a guide to safe food temperatures for a variety of foods.

Cooking Temperatures

Food	Temperature (°F)
Pork	145
Poultry	165
Red meat, ground	160
Red meat, whole	145
Seafood	145

Dangerous bacteria and toxins can flourish even in cool temperatures. It's important to understand the danger zone, the temperature range where most bacteria thrives. The danger zone is 40 to 140 degrees. Store foods in the refrigerator below 40 degrees and in the freezer below 10 degrees to preserve foods.

WARNING

Thawing frozen foods on the counter is not safe because different parts will enter the danger zone at different times. Here are the safest ways to defrost food:

>> **In the refrigerator overnight:** This method is ideal, but you need to plan ahead.

>> **Submerged in cold water:** Place the food in a leak-proof plastic bag and submerge the bag in cold water for 30 minutes. Change the water and repeat until the food is thawed.

>> **In the microwave:** This method requires foods to be cooked immediately. Do not store foods that have been defrosted in the microwave in the refrigerator.

TIP

Here are a few additional tips for keeping foods safe:

>> Don't let prepared foods sit outside of the refrigerator for more than 2 hours.

>> To store leftovers, place them in shallow containers and refrigerate. Make sure they're below 40 degrees within 2 hours, or the food risks having bacterial growth.

>> To reheat leftovers, make sure that the foods reach a temperature of 165 degrees.

Cross-Contamination

Cross-contamination is another area where foods can be exposed to bacteria and make you sick. If you cut meat and then use that same knife or cutting board, or you forget to wash your hands, you can cross-contaminate anything you cut after the meat.

When preparing foods, keep in mind the following tips to avoid cross-contamination:

>> **Wash your hands, produce, cookware, and surfaces during food prep.**
Even melons need to be washed — slicing through a cantaloupe without washing it first can contaminate the inside fruit from the bacteria on the outside of the melon.

>> **Store raw meats on a plate or in a bowl or on the lowest possible shelf without anything beneath the meat.** As the meat defrosts, meat juices can drip down and contaminate other items in your refrigerator.

>> **Use separate cutting boards.** Keep your foods safe by having designated cutting boards for different foods. An example would be a red cutting board for meat, a white one for poultry, a green one for vegetables, a yellow one for fish, and a wood one for breads.

>> **Skip washing the chicken.** Yes, your grandmother may still do this, but studies have found that washing raw poultry in the sink contaminates more items — from the sink to the countertop where water splashes. It's best to skip the rinsing and just cook the chicken to the proper temperature instead.

Index

A

aguachile, 118
allergen-free diet, 40–41
almonds as topping, 230
amaretti cookies, 210
Ambrosia, 208
antipasto
  Antipasto Pantry Salad, 169
  Antipasto Salad, 154
apples
  Apple, Candied Pecan, and Orange Salad, 190
  Apple and Walnut Salad, 189
  Delicata Squash and Apple Salad, 200
arugula
  Arugula Parmesan Crisps and Bacon-Wrapped Date Salad, 159
  Italian Arugula and Lox Salad, 104
  Orange Arugula Salad with Pistachio-Crusted Date Croutons, 204
  Roasted Mushroom, Arugula, and Buckwheat Salad, 182
Asian Ground Beef and Rice Bowls, 128
asparagus
  Asparagus and Crumbled Egg Salad, 86
  Shaved Asparagus and Walnuts Salad, 146
avocados
  Avocado and Crunchy Corn Salad, 158
  Blood Orange, Avocado, and Pistachio Salad, 192
  Zesty Avocado Dressing, 62
azifa, 112

B

bacon
  Arugula Parmesan Crisps and Bacon-Wrapped Date Salad, 159
  Cali BLT Panzanella Salad, 181
  Crispy Bacon Wedge Salad, 67
  Grilled Romaine Salad with Warm Bacon Vinaigrette, 160
  as topping, 232
Balsamic Berry and Mozzarella Salad, 191
Balsamic Vinaigrette, 46
barbecue sauce, 129
barley
  Barley and Lemon Chive Salad, 184
  Bean and Barley Canadian Salad, 90
  Egyptian Barley and Pomegranate Salad, 111
  Roasted Grape and Barley Salad, 194
beans
  Bean and Barley Canadian Salad, 90
  Bean Fritters with Pesto Couscous Salad, 143–144
  Italian Tortellini and Bean Salad, 179
  Layered Bean Salad, 153
  Lentil Salad, 167
  Quinoa, Herbed Bean, and Olive Salad, 175
  Shaved Brussels Sprouts and White Bean Salad, 137
  Southwestern Black Bean Salad, 172
  storing, 246–247
  Three Bean Salad, 168
  as topping, 231
beef
  Asian Ground Beef and Rice Bowls, 128
  defrosting, 250
  Fiesta Bowls, 123
  food safety, 249
  storing, 245
  Wurstsalat, 103
  Zesty Thai Steak Bowls, 122
beets, 177

berries
  Balsamic Berry and Mozzarella Salad, 191
  Bold Berry Salad, 188
  storing, 236, 247
black beans, 172
blenders, 17
blood oranges
  Blood Orange, Avocado, and Pistachio Salad, 192
  Italian Radicchio and Blood Orange Salad, 107
blue cheese, 52
Blushed Strawberry and Spinach Salad, 72
Bold Berry Salad, 188
bowls
  Asian Ground Beef and Rice Bowls, 128
  Chinese Chicken Slaw Bowls, 126
  Cold Ramen Noodle Bowls, 132
  Creamy Coconut Chicken Bowls, 125
  Crunchy Southwestern Bowls, 120
  Fiesta Bowls, 123
  Grilled Chicken Shawarma Bowls, 130
  Mediterranean Farro Bowls, 124
  Moroccan Spiced Veggie Bowls, 127
  Nutty Chinese Noodle Bowls, 131
  overview, 10, 119
  Roasted Veggie Bowls with Peanut Dressing, 140
  styling, 20–21
  Tangy Barbecue Chicken Bowls, 129
  Texas-Style Chopped House Bowls, 121
  Zesty Thai Steak Bowls, 122
bread
  croutons, 229–230
  Korean Bun Noodle Salad, 109
  Orange Arugula Salad with Pistachio-Crusted
    Date Croutons, 204
broccoli
  Broccoli and Feta Salad, 88
  Sunflower Seed and Broccoli Salad, 152
brussels sprouts, 137
buckwheat, 182
bulgur, 185

buns, Korean, 109
butternut squash, 141

C

cabbage
  Canadian Maple, Cabbage, and Cranberry
    Salad, 116
  Chinese Chicken Slaw Bowls, 126
Caesar Salad
  recipe, 65
  salad kits, 224
Cali BLT Panzanella Salad, 181
Canadian Maple, Cabbage, and Cranberry
    Salad, 116
candied pecans, 230
canned salads
  Antipasto Pantry Salad, 169
  Chickpea and Sunflower Smashed Salad, 171
  Lentil Salad, 167
  overview, 165–166
  Pantry Pasta Salad, 170
  Southwestern Black Bean Salad, 172
  Three Bean Salad, 168
caprese, 98
carrots
  Carrot Crunch Salad, 228
  Honey Mustard Grated Carrot Salad, 84
  Pineapple and Carrot Sweet Slaw, 206
  Roasted Carrot Vinaigrette, 48
  Sesame and Carrot Dressing, 59
  storing, 235
cauliflower, 145
celery, 235
ceviche, 117
charcuterie, 20
cheese. *See also by type*
  in jarred salad, 221
  storing, 237, 246
  as topping, 231
cherries, 207

chicken
    Chicken Curry Salad, 77
    Chinese Chicken Slaw Bowls, 126
    Creamy Coconut Chicken Bowls, 125
    Crunchy Chicken Salad with Orange Ginger Dressing, 155
    defrosting, 250
    food safety, 249
    Grilled Chicken Shawarma Bowls, 130
    storing, 245
    Tangy Barbecue Chicken Bowls, 129
    washing, 250
chickpeas
    Chickpea and Cucumber Dill Salad, 156
    Chickpea and Sunflower Smashed Salad, 171
    as topping, 231
chips as topping, 231
chives, 184
Chopped House Salad, 68
cilantro
    Fiesta Grilled Sweet Potato and Cilantro Salad, 161
    Spicy Cilantro Vinaigrette, 50
circular serving style, 20–21
Citrus Salad, 193
classic salads
    Blushed Strawberry and Spinach Salad, 72
    Caesar Salad, 65
    Chicken Curry Salad, 77
    Chopped House Salad, 68
    Classic Italian Vinaigrette, 47
    Classic Macaroni Salad, 151
    Cobb Salad, 69
    Creamy Egg Salad, 75
    Crispy Bacon Wedge Salad, 67
    English Pea Salad, 71
    Greek Salad, 66
    Green Goddess Salad, 70
    overview, 63
    Simple American Pasta Salad, 74
    Simple Side Salad, 64
    Taco Salad, 73
    Zesty Tuna Salad, 76

Cobb Salad
    recipe, 69
    salad kits, 224
    Vegetarian Cobb Salad, 134
coconut
    Creamy Coconut Chicken Bowls, 125
    Creamy Filipino Coconut Salad, 213
Cold Ramen Noodle Bowls, 132
Cold Soba and Edamame Salad, 180
community-supported agriculture (CSA), 13, 24
cookies, 210
corn, 158
cottage cheese, 214
couscous, 143–144
cranberries
    Canadian Maple, Cabbage, and Cranberry Salad, 116
    Cranberry and Pecan Salad, 225
Creamy Coconut Chicken Bowls, 125
Creamy Egg Salad, 75
Creamy Filipino Coconut Salad, 213
Creamy Green Herb Dressing, 53
Creamy Green Macaroni Salad, 178
Creamy Tahini Dressing, 54
Crispy Bacon Wedge Salad, 67
Crispy Spring Salad, 94
cross-contamination, 250–251
croutons
    Orange Arugula Salad with Pistachio-Crusted Date Croutons, 204
    overview, 229–230
Crunchy Chicken Salad with Orange Ginger Dressing, 155
Crunchy Peanut Zoodle Salad, 136
Crunchy Southwestern Bowls, 120
CSA (community-supported agriculture), 13, 24
cucumbers
    Chickpea and Cucumber Dill Salad, 156
    Cucumber, Tomato, and Goat Cheese Salad, 85
    storing, 234–235, 247
    Yogurt Cucumber Salad, 83
curry, 77

D

dairy
 Creamy Coconut Chicken Bowls, 125
 Creamy Egg Salad, 75
 Creamy Filipino Coconut Salad, 213
 Creamy Green Herb Dressing, 53
 Creamy Green Macaroni Salad, 178
 Creamy Tahini Dressing, 54
 Ranch Dressing, 58
 storing, 246
 Yogurt Cucumber Salad, 83
dates
 Arugula Parmesan Crisps and Bacon-Wrapped
  Date Salad, 159
 Orange Arugula Salad with Pistachio-Crusted
  Date Croutons, 204
defrosting food, 250
Delicata Squash and Apple Salad, 200
Dijon mustard, 56
dill
 Chickpea and Cucumber Dill Salad, 156
 Tomato and Feta with Dill Salad, 82
dressings. *See also* vinaigrettes
 Blue Cheese Dressing, 52
 Creamy Green Herb Dressing, 53
 Creamy Tahini Dressing, 54
 Fire-Roasted Tomato Dressing, 55
 Honey Dijon Dressing, 56
 in jarred salad, 217–219
 overview, 12, 45
 Poppyseed Dressing, 57
 Ranch Dressing, 58
 Sesame and Carrot Dressing, 59
 Spicy Peanut Dressing, 60
 Turmeric-Spiced Cauliflower Salad with Tahini
  Dressing, 145
 Vegan Nutty Dressing, 61
 Zesty Avocado Dressing, 62

E

edamame
 Cold Soba and Edamame Salad, 180
 Edamame, Crispy Onions, and Farro Salad, 147

eggs
 Asparagus and Crumbled Egg Salad, 86
 Creamy Egg Salad, 75
Egyptian Barley and Pomegranate Salad, 111
endive, 108
English Garden Salad, 115
English Pea Salad, 71
Ethiopian Azifa Salad, 112

F

fall salads
 Apple, Candied Pecan, and Orange Salad, 190
 Apple and Walnut Salad, 189
 Fall Harvest Salad, 92
 Harvest Salad, 227
farro
 Edamame, Crispy Onions, and Farro Salad, 147
 Fennel and Orange Beet Farro Salad, 177
 Mediterranean Farro Bowls, 124
fattoush, 96–97
Fennel and Orange Beet Farro Salad, 177
feta cheese
 Broccoli and Feta Salad, 88
 Roasted Butternut Squash, Pumpkin Seed, and
  Feta Salad, 141
 Tomato and Feta with Dill Salad, 82
Fiesta Bowls, 123
Fiesta Grilled Sweet Potato and Cilantro Salad, 161
figs, 203
Fire-Roasted Tomato Dressing, 55
fish
 French Tuna Niçoise Salad, 105
 Italian Arugula and Lox Salad, 104
 Spicy Filipino-Style Ceviche, 117
 storing, 245
 Zesty Tuna Salad, 76
food safety
 allergens and, 41
 cross-contamination, 250–251
 overview, 249–251
 proteins, 219
 salad kits, 223–228
 storing food, 245–248

storing produce, 233–237

storing salads, 21

temperature, 149, 249–250

freekeh, 183

French Endive Salad, 108

French Tuna Niçoise Salad, 105

fritters, 143–144

fruits. *See also by type*

Ambrosia, 208

Citrus Salad, 193

Fruity Cottage Cheese and Jell-O Salad, 214

salads, 9

storing, 233–237, 246–247

as topping, 232

Tropical Fruit Salad, 195

G

garbanzo beans

Chickpea and Cucumber Dill Salad, 156

Chickpea and Sunflower Smashed Salad, 171

as topping, 231

garnishes, 19–20

German Radish Salad, 102

German Swabian Potato Salad, 100–101

ginger

Crunchy Chicken Salad with Orange Ginger Dressing, 155

Grilled Tofu with Soy and Ginger Salad, 135

gluten-free diet, 39–40

goat cheese

Cucumber, Tomato, and Goat Cheese Salad, 85

Grilled Fig and Pistachio-Crusted Goat Cheese Salad, 203

Spring Pea, Bulgur, and Goat Cheese Salad, 185

gorgonzola cheese, 199

grains

Barley and Lemon Chive Salad, 184

Bean and Barley Canadian Salad, 90

Egyptian Barley and Pomegranate Salad, 111

protecting delicate ingredients with, 219

Roasted Grape and Barley Salad, 194

Roasted Mushroom, Arugula, and Buckwheat Salad, 182

in salads, 11

Spring Pea, Bulgur, and Goat Cheese Salad, 185

grapes

Grape and Melon Mojito Salad, 209

Roasted Grape and Barley Salad, 194

Greek Salad, 66

green beans, 236, 247

Green Goddess Salad, 70

green onions, 247

greens

Arugula Parmesan Crisps and Bacon-Wrapped Date Salad, 159

Bean Fritters with Pesto Couscous Salad, 143–144

Blushed Strawberry and Spinach Salad, 72

Cali BLT Panzanella Salad, 181

Canadian Maple, Cabbage, and Cranberry Salad, 116

Chinese Chicken Slaw Bowls, 126

Creamy Green Macaroni Salad, 178

Edamame, Crispy Onions, and Farro Salad, 147

Green Goddess Salad, 70

Grilled Romaine Salad with Warm Bacon Vinaigrette, 160

Grilled Tofu with Soy and Ginger Salad, 135

Italian Arugula and Lox Salad, 104

Japanese Seaweed Salad, 99

in jarred salad, 221

Lemon Miso Quinoa Crunch Salad, 139

Lemony Kale and Parmesan Salad, 87

Loaded Roasted Potato and Kale Salad, 186

microgreens, 34

Orange Arugula Salad with Pistachio-Crusted Date Croutons, 204

Orange-Glazed Tempeh with Noodles Salad, 138

overview, 8, 11

Roasted Butternut Squash, Pumpkin Seed, and Feta Salad, 141

Roasted Mushroom, Arugula, and Buckwheat Salad, 182

Roasted Veggie Bowls with Peanut Dressing, 140

greens *(continued)*
  in salad kits, 223
  Spinach and Orzo Salad, 157
  storing, 234, 248
  Turmeric-Spiced Cauliflower Salad with Tahini Dressing, 145
  Vegetarian Cobb Salad, 134
Grilled Chicken Shawarma Bowls, 130
Grilled Fig and Pistachio-Crusted Goat Cheese Salad, 203
Grilled Pineapple and Macadamia Nut Salad, 211
Grilled Romaine Salad with Warm Bacon Vinaigrette, 160
Grilled Tofu with Soy and Ginger Salad, 135
grocery shopping
  making list, 24–27
  options, 23–24
  salad kits, 223–228
  storing produce, 233–237

H

Harvest Salad, 227
herbs
  Bean Fritters with Pesto Couscous Salad, 143–144
  Creamy Green Herb Dressing, 53
  Fiesta Grilled Sweet Potato and Cilantro Salad, 161
  Minty Melon Salad, 196
  Pesto Tortellini Salad, 89
  Quinoa, Herbed Bean, and Olive Salad, 175
  Spicy Cilantro Vinaigrette, 50
  storing, 235
honey
  Honey Dijon Dressing, 56
  Honey Mustard Grated Carrot Salad, 84

I

international recipes
  Asian Ground Beef and Rice Bowls, 128
  Bean and Barley Canadian Salad, 90
  Caesar Salad, 65
  Cali BLT Panzanella Salad, 181
  Canadian Maple, Cabbage, and Cranberry Salad, 116
  Chinese Chicken Slaw Bowls, 126
  Classic Italian Vinaigrette, 47
  Cold Ramen Noodle Bowls, 132
  Creamy Filipino Coconut Salad, 213
  Creamy Tahini Dressing, 54
  Egyptian Barley and Pomegranate Salad, 111
  English Garden Salad, 115
  English Pea Salad, 71
  Ethiopian Azifa Salad, 112
  French Endive Salad, 108
  French Tuna Niçoise Salad, 105
  German Radish Salad, 102
  German Swabian Potato Salad, 100–101
  Greek Salad, 66
  Grilled Chicken Shawarma Bowls, 130
  Italian Arugula and Lox Salad, 104
  Italian Caprese Salad, 98
  Italian Panzanella Salad, 106
  Italian Radicchio and Blood Orange Salad, 107
  Italian Tortellini and Bean Salad, 179
  Japanese Seaweed Salad, 99
  Korean Bun Noodle Salad, 109
  Laotian Ground Pork Larb, 114
  Lebanese Tabbouleh Salad, 110
  meal plan, 38
  Mediterranean Farro Bowls, 124
  Mexican Zesty Shrimp Aguachile with Peanuts, 118
  Middle Eastern Fattoush Salad, 96–97
  Moroccan Spiced Veggie Bowls, 127
  Nutty Chinese Noodle Bowls, 131
  overview, 95
  Simple American Pasta Salad, 74
  Spicy Filipino-Style Ceviche, 117
  Taco Salad, 73
  Thai Green Papaya with Shrimp Salad, 113
  Thai Salad, 227
  Wurstsalat, 103
  Zesty Thai Steak Bowls, 122

Italian Arugula and Lox Salad, 104
Italian Caprese Salad, 98
Italian Panzanella Salad, 106
Italian Radicchio and Blood Orange Salad, 107
Italian Tortellini and Bean Salad, 179

J

Japanese Seaweed Salad, 99
jarred salads, 217–221
Jell-O
    Fruity Cottage Cheese and Jell-O Salad, 214
    Nutty Strawberry Jell-O Salad, 212
Jicama, 201
Jump into Summer Salad, 91

K

kale
    Lemony Kale and Parmesan Salad, 87
    Loaded Roasted Potato and Kale Salad, 186
    storing, 248
kitchen equipment, 15–17, 250
knives
    cutting techniques, 18–19
    overview, 16
Korean Bun Noodle Salad, 109

L

Laotian Ground Pork Larb, 114
larb, 114
Layered Bean Salad, 153
layered serving style, 21
Lebanese Tabbouleh Salad, 110
leftovers, 250
legumes
    Bean and Barley Canadian Salad, 90
    Bean Fritters with Pesto Couscous Salad, 143–144
    Italian Tortellini and Bean Salad, 179
    Layered Bean Salad, 153
    Lentil Salad, 167

Quinoa, Herbed Bean, and Olive Salad, 175
Shaved Brussels Sprouts and White Bean Salad, 137
Southwestern Black Bean Salad, 172
storing, 246–247
Three Bean Salad, 168
as topping, 231
lemons
    Barley and Lemon Chive Salad, 184
    Citrus Salad, 193
    Lemon Miso Quinoa Crunch Salad, 139
    Lemony Kale and Parmesan Salad, 87
    Lemony Orzo Pasta Salad, 81
    Simple Citrus Vinaigrette, 49
    storing, 237
Lentil Salad, 167
lettuce
    Cali BLT Panzanella Salad, 181
    storing, 247
Lime, Jicama, and Mango Salad, 201
linear serving style, 21
Loaded Roasted Potato and Kale Salad, 186
localharvest.org website, 13
low-carb diet, 40
lox, 104

M

macadamia nuts, 211
macaroni pasta
    Classic Macaroni Salad, 151
    Creamy Green Macaroni Salad, 178
mangos
    Lime, Jicama, and Mango Salad, 201
    Spicy Pineapple and Mango Salad, 202
maple syrup, 116
Mayo and Mustard Potato Salad, 150
meal plans
    diets and, 38–41
    international salads, 38
    seasonal, 35–37

meat
  Asian Ground Beef and Rice Bowls, 128
  defrosting, 250
  Fiesta Bowls, 123
  food safety, 249
  storing, 245
  Wurstsalat, 103
  Zesty Thai Steak Bowls, 122
Mediterranean diet, 39
Mediterranean salads
  Mediterranean Farro Bowls, 124
  Mediterranean Potato Salad, 174
  Mediterranean Salad, 226
  Mediterranean Watermelon Salad, 197
melons
  Grape and Melon Mojito Salad, 209
  Mediterranean Watermelon Salad, 197
  Minty Melon Salad, 196
metric conversion guide, 241–243
Mexican Zesty Shrimp Aguachile with Peanuts, 118
microgreens, 34
microwaves, 250
Middle Eastern Fattoush Salad, 96–97
Minty Melon Salad, 196
mirepoix, storing, 235
miso, 139
mojito, 209
Moroccan Spiced Veggie Bowls, 127
mozzarella cheese, 191
mushrooms, 182
mustard
  Honey Dijon Dressing, 56
  Honey Mustard Grated Carrot Salad, 84
  Mayo and Mustard Potato Salad, 150

N

Niçoise salad, 105
noodles. *See also* pasta
  Cold Ramen Noodle Bowls, 132
  Cold Soba and Edamame Salad, 180
  Korean Bun Noodle Salad, 109

  Orange-Glazed Tempeh with Noodles Salad, 138
  as topping, 232
nutrition, 31–34
nuts. *See also by type*
  in jarred salad, 220
  Nutty Chinese Noodle Bowls, 131
  Nutty Strawberry Jell-O Salad, 212
  storing, 237, 248
  as topping, 230
  Vegan Nutty Dressing, 61

O

olives, 175
onions
  Edamame, Crispy Onions, and Farro Salad, 147
  storing, 235, 247–248
  as topping, 230
oranges
  Apple, Candied Pecan, and Orange Salad, 190
  Blood Orange, Avocado, and Pistachio Salad, 192
  Citrus Salad, 193
  Crunchy Chicken Salad with Orange Ginger Dressing, 155
  Fennel and Orange Beet Farro Salad, 177
  Italian Radicchio and Blood Orange Salad, 107
  Orange Arugula Salad with Pistachio-Crusted Date Croutons, 204
  Orange Pomegranate Salad, 198
  Orange Poppyseed Salad, 228
  Orange-Glazed Tempeh with Noodles Salad, 138
orzo pasta
  Lemony Orzo Pasta Salad, 81
  Spinach and Orzo Salad, 157
overview, 95

P

Pantry Pasta Salad, 170
panzanella
  Cali BLT Panzanella Salad, 181
  Italian Panzanella Salad, 106
papaya, Thai green, 113

parmesan cheese
   Arugula Parmesan Crisps and Bacon-Wrapped
      Date Salad, 159
   Lemony Kale and Parmesan Salad, 87
   as topping, 231
party platters
   Antipasto Salad, 154
   Arugula Parmesan Crisps and Bacon-Wrapped
      Date Salad, 159
   Avocado and Crunchy Corn Salad, 158
   Chickpea and Cucumber Dill Salad, 156
   Classic Macaroni Salad, 151
   Crunchy Chicken Salad with Orange Ginger
      Dressing, 155
   Fiesta Grilled Sweet Potato and Cilantro
      Salad, 161
   Grilled Romaine Salad with Warm Bacon
      Vinaigrette, 160
   Layered Bean Salad, 153
   Mayo and Mustard Potato Salad, 150
   overview, 10
   Spinach and Orzo Salad, 157
   Sunflower Seed and Broccoli Salad, 152
pasta. See also noodles
   Classic Macaroni Salad, 151
   Creamy Green Macaroni Salad, 178
   Italian Tortellini and Bean Salad, 179
   Lemony Orzo Pasta Salad, 81
   Pantry Pasta Salad, 170
   Pesto Tortellini Salad, 89
   Protein-Packed Pasta Salad, 142
   Simple American Pasta Salad, 74
   Spinach and Orzo Salad, 157
   as topping, 232
Peach and Amaretti Cookie Salad, 210
peanuts
   Crunchy Peanut Zoodle Salad, 136
   Mexican Zesty Shrimp Aguachile with
      Peanuts, 118
   Roasted Veggie Bowls with Peanut Dressing, 140
   Spicy Peanut Dressing, 60
Pear Gorgonzola Salad, 199

peas
   Chickpea and Cucumber Dill Salad, 156
   English Pea Salad, 71
   Spring Pea, Bulgur, and Goat Cheese Salad, 185
pecans
   Apple, Candied Pecan, and Orange Salad, 190
   Cranberry and Pecan Salad, 225
   as topping, 230
Perfect Side Salad, The, 80
pesto
   Bean Fritters with Pesto Couscous Salad,
      143–144
   Pesto Tortellini Salad, 89
pineapples
   Grilled Pineapple and Macadamia Nut Salad, 211
   Pineapple and Carrot Sweet Slaw, 206
   Spicy Pineapple and Mango Salad, 202
pistachios
   Blood Orange, Avocado, and Pistachio Salad, 192
   Grilled Fig and Pistachio-Crusted Goat Cheese
      Salad, 203
   Orange Arugula Salad with Pistachio-Crusted
      Date Croutons, 204
plating, 17–21
pomegranates
   Egyptian Barley and Pomegranate Salad, 111
   Orange Pomegranate Salad, 198
poppyseeds
   Orange Poppyseed Salad, 228
   Poppyseed Dressing, 57
pork
   Arugula Parmesan Crisps and Bacon-Wrapped
      Date Salad, 159
   Crispy Bacon Wedge Salad, 67
   defrosting, 250
   food safety, 249
   Grilled Romaine Salad with Warm Bacon
      Vinaigrette, 160
   Laotian Ground Pork Larb, 114
   storing, 245
   as topping, 232

potatoes
  Fiesta Grilled Sweet Potato and Cilantro
    Salad, 161
  German Swabian Potato Salad, 100–101
  Loaded Roasted Potato and Kale Salad, 186
  Mayo and Mustard Potato Salad, 150
  Mediterranean Potato Salad, 174
  storing, 236, 248
  as topping, 232
proteins
  Bean Fritters with Pesto Couscous Salad,
    143–144
  Crunchy Peanut Zoodle Salad, 136
  Edamame, Crispy Onions, and Farro Salad, 147
  food safety and, 219
  Grilled Tofu with Soy and Ginger Salad, 135
  in jarred salad, 219–220
  Lemon Miso Quinoa Crunch Salad, 139
  Orange-Glazed Tempeh with Noodles Salad, 138
  overview, 34
  Protein-Packed Pasta Salad, 142
  Roasted Butternut Squash, Pumpkin Seed, and
    Feta Salad, 141
  Roasted Veggie Bowls with Peanut Dressing, 140
  in salads, 12
  Shaved Asparagus and Walnuts Salad, 146
  Shaved Brussels Sprouts and White Bean
    Salad, 137
  Turmeric-Spiced Cauliflower Salad with Tahini
    Dressing, 145
  Vegetarian Cobb Salad, 134
pumpkin seeds
  Roasted Butternut Squash, Pumpkin Seed, and
    Feta Salad, 141
  as topping, 231

Q
quinoa
  Lemon Miso Quinoa Crunch Salad, 139
  Quinoa, Herbed Bean, and Olive Salad, 175
  Southwestern Quinoa Salad, 176

R
radishes, 102
ramen, 132
Ranch Dressing, 58
Rancher's Delight Salad, 225
raspberry vinaigrette, 51
reheating food, 250
rice, 128
Roasted Butternut Squash, Pumpkin Seed, and
  Feta Salad, 141
Roasted Carrot Vinaigrette, 48
Roasted Grape and Barley Salad, 194
Roasted Mushroom, Arugula, and Buckwheat
  Salad, 182
Roasted Veggie Bowls with Peanut Dressing, 140
romaine lettuce, 160
rosemary almonds, 230

S
salad kits
  Caesar Salad, 224
  Carrot Crunch Salad, 228
  Cobb Salad, 224
  Cranberry and Pecan Salad, 225
  Harvest Salad, 227
  Mediterranean Salad, 226
  Orange Poppyseed Salad, 228
  Rancher's Delight Salad, 225
  Southwestern Salad, 226
  Thai Salad, 227
salad spinners, 16
salads
  composed, 10
  including at lunchtime, 34
  making in jars, 217–221
  nutrition, 31–34
  overview, 11–12
  plating, 17–21
  storing, 21
  styling, 20–21

toppings in, 12
tossing, 21
types of, 8–11
seafood
  defrosting, 250
  food safety, 249
  Mexican Zesty Shrimp Aguachile with Peanuts, 118
  storing, 245
  Thai Green Papaya with Shrimp Salad, 113
seasonal salads
  grocery shopping and, 27
  meal plans, 35–37
  overview, 12–13
seaweed, 99
seeds. *See also* poppyseeds; pumpkin seeds; sunflower seeds
  in jarred salad, 220
  storing, 237, 248
Sesame and Carrot Dressing, 59
Shaved Asparagus and Walnuts Salad, 146
Shaved Brussels Sprouts and White Bean Salad, 137
shrimp
  Mexican Zesty Shrimp Aguachile with Peanuts, 118
  Thai Green Papaya with Shrimp Salad, 113
side salads
  Asparagus and Crumbled Egg Salad, 86
  Bean and Barley Canadian Salad, 90
  Broccoli and Feta Salad, 88
  Crispy Spring Salad, 94
  Cucumber, Tomato, and Goat Cheese Salad, 85
  Fall Harvest Salad, 92
  Honey Mustard Grated Carrot Salad, 84
  Jump into Summer Salad, 91
  Lemony Kale and Parmesan Salad, 87
  Lemony Orzo Pasta Salad, 81
  overview, 10, 79
  The Perfect Side Salad, 80
  Pesto Tortellini Salad, 89
  Simple Side Salad, 64

Tomato and Feta with Dill Salad, 82
  Warming Winter Salad, 93
  Yogurt Cucumber Salad, 83
Simple American Pasta Salad, 74
Simple Citrus Vinaigrette, 49
Simple Side Salad, 64
Smoky Sumac and Freekeh Salad, 183
soba noodles, 180
Southwestern Black Bean Salad, 172
Southwestern Quinoa Salad, 176
Southwestern Salad, 226
soy, 135
Spicy Cilantro Vinaigrette, 50
Spicy Filipino-Style Ceviche, 117
Spicy Peanut Dressing, 60
Spicy Pineapple and Mango Salad, 202
spinach
  Blushed Strawberry and Spinach Salad, 72
  Spinach and Orzo Salad, 157
  storing, 248
spiralizing, 17, 19
spring salads
  Crispy Spring Salad, 94
  Spring Pea, Bulgur, and Goat Cheese Salad, 185
starchy salads
  Barley and Lemon Chive Salad, 184
  Cali BLT Panzanella Salad, 181
  Cold Soba and Edamame Salad, 180
  Creamy Green Macaroni Salad, 178
  Fennel and Orange Beet Farro Salad, 177
  Italian Tortellini and Bean Salad, 179
  Loaded Roasted Potato and Kale Salad, 186
  Mediterranean Potato Salad, 174
  overview, 8–9
  Quinoa, Herbed Bean, and Olive Salad, 175
  Roasted Mushroom, Arugula, and Buckwheat Salad, 182
  Smoky Sumac and Freekeh Salad, 183
  Southwestern Quinoa Salad, 176
  Spring Pea, Bulgur, and Goat Cheese Salad, 185
storing salads, 21

strawberries
  Blushed Strawberry and Spinach Salad, 72
  Nutty Strawberry Jell-O Salad, 212
styling salads and bowls, 20–21
sumac, 183
summer salads
  Citrus Salad, 193
  Jump into Summer Salad, 91
sunflower seeds
  Chickpea and Sunflower Smashed Salad, 171
  Sunflower Seed and Broccoli Salad, 152
sweet potatoes
  Fiesta Grilled Sweet Potato and Cilantro Salad, 161
  storing, 236
Sweet Raspberry Vinaigrette, 51
sweet salads
  Ambrosia, 208
  Apple, Candied Pecan, and Orange Salad, 190
  Apple and Walnut Salad, 189
  Balsamic Berry and Mozzarella Salad, 191
  Blood Orange, Avocado, and Pistachio Salad, 192
  Bold Berry Salad, 188
  Cherry Waldorf Salad, 207
  Citrus Salad, 193
  Creamy Filipino Coconut Salad, 213
  Delicata Squash and Apple Salad, 200
  Fruity Cottage Cheese and Jell-O Salad, 214
  Grape and Melon Mojito Salad, 209
  Grilled Fig and Pistachio-Crusted Goat Cheese Salad, 203
  Grilled Pineapple and Macadamia Nut Salad, 211
  Lime, Jicama, and Mango Salad, 201
  Mediterranean Watermelon Salad, 197
  Minty Melon Salad, 196
  Nutty Strawberry Jell-O Salad, 212
  Orange Arugula Salad with Pistachio-Crusted Date Croutons, 204
  Orange Pomegranate Salad, 198
  overview, 11
  Peach and Amaretti Cookie Salad, 210
  Pear Gorgonzola Salad, 199
  Pineapple and Carrot Sweet Slaw, 206

Roasted Grape and Barley Salad, 194
Spicy Pineapple and Mango Salad, 202
Tropical Fruit Salad, 195
Swiss/German Meat Salad (Wurstsalat), 103

T

tabbouleh, 110
Taco Salad, 73
Tahini dressing, 145
Tangy Barbecue Chicken Bowls, 129
tempeh, 138
Texas-Style Chopped House Bowls, 121
Thai Green Papaya with Shrimp Salad, 113
Thai Salad, 227
Three Bean Salad, 168
tofu, 135
tomatoes
  Cali BLT Panzanella Salad, 181
  Cucumber, Tomato, and Goat Cheese Salad, 85
  Fire-Roasted Tomato Dressing, 55
  storing, 234, 248
  Tomato and Feta with Dill Salad, 82
toppings
  bacon, 232
  beans, 231
  croutons, 229–230
  fruits, 232
  in jarred salad, 220
  noodles, 232
  nuts, 230
  onions, 230
  parmesan crisps, 231
  potato chips, 232
  in salads, 12
  seeds, 231
  storing, 237
tortellini pasta
  Italian Tortellini and Bean Salad, 179
  Pesto Tortellini Salad, 89
tossing salads, 21
Tropical Fruit Salad, 195
tuna

French Tuna Niçoise Salad, 105
Zesty Tuna Salad, 76
Turmeric-Spiced Cauliflower Salad with Tahini Dressing, 145

V

Vegan Nutty Dressing, 61
vegetable peelers, 16
vegetables, storing, 233–237, 246–247
vegetarian recipes
Ambrosia, 208
Apple, Candied Pecan, and Orange Salad, 190
Apple and Walnut Salad, 189
Asparagus and Crumbled Egg Salad, 86
Avocado and Crunchy Corn Salad, 158
Balsamic Berry and Mozzarella Salad, 191
Balsamic Vinaigrette, 46
Barley and Lemon Chive Salad, 184
Bean and Barley Canadian Salad, 90
Bean Fritters with Pesto Couscous Salad, 143–144
Blood Orange, Avocado, and Pistachio Salad, 192
Blue Cheese Dressing, 52
Blushed Strawberry and Spinach Salad, 72
Bold Berry Salad, 188
Broccoli and Feta Salad, 88
Canadian Maple, Cabbage, and Cranberry Salad, 116
Cherry Waldorf Salad, 207
Chickpea and Cucumber Dill Salad, 156
Citrus Salad, 193
Classic Italian Vinaigrette, 47
Classic Macaroni Salad, 151
Cold Ramen Noodle Bowls, 132
Cold Soba and Edamame Salad, 180
Creamy Egg Salad, 75
Creamy Filipino Coconut Salad, 213
Creamy Green Herb Dressing, 53
Creamy Green Macaroni Salad, 178
Creamy Tahini Dressing, 54
Crispy Spring Salad, 94
Crunchy Peanut Zoodle Salad, 136

Cucumber, Tomato, and Goat Cheese Salad, 85
Delicata Squash and Apple Salad, 200
Edamame, Crispy Onions, and Farro Salad, 147
Egyptian Barley and Pomegranate Salad, 111
English Garden Salad, 115
Ethiopian Azifa Salad, 112
Fall Harvest Salad, 92
Fennel and Orange Beet Farro Salad, 177
Fiesta Grilled Sweet Potato and Cilantro Salad, 161
Fire-Roasted Tomato Dressing, 55
French Endive Salad, 108
Fruity Cottage Cheese and Jell-O Salad, 214
German Radish Salad, 102
Grape and Melon Mojito Salad, 209
Greek Salad, 66
Green Goddess Salad, 70
Grilled Fig and Pistachio-Crusted Goat Cheese Salad, 203
Grilled Pineapple and Macadamia Nut Salad, 211
Grilled Tofu with Soy and Ginger Salad, 135
Honey Dijon Dressing, 56
Honey Mustard Grated Carrot Salad, 84
Italian Caprese Salad, 98
Italian Panzanella Salad, 106
Italian Radicchio and Blood Orange Salad, 107
Japanese Seaweed Salad, 99
Jump into Summer Salad, 91
Layered Bean Salad, 153
Lebanese Tabbouleh Salad, 110
Lemon Miso Quinoa Crunch Salad, 139
Lemony Kale and Parmesan Salad, 87
Lemony Orzo Pasta Salad, 81
Lime, Jicama, and Mango Salad, 201
Mayo and Mustard Potato Salad, 150
Mediterranean Farro Bowls, 124
Mediterranean Watermelon Salad, 197
Middle Eastern Fattoush Salad, 96–97
Minty Melon Salad, 196
Moroccan Spiced Veggie Bowls, 127
Nutty Chinese Noodle Bowls, 131
Nutty Strawberry Jell-O Salad, 212

vegetarian recipes *(continued)*

Orange Arugula Salad with Pistachio-Crusted Date Croutons, 204

Orange Pomegranate Salad, 198

Orange-Glazed Tempeh with Noodles Salad, 138

Peach and Amaretti Cookie Salad, 210

Pear Gorgonzola Salad, 199

The Perfect Side Salad, 80

Pesto Tortellini Salad, 89

Pineapple and Carrot Sweet Slaw, 206

Poppyseed Dressing, 57

Protein-Packed Pasta Salad, 142

Quinoa, Herbed Bean, and Olive Salad, 175

Ranch Dressing, 58

Roasted Butternut Squash, Pumpkin Seed, and Feta Salad, 141

Roasted Carrot Vinaigrette, 48

Roasted Grape and Barley Salad, 194

Roasted Mushroom, Arugula, and Buckwheat Salad, 182

Roasted Veggie Bowls with Peanut Dressing, 140

Sesame and Carrot Dressing, 59

Shaved Asparagus and Walnuts Salad, 146

Shaved Brussels Sprouts and White Bean Salad, 137

Simple Citrus Vinaigrette, 49

Simple Side Salad, 64

Smoky Sumac and Freekeh Salad, 183

Southwestern Quinoa Salad, 176

Spicy Cilantro Vinaigrette, 50

Spicy Peanut Dressing, 60

Spicy Pineapple and Mango Salad, 202

Spinach and Orzo Salad, 157

Spring Pea, Bulgur, and Goat Cheese Salad, 185

Sweet Raspberry Vinaigrette, 51

Tomato and Feta with Dill Salad, 82

Tropical Fruit Salad, 195

Turmeric-Spiced Cauliflower Salad with Tahini Dressing, 145

Vegan Nutty Dressing, 61

Vegetarian Cobb Salad, 134

Warming Winter Salad, 93

Yogurt Cucumber Salad, 83

Zesty Avocado Dressing, 62

vinaigrettes

Classic Italian Vinaigrette, 47

Grilled Romaine Salad with Warm Bacon Vinaigrette, 160

Roasted Carrot Vinaigrette, 48

Simple Citrus Vinaigrette, 49

Spicy Cilantro Vinaigrette, 50

Sweet Raspberry Vinaigrette, 51

W

walnuts

Apple and Walnut Salad, 189

Shaved Asparagus and Walnuts Salad, 146

watermelons, 197

white beans, 137

winter salads

Apple, Candied Pecan, and Orange Salad, 190

Apple and Walnut Salad, 189

Citrus Salad, 193

Warming Winter Salad, 93

Wurstsalat (Swiss/German Meat Salad), 103

Y

Yogurt Cucumber Salad, 83

Z

zesting, 19

Zesty Avocado Dressing, 62

Zesty Thai Steak Bowls, 122

Zesty Tuna Salad, 76

zucchini, 136

About the Author

Wendy Jo Peterson, MS, RDN, is an award-winning author, speaker, culinary nutritionist, proud military wife, and mom. Whether at work or at the table, Wendy Jo believes in savoring life. Check out her other *For Dummies* titles: *Meal Prep Cookbook For Dummies, Bread Making For Dummies, Mediterranean Diet Cookbook For Dummies, Air Fryer Cookbook For Dummies,* and *Instant Pot Cookbook For Dummies.* When she's not in her kitchen, you can find Wendy Jo globetrotting around Europe, strolling a SoCal beach with her pups, or exploring the great outdoors with her family. You can catch her on social media at @just_wendyjo or check out her website, www.justwendyjo.com.

Dedication

To my mom, who gave me the love of greens.

Authors' Acknowledgments

Thanks to my mom, who always had a garden and crafted delicious salads right from our backyard.

If you were to ask my husband his favorite meal, he'd quickly declare my salads. He adores even the simplest of salads. Thank you for always letting me throw together something crazy from my garden and telling me you love it, Brandon!

I'm thankful that my 7-year-old tries all my salads, too! Anya, you are an adventurous eater, and I love sharing meals with you!

For me, writing a book is never a solo endeavor — my village of friends, family, and colleagues helps along the way. Thanks to my mom, sister, and sister-in-law for always stepping up to try my recipes and give me feedback. Thanks to Kathie, Nadine, Heather, and Sarah for helping me with salad ideas. Thanks to Heather Wosoogh for being a friend who shares my love of salads and always opens her door for playdates so I can keep my writing deadlines. Thanks to Leslie Schilling for being my sounding board in the writing process. Thanks to Shai Espino for being my assistant and helping me keep my deadlines. Thanks to Geri Goodale for helping me capture the right images for this book and for her ever-positive energy along the way. It takes a village, especially during a pandemic!

No book is ever achieved without a great team, and I'm blessed to have worked with this team on many books. Thanks to my agent, Matt Wagner, for continually advocating for me as the writer. I'm forever grateful for Tracy Boggier, senior acquisitions editor at Wiley, who believes in me and my recipes. Thanks to my project and copy editor, Elizabeth Kuball, for keeping me on track with deadlines and helping me better express my creative ideas. I thoroughly enjoy the creative process working with each of you. Thank you for your collaboration!

Publisher's Acknowledgments

Senior Acquisitions Editor: Tracy Boggier

Project Editor: Elizabeth Kuball

Copy Editor: Elizabeth Kuball

Recipe Tester: Rachel Nix, RDN

Nutrition Analyst: Rachel Nix, RDN

Production Editor: Tamilmani Varadharaj

Photographers:
Wendy Jo Peterson and Geri Goodale

Cover Image: Courtesy of Wendy Jo Peterson